About t

This is a true and honest account ＿ Lin Xiangbei, an ordinary Chinese man from Sic ＿ Province, who celebrated his 100th birthday in 2018. In his memoir, he documents his passion for the ideals of Communism and the tumultuous changes that China has undergone within the last century. (Originally named Lin Xianli, he changed his name at his Communist Party membership ceremony in 1938 to Xiangbei, which means 'Towards the North', because the Communist Party's base was in Yanan in the north of China at that time.)

His book has been translated and compiled by his youngest daughter, Lin Ping, who is an accomplished artist in various media ranging through sculpture, oil painting and photography, specialising in portraits. She currently lives in London.

To Survive is Victory

To Survive is Victory

One Man's Struggle to Forge a New China 1918–1980

Lin Xiangbei

Translated and compiled by Lin Ping

unbound

This edition first published in 2019

Unbound
6th Floor Mutual House, 70 Conduit Street, London W1S 2GF
www.unbound.com

© Lin Xiangbei and Lin Ping, 2019

ISBN (eBook): 978-1-78965-060-0
ISBN (Paperback): 978-1-78965-059-4

Cover design by Mecob

Printed and bound in Great Britain by Clays Ltd, Elcograf S.p.A.

To my father:
I love you dearly and respect you with all my heart.

To my mother:
My memories of you are in my heart forever. I only wish there had been more time to spend with you. I am proud to be your daughter.

To my grandmother:
You were not only a remarkable woman in our family, but in Chinese history too.

To my grandfathers:
I wish I had met you both.

– Lin Ping

Super Patrons

Ellen Aquing
Felix Aquing
Anthony Aquing
Georgia Aquing
Kenneth Noggle
Tony Laws
Shula-Mit-Laws
Adam Laws
Debbie Terrell
Paul Bedding
Xinran
Lin Mingtao
Lin Bo
Lin He
Lin Zi
Lin Ying
Lin Xi
Lin TingTing
Lin Xiaoke
Li Li
Liu Xiangrong

Liu Jiangyi
Lu Shang
Lu Jiangyue
Lu Zimo
Xu Ying

*

Nasir Abdillahi
Ashley Allen
Trish Amichi
Roderick Andrew
Xinying Baker
Liping Balkwill
James Bradburn
Martin Brame
Margaret JC Brown
Jonathan Buckle
Tom Callaghan
Stephen Carlaw
Li Chenghua
David A P Cooke
Phil Cox
Mark Davis
Graham Duncan
Steve Duncan
Jean Farah
Franz-Bernd Frechen
Paul Gavan
Tim Gee
Bernie Greene
Julian Gruin
Gong Guobi

Edwina Huawen Li
Muhammad Imran
Chen Jian
Luo Jiyuan
Arpheel John
Dan Kieran
Felicity Lane
Lu Liangjun
Bi Lijun
Guo Liwei
Aimili Low-Foon
Richard Low-Foon
Abdul Malik
Xingwei McArthur
Julian Meacher
John Mitchinson
Katrina Moseley
Wai Yue Neep
Phill Patel
Geoff Patterson
Desmond M Phillips
Justin Pollard
David Prew
Carlos Rehaag
Ruel Reid
Meg Ryan
Lily Shang
Andrew Shead
Michael TA Smith
Lili Soh
Ben Squibb
David Stevens
Bin Tan

Contents

Foreword

By Lin Ping

For many years I had promised Father that I would paint his portrait. I don't know why it took so long before we both made time to do it, but he was in his late eighties before he sat for me. In the process, it gave us valuable time together to talk about his past life and, by the end of that day, my father had asked me to write down the story of his life.

It all started with him picking up the photograph, dear to all of our family, which was taken in Chongqing in 1939. It is in black and white and holds the solemn images of my father and his father and my mother and her mother. His face suddenly clouded with sadness and he heaved such a heavy sigh. I went to sit down next to him to comfort him and he said: 'It's not easy being the only one left alive – not easy at all. I miss the other people in this photograph so much.'

Then Father started pointing out details of the photo, which I hadn't been told about before, and he cheered up considerably.

'You can't tell from this photo, but we were a happy group dressed very colourfully. Your *yeye* [paternal grandfather] was wearing his Nationalist Army uniform. The first time I remember him, when I was a child, he was in uniform. Look at me – don't you think I was handsome when I was a young man! You know – there were lots of girls after me then and your mother wasn't even the prettiest one! My Sun Yat-sen style suit was in metallic blue – that style was most fashionable at the time. Your mother was wearing a long, red silk cheongsam [gown] and your *waipo* [maternal grandmother] was in a long, dark blue one. They look more like sisters in this photo than mother and daughter.'

From left: Shibo (Chen Lianshi), Lin Zhuxi, Lin Xiangbei (then Xianli) and Liao Ninjun

It was true. Everybody said that if you didn't know anything about the people in the photo, you would find it hard to tell which person was my grandmother and which one was my mother.

'Ever since the day I met your *waipo* I thought she was the most wonderful person on this earth. My father obviously thought so too and it was plain that he was in love with her, and she with him. But she had made a vow after her husband was executed – sworn in front of two hundred guerrilla fighters – that she would never marry again. She also swore that she would never betray his memory.'

Father sighed again. 'What an incredible woman she was! At the time, all your *yeye*'s friends assumed that they would marry each other, but life is strange – in the end she became my mother-in-law rather than my stepmother. The two of them were the most influential people in my life – actually there were three. Firstly there was Seventh Aunt. When I was about seven or eight, I went to live with my father in the army barracks, but then Seventh Aunt took me in with her family and she taught me to work hard, be determined and to strive for success in everything I did.'

I had never heard him mention his Seventh Aunt, one of his father's sisters, before.

'Your *yeye* was also an exceptional person. In his day he became a loyal Sun Yat-sen supporter and he was the one to set me on the path of revolution. Then, when he came across your *waipo* and her husband, they were the ones to show him the path of Communism. The Communist philosophy was a perfect match with his ideals. My father was one of life's innocents though – everybody said it. He was called "Lunatic Lin" by all those corrupt officials he came up against because he remained incorruptible to the very end. I miss him and I hate the unfairness of life because he died too early. He once said to me: "A family with no children is like a street with no lamplight." If only he had lived to see my "five golden flowers" – like you!'

Father swiftly, but gently, swiped my nose with his finger, just like he used to do when I was a small child. I knew that he was truly happy at that moment and I'm sure he was imagining a happy scene where we were all surrounding his father, listening to his stories.

'Your *waipo*, however, was probably the one who shaped and influenced my life the most. I loved and respected her greatly. If she were alive today, I think she would be very proud to see that you have become an artist. She was very talented herself, but only managed to do much painting in the last two years of her life. It's hard to believe the same person who created such beautiful artwork was also a sharpshooter known as "Double Gun Woman".'

It was true that I had always heard my grandmother described as having been a skilful artist one moment and a fearless warrior the next. There are a few of her paintings, which escaped the scourge of the Cultural Revolution, hanging on the wall opposite my father's rocking chair. They are of flowers, mainly orchids, other plants, birds and butterflies. They are so beautiful, and the birds and iridescent butterflies almost look ready to take flight into the room.

'She became a legend in her own lifetime, but she started out as a very unusual little girl. She refused to have her feet bound – every time somebody bound them up she always found a way of taking off the bandages. She was born into a rich, scholarly family and had been given a very good education, but then she chose to marry beneath her class and was disowned. Only one of her sisters stood by her. She led a hard life. She really was an extraordinary woman – fearless too. I saw her riding a horse bareback once and the way she rode was a lot more handsome than the way you see it in those American westerns. She could assemble a pistol in the dark in just over ten seconds. It is rare to hear about a woman like her in Chinese history. Have you ever heard about another woman like her anywhere? I think probably not!'

Father looked at me doubtfully and shook his head.

'Although your *waipo* was so renowned, I can safely boast that I knew her better than anyone else, even your mother. Oh!

I have so many stories I could tell you about her and my father – I am overflowing with memories. If you wanted to write a book about them, it would have to be this thick.'

Father indicated a large distance between his thumb and forefinger.

'Hah! Why don't you tell your Western world all about them! Tell them about how we lived here in China in the '20s, '30s and '40s of the last century. Come with me.'

Father suddenly got up from his chair, moving quickly for such an old man, and beckoned to me. I followed him to his bedroom. He opened a drawer, pulled out a pile of papers and presented them to me.

'You see how busy I've been! I have been writing about my life for the past couple of years – this is my legacy to you and your sisters – there is nothing else to leave behind when I go.'

'But, Baba…'

'*But?* I know what you are going to say – you want to tell me that you are an artist, not a writer, and that you can't do this. You would never have heard your grandparents say "I can't". If you do this for me, you will come to understand us all better. In fact, don't do it just for me – do it for your *waipo*, *waigong* [maternal grandfather], *yeye* and your mother, and for all the millions of people who died for the Liberation and whose lives and deaths were never recorded.'

I couldn't answer my father straight away as I hadn't expected that painting his portrait would lead me to such a huge task as this. I felt unsure of myself, but I had to decide whether I was prepared to disappoint my elderly father by saying no. He was right in the fact that, if I did this, I would come to understand them all better and why certain things happened. There was, indeed, so much that I didn't understand. I remembered that I once asked my father the question: if the Communist Party had asked him to abandon his children, would he have done so? His answer was expected, but still, it was difficult to hear. He said very gravely and after a long silence: 'If you want the truth, then the answer is "yes". If it had been for the sake of the Revolution, then yes.'

Then, as if my father was reading my mind, he said to me: 'You know, in those days we dedicated our whole lives to the Party. We put it first, before anything else, whether that was family, love, or even life itself. We felt it was for the good of the whole of China and her people. Life isn't as simple as just being happy, or in love, or doing as you please. I will tell you a fact about the path my life has taken – to survive is victory!'

I turned over the first page in the bundle of papers Father had given me and was met by the familiar style of his handwriting. It read:

My Life

By Lin Xiangbei

To all my children and grandchildren
I am an ordinary Chinese man
Neither a hero nor a coward
I have no legendary stories or great achievements
But if you are curious to know more
About a small corner of a country in upheaval during the twentieth century
About the distress and hardship of resurrecting a nation
Through the eyes of a 'red' intellectual
Then please read this book.

A Note on Names

Each Chinese name has three components: family, generational and given name. Thus, Lin Xianli comprises the family name Lin, the generational name Xian and the given name Li. Unlike in English, the family name is given first.

This book uses the standard Pinyin spelling and presentation (without hyphens), as in Lin Xianli, except in rare cases where the older Wade-Giles format, as in Sun Yat-sen and Chiang Kai-shek, is still in wide usage.

Introduction

By Lin Xiangbei

I have always loved writing and am still doing so today at the age of 101.

When I was young I worked as a newspaper journalist and, as well as writing the usual reports and articles, I wrote many stories and poems. Writing and playing tennis were my passions and longed-for careers, but events got in the way of their fulfilment. There was a long period of time, a very dark period, when I didn't have any opportunity even to pick up a pen, let alone write with it.

I started writing again after my retirement. The Communist Party History Department invited me to write for them on a volunteer basis. I wrote many articles for their publications. At that time friends suggested to me that I should write my autobiography, but I didn't as I thought I was too ordinary, with nothing to write about.

In the late 1990s my youngest daughter, Ping, brought Toby Eady, a literary agent from London, to visit me. He was interested in the story of the life of my mother-in-law, Chen Lianshi, Double Gun Woman. On his subsequent visits he encouraged me, with a great deal of enthusiasm, to write about my own life.

I didn't find it easy to recall the details of time, places and people, but, as I unearthed my memories one by one, many moving stories emerged. I started by recording everything I remembered on tapes, sixty of them in the end, which took three months, before I started writing. I remember how my beloved mother-in-law recorded her life. Each night she searched the depths of her mind and during the daytime she asked people to record her memories. Sometimes she laughed and sometimes she cried. Three months later, she was spitting blood and then she died in a hospital bed. My memories brought out all the emotions too and gave me many, many sleepless nights; sometimes I couldn't hold back my tears. I tried to control my feelings, but at times it got too much to bear so I would have to stop for a little while, but I came to realise that it was time for me to tell my children about my life otherwise I would regret it. It took me two years to write 400,000 words, but that only brought me up to 1950.

I see my life as being in three distinct parts.

The first thirty years took me from childhood into adulthood, firmly following a path which would lead me to Communism. Once I became a member of the Party I dedicated my body and soul to it. I did my utmost to carry out whatever they told me to do. We lived in hardship and danger, but the goals seemed clear. We were fighting for a new China and we knew our enemies were the Guomingdan, Chiang Kai-shek and the Japanese. The years 1920 to 1949 were extraordinary times for ordinary people. These ordinary people turned into heroes and heroines with moving stories of bravery and personal sacrifice. Finally, victory was ours and our Communist Party ruled a new China.

The second thirty years, but especially from 1957 to 1978, were harder than anything we had encountered before. The distinction between right and wrong blurred and became confused. So many people seemed transformed or had been forced to change themselves beyond recognition. I was one of hundreds of thousands of Chinese who existed in a dark, frightening place in limbo between humans and ghosts. We suffered endless humiliation and were terrified, day and night, of what might happen next. Each time my thoughts turn to my dear loved ones and friends whose deaths were unjustified, I cry with my heart aching.

The third part of my life is up until today and it finds me happy to be surrounded by my children, grandchildren and great-grandchildren. As one of the oldest members of the Communist Party alive today, I would like to say that I never regretted anything in my life: I kept my integrity and I never falter in being proud to be Chinese.

I want to sincerely thank Toby Eady for recognising my contribution and for putting trust in me. I want to thank Xue, my eldest daughter, who has spent much time in helping me publish all my writing in China, and Ping, my youngest daughter, who has been working on this English version of this book. Sincere thanks to Xinran for helping Ping over the years and having faith in her to complete the project. My thanks and gratitude to Ping's friend, Ellen Aquing, who not only helped her with her English, but went through every word with her and never let her give up. Thanks to all Ping's foreign friends, to whom she introduced me over the years – they broadened my horizons. Thanks to all my children, who love me and look after me so well in my old age, and to my grandchildren and great-grandchildren who have brought me so much joy. Sincere thanks to John Mitchinson for thinking my story is worthy of publication and to all the staff at Unbound in making it happen in my lifetime.

This book is for my beloved father, my mother-in-law Shibo (Chen Lianshi), my wife Ninjun, and my friends.

Lin Xiangbei, March 2019

Lin Xiangbei at 100

狂風惡浪一小舟

'I feel my life is reflected in this drawing: a small boat being tossed around in the turbulent ocean struggling to survive. Through the dark cloud is a ray of light – THAT IS HOPE.'
– Lin Xiangbei

(Drawing by Huang Zhenghai,
Calligraphy by Huang Zhenguo)

Prologue: An Uncertain Beginning

The eighth day of the first lunar month of 1918 brought exceptionally cold weather to the small town of Yunan. Yunan lies on the banks of the Qu River, a tributary of the Yangtze River, in the mountainous eastern region of Sichuan Province. The area is called 'Silver Nest' because of its network of salt mines and wells, both ancient and modern. Salt extraction began here over two thousand years ago.

As the night drew in the temperature plummeted and silenced the streets and alleyways of the small town. Behind the closed doors of each house there would, no doubt, be a story to tell, but one story in particular was unfolding in the house of the Lin family. On this night they were waiting to welcome a new life into their midst. They had been waiting anxiously, but anxiety had long since turned to alarm.

The midwife had been summoned days ago to attend the labour of the youngest daughter-in-law in the household. As soon as the overdue labour started, the midwife ushered the men out of the room. The mother-in-law and the second daughter-in-law remained to help. For hours on end the cries and moans of the young girl filled the air as she tossed and turned on the bed. She grew more and more exhausted, but finally the baby's head was showing and surely it would only take one more push for the baby to be born. The three concerned women almost held their breath as they waited for the young girl to muster her last bit of energy. At this crucial moment a woman burst into the room. She threw the door open and it crashed against its hinges, caught by an icy gust of wind. The warmth in the room was sucked out immediately and the oil lamps flickered.

'Aah! I come to congratulate our Lin family who have a new root.' Her voice was loud and harsh. Then she shovelled a handful of sunflower seeds into her mouth and looked surprised when she didn't receive a welcome.

The midwife spun around in anger: 'You! You! I should chop your head off. You frightened her. The baby has gone back. The baby has gone back into the womb. Now what am I expected to do! Oh my heavenly God, the poor thing!'

The mother-in-law raged too as she pushed the woman back out of the door, hampered somewhat by her tiny, bound feet: 'Get out! Get out! You're always making trouble. This has nothing to do with you. You don't even realise what you've done. Get out now and stay out!'

The intruder was the eldest daughter-in-law. She was in her mid-twenties and was the spoiled daughter of a local landowner and salt merchant. After she married into the Lin family she remained lazy and idle. She never contributed to any of the work of the household, not even the needlework, normally expected of girls. She had a round, plump face and too much loose flesh hung from her short frame. She ate so many sunflower seeds each day, shelled for her by her maid, that she earned the nickname 'seed mouth'. This wasn't the only reason for the nickname, however. People said that her mouth spread the seeds of bad news and unhappiness wherever she went. Smoking opium was her main pleasure.

2

The young girl on the bed was in shock and lying motionless. Two more hours passed by interminably and her contractions stopped. She was utterly spent. Her sad eyes sought her mother-in-law's and seemed to apologise for failing to deliver the baby. Hope had left her. The mother-in-law loved her as much as one of her own daughters and her heart ached at seeing her in such pain.

It was only just over a year ago that this girl had married into the Lin family and she proved herself to be hard working, virtuous, quiet and well mannered. She came from a respectable family. Her father was a doctor working in the next town. The first daughter-in-law had been chosen by the matchmakers and the mother-in-law hadn't wanted to trust them again to find a wife for her second son. Instead, a trusted friend had introduced the second daughter-in-law and this had turned out well. She was sensible, dependable and an asset to the family. So the mother-in-law had asked the second daughter-in-law to find the third. The mother-in-law took a liking to the girl as soon as she saw her and happily ordered the betrothal banquet to be arranged. It was decided that the family's youngest son, aged fifteen, would do very well to marry this girl.

The mother-in-law exchanged glances with the midwife and said quietly: 'Save the big one.'

The midwife sighed and bit her lip. She didn't hold much hope of being able to save either one. The girl remained ashen faced, but knew what was happening. The midwife rolled up her sleeves once more in readiness for the necessary intervention. She managed to get hold of the baby's head within the womb and pulled. As soon as the baby was out, the girl lost consciousness.

It was a boy, but his body was blue and he made no sound. The mother-in-law, already mourning the loss of a grandson, sorrowfully wrapped the infant in a blanket and put him in a basket near the fire. She told her second daughter-in-law to go and inform the Master and her youngest son of what had happened.

The midwife was tending to the young mother to save her life. When she had done all she could for her, the woman's attention turned back to the baby. The midwife examined him and detected a very faint, but erratic, heartbeat and a bit of warmth coming from his mouth. It wasn't enough to ensure that the baby would survive, however, and they wrapped him up again and returned him to the basket by the fire.

Whilst still bending over the baby they were surprised and relieved to hear the voice of the young mother: 'Give me my baby. Give him to me. Please let me warm him with my body. I beg you, let me hold him. Just let me hold him, please.'

The matriarch's word was final: 'To have a dying baby by your side is a bad omen. It will adversely affect your recovery. It is up to the Fates to decide whether the baby lives or dies.'

They stoked up the fire and settled down to get some much needed rest. The night returned to its silence. The new mother was bereft and could only glance in the direction of the fireplace. As dawn broke she heard a faint sound coming from her baby. The sound was weak and only loud enough to alert a mother who yearned for her baby with every cell of her body.

'The baby is alive! The baby is alive!' she shouted, or so she thought. Her cry was as feeble as the baby's, though, and she couldn't rouse the other exhausted people in the room. In desperation she struggled to get up. She managed to reach her baby and pick him up, but she collapsed with him in her arms before she could get back to her bed.

My grandmother told me that story. I was that baby: a fugitive from death. There is an old saying: 'A life escaped from death

4

is a life destined to follow a lucky star.' When I look back on my life, I would say that I have been a lucky man. I am still healthy in my nineties. I have survived countless hardships and there have been many times when death has hovered over my head.

My father named me 'Xianli'. Xian is my generational name and means 'First'. Li means 'Ritual'.

Part 1:
Turning China Red
(1918–1949)

The Lin Family

My grandfather was known as 'The Big Master Lin' by the local people. He was a kind and honest man who worked hard for his family of five surviving children: three sons and two daughters. As a young man he started out in business as an itinerant pedlar of any articles he could carry. He would announce his arrival in city streets and rural lanes alike by beating a drum and shouting out his wares. In the summertime he went barefoot and in the wintertime he made sandals for himself out of straw. On occasions he wandered too far to get home at night, but he would always be offered shelter by one of his customers due to his popularity.

Over the years, Grandfather saved enough money to open a store selling general goods and textiles. Sometime later he could afford to buy a working salt well. Salt production in this area was by means of digging wells and scooping up the subterranean brine in buckets. The brine was transferred to shallow pools to concentrate in the sunshine and air before being further evaporated on huge stoves, fuelled by coal, to leave salt crystals. This turned out to be a very profitable business.

With his new-found wealth, Grandfather set about rebuilding the Lin family yard on the best plot in the high street. On the roadside he built two shops with a wide frontage: one for textiles, mainly silk, and the other for general goods. Over the shopfront was a banner, painted with gold lettering, which said 'Leadership, Prosperity, Glory'. This banner was given to Grandfather by the county governor and he was very proud of it.

The family house was built directly behind and consisted of a reception hall, three living rooms and a courtyard with the family bedrooms running down one side and the servants' rooms down the other, squared off with a large kitchen. There were two acres of garden mostly given over to growing fruit and vegetables. I still remember the delicious grapefruit: they were juicy, sweet and fragrant. Grandfather had also planted a grove of many different species of bamboo especially for his third and favourite son, my father, who had been named Zhuxi, which means 'Roosting by the Bamboo'. My father had been the only one of the boys willing to accompany Grandfather when he was still a pedlar. After finishing the family property, Grandfather went on to build about twenty other houses in the high street for rental.

The Lin family, with my grandfather at its head, gained in wealth and reputation and in this prosperous period he bought himself an official title and became a fifth-rank bureaucrat without duties. His eldest son, my Big Uncle, was elected as the chairman of the Salt Mining Union, which had over ten thousand members. My Second Uncle was elected as the president of the Association of the Chamber of Commerce and he later became the County Police Minister. My Seventh Aunt married into the richest branch of the Tang family in the region. However, my grandfather never forgot what it was like to be poor and was always quick to offer help where needed. Each winter he set up large woks in the street and cooked rice porridge for anyone who wanted it. People often asked him to sort out family and neighbour disputes and he could be relied upon to be fair and impartial. He spent a lot of his personal fortune on projects for the community, such as building roads and a bridge.

But then a series of events shook our comfortable existence. The salinity level of the salt wells gradually decreased until it was no longer a viable business. Salt production was the mainstay of the family's income, but the real disaster was when Grandfather was paralysed by a stroke and wasn't able to look after any of the other businesses. The shops started to lose money and the income from the rental properties, which were mainly occupied by the extended family, fell below the cost of repairs. Both my uncles eventually lost their government positions. Big Uncle should have taken over the family businesses, but by then he had become an opium addict, along with his wife, and wasn't interested. Second Uncle had a mistress, who lived in the city, and came home less and less. My grandmother was reduced to selling salt and her home-made bean curd on the high street to support us all.

I was born in this period of family decline. It was the period when the old Qing Empire had been swept away and the Chinese Republic had been established by Dr Sun Yat-sen: a time when China was preoccupied with social reform.

My parents were both fifteen years old when they got married. It was an arranged marriage as was the norm, but they loved each other nonetheless. I survived my difficult and protracted birth, but my mother never left her bed afterwards and died nearly a year later. When she finally died my father was grief stricken. He was like a wraith wandering around the house until he finally shut himself in his room and wouldn't come out.

With Grandfather lying paralysed in bed and me barely one year old, Grandmother needed some help. She hired a young girl from the Li family who lived in the neighbourhood. As she was the eldest child in her family she was called 'Big Li'. Big

Li's main task was to take food to my father and to keep a general eye on him. Gradually the two young people became very close and affectionate to each other. Soon Big Li fell pregnant. When Grandmother found out she sacked Big Li.

My father realised that he couldn't hide from life any more and needed to take responsibility. He pleaded with my grandmother to be allowed to marry Big Li. But Grandmother was furious and said:

'Firstly, your wife's bones aren't even cold yet and you have done such an immoral thing. Secondly, the Li family is poor and has no standing in society. Nothing about them matches our family. Even worse, she came to my house as a maid. How dare she entice you and embark on an illicit affair. Just sacking her is merciful. How could you even ask to officially marry her – you would ruin the Lin family name. People would never respect us again.'

The whole family was against Father marrying Big Li and he gave in to their pressure. However, he tried to give some support to the Li family, who were humiliated by the scandal. It now meant that Big Li would not be eligible for marriage and life became very hard for them all. My father begged my grandmother to allow the Li family to gather the coal cinders left over from boiling the salt, so that they might be able to supplement their now-meagre income. Grandmother agreed as she had to acknowledge that their situation was partially her son's fault too. When Big Li gave birth to a girl, my father named his daughter Liuqing, which means 'Evergreen Willow Tree'.

My father watched Big Li sorting through those dirty cinders, whilst holding the baby, day in and day out. He blamed himself for bringing such troubles onto them. He wrote a poem, which I remember even today:

Left hand holds the baby
Right hand picks the carbon
Baby, baby, don't cry
Sell the cinders to buy rice and mutton.

There was a strong bond between Big Li and Father and their desire to be together gave them courage to continue their relationship. Father secretly rented a room in the town and hid Big Li and their baby there. Being a small town though, it wasn't long before word came to Grandmother's ears. Her anger knew no bounds and once again Father had to bow to family pressure and uphold traditional morals. Everyone made it impossible for the two young people to stay together. Big Li was sent out of the area and married off to a peasant, whose wife had died, as his 'fill-in wife'. This was a very lowly position. She had to take Liuqing with her and my father was powerless to prevent it.

Once again my father's heart was turned to ashes. The only person he wanted to talk to was his own father, but not only was his father paralysed he had also lost the power of speech. My father's only pleasure was going to the pagoda at the top of the hill to read. From the top, there was a wonderful view of the Qu River. Whilst there he met two young men from the town whose thinking was very radical. With them, my father engaged in many discussions about the country's state of affairs, the inequality of society, political corruption and invasion by foreigners. Through these young men my father was introduced to a vision of a different China. They discussed and planned for an idealistic future society and so the scene was set for my father's pathway through life. He vowed to his new friends: 'The day my father passes away is the day I leave home.'

Grandfather died after enduring two years of illness. On the third day of his funeral, my father packed a few clothes and some sandals and, with only a small amount of money, which was given to him by his younger sister, he left without saying goodbye to anyone. When Grandmother came back from the graveyard she found his letter announcing that he had left home. She was heartbroken and couldn't believe that her youngest son, whom she had thought she would be able to rely on, would leave his three-year-old son and ageing mother. The letter read:

Mother,

I am leaving home. I could not tell you before of my intention, face to face, because I knew that you would never agree. I have made my decision and I am not going to change my mind. I cannot get used to the way our lives have turned out and having to watch my brothers lay waste to all my father's hard work. I don't want to live like a drunkard stumbling around in the dark. I want to find a useful life and make my own future. Please do not worry. I will not do anything to dishonour you and my ancestors.

During the past two years I have done my best to look after Father and to fulfil my duty as a son. Now Father has gone to heaven and I do not need to have any more concern for him. I know that you will be looked after by my other siblings. Xianli is still small. I am not able to look after him myself and so I ask you to bring him up. Please do not spoil him. Liuqing is part of the Lin family too. If there is a chance, please bring her back, and I hope that you will be able to find it in your heart to treat her like your own granddaughter.

When the time is right I will write to you.

Your son,

Zhuxi

Mischievous Childhood

My grandfather had never been educated, but he recognised the importance of education. Once he had gained wealth and status he declared that, from then on, all the Lin children must attend school. There were no state schools in our locality, so Big Uncle set up a school in one of the family's rented houses and engaged a teacher. The neighbourhood children were invited to attend free of charge. Our teacher's name was Zhao and he was given accommodation and board at the school in addition to his salary.

The classroom was simple with just a few long, wooden desks and benches lined up in rows. Attending school was new and exciting for me. We started with the classic reading books like *One Thousand Characters*, *One Hundred Surnames* and *The Three Characters*. I had an excellent memory and found that after having something read to me only a couple of times I could remember all of the words. Teacher Zhao was very fond of me and often said to the others: 'Why can't you all be clever and good learners like Xianli?'

I was always the first one to finish the lessons, but I soon got bored of sitting there waiting for the others to catch up, so I started being disruptive in the classroom. Most of the time I would be late for school, get behind with homework and often pick fights during the lessons. Then, when I was especially bored, I would pretend to be desperate to go to the latrine. I would wriggle around so much that Teacher Zhao would have to excuse me from the classroom, but then I wouldn't return afterwards.

During the spring I would sometimes run up the hill to pick mulberries instead of going to school at all. I hid from anyone sent by Teacher Zhao to find me. One afternoon, Teacher Zhao himself came to our house and hauled me out from under my bed where I was hiding. Grasping my ear in what felt like an iron clamp, he pulled me all the way back to the classroom. I hated him after that, firstly for humiliating me in front of everyone on the street and secondly for hurting my ear. On the following day, while he was taking his lunch, I threw his teapot, cup and tobacco pipes into the latrine pit. All the way through the afternoon lessons he was searching for his possessions until he finally asked each one of us in turn if we had seen them. When he got to me, I answered him forthrightly that I had thrown them into the latrine. Teacher Zhao was so angry. I can still remember his twisted face as he picked up the thick bamboo stick and started to beat my hand with it. Then he tried to thrash me on the behind, but I fought my way out and ran, crying and screaming, to report to Big Uncle.

Big Uncle took me gently by the hand and went straight to Teacher Zhao to confront him: 'You are a teacher and should set a worthy example. Why did you beat this child? He doesn't have any parents and even we never touch him.'

In fact everyone knew that a teacher had a right to beat pupils and they commonly did so. Each family's shrine would display the deities representing Heaven, Earth, Supreme Ruler, Kin and Educator. The teacher was held in high regard and had a very important position in society; no one should dare to disrespect a teacher. What I did was intolerable to Teacher Zhao and the fact that Big Uncle had tried to protect me made the situation worse. Teacher Zhao was trembling violently, but with great dignity and in silence he proceeded to pack up his few remaining possessions. He left, still without a word, and he never came back. He must have recovered his voice soon, though, as my bad reputation became widely known and no one wanted to come and teach us.

No more school. I was totally free and became more than mischievous: wicked and uncontrollably wild. There was plenty of time to go to the bamboo grove to shoot the sparrows and turtle doves with a catapult. I gave my little victims to our family storekeeper so that he could roast and eat them. He praised my accuracy and spurred me on. I used anything as a target in order to practise my aim. Once I catapulted a stone at a child passing by and nearly blinded him. Grandmother was particularly scared on this occasion and, tired of apologising to others for me, she prohibited me from leaving our yard.

Grandmother was a very devout and conventional Buddhist. Every morning I was used to seeing her kowtowing and praying in front of the shrine in the altar room. On our shrine stood the usual deities – in addition to those we had the Buddha of Mercy, the Buddha of Wealth, the Buddha of Protection and, specifically important to our family, our genealogy written on a scroll. Grandfather had reverently placed this scroll in a very finely carved, lined, oak box. The Lin family were extremely proud of their genealogy and our long-held motto was: 'Loyalty to your country and filial piety to your home.' Grandmother noticed my interest in the deities and undertook to teach me, step by step, how to worship. She told me about the strict order in which the Buddhas had to be attended to, when to kowtow on the prayer cushion and when to light the sticks of incense. In all there were about twenty kowtows to perform each day. The procedure of worship was something new and fun to me. Grandmother was thrilled when I started to show an interest in doing something worthy, so I was chosen to represent the whole family in prayer each morning.

For the first few days I solemnly did what I had been told to do whilst Grandmother watched me. When she felt satisfied that my wicked spirit had been tamed at last she left me to my duties. However, my new-found virtue didn't last more than a week or two and I was soon bored of the whole thing. What I could do in the hall to pass the time more interestingly was limited. I could not move, or even touch, the deities, as I knew how holy they were considered to be. I lit the incense, but instead of kowtowing, I started doing cartwheels, handstands and somersaults from one side of the room to the other whilst happily humming folk tunes. I knew roughly how much time was needed to finish the prayers and then I went to Grandmother to report my task completed. To reward me she would give me a rice cake, a yellow pea cake or some other little treat to pop into my mouth and then I would skip away.

There is an old Chinese saying: 'The longer you walk in the darkness, the greater chance of bumping into a ghost.' For many weeks I contentedly 'did' my important family job and thought that I would never be found out. Then one day, whilst in the middle of performing a handstand on the prayer cushion, I was amazed to see a pair of upside-down, tiny, pointed silk shoes appear before me. I just had time to admire the pretty embroidery of red flowers entwined with golden leaves before I realised what they meant. My heart leaped, my stomach lurched and I choked on my happy song. I quickly sprang upright and saw that Grandmother's face had become contorted by her anger and, for the first time in my life, I was scared. Grandmother was a genuinely kind person and I had never experienced anything except gentleness from her, but in that moment I saw her eyes dancing with fire. What I had done insulted the ancestors and the holy spirits. It was an unforgivable thing to do, and I knew I was in trouble. Grandmother was holding a feather duster in her hand and, as soon as she started to wave it in the air, I fled like a wild animal seeing the hunters raise their guns. Her three-inch bound feet didn't allow her to run after me, but she still managed to deliver a painful blow to the back of my hand before I managed to get away. In my memory this was the first and only time that she beat me. After that I was excluded from worshipping at the shrine.

As punishment I wasn't allowed to go outside at all and there was nothing to do inside the house. I knew that I ought to do something good to please Grandmother in the hope that she would soon forget my bad deeds, so I volunteered to help her in the shop. I didn't have any wicked thoughts at first, until my cousin, who was three years older than me, told me I could easily steal money when helping Grandmother. I was still innocent about money because I almost always got everything I asked for, but my cousin tempted me. He told me that if I had money I would be able to buy my favourite yellow pea cake whenever I wanted and wouldn't have to wait to be given it. It was temptation indeed! The money box was a bamboo tube and it was put on the table about three arms' length away from the scales. Whenever I helped Grandmother to serve a customer, I would take the payment then turn around and throw the coins into the bamboo tube. Nine times out of ten I hit the target, but every so often I deliberately missed. The bronze coins, which were the smallest, were the least likely to be missed when calculating the day's takings, so these were the ones which I saw as being mine. I made a note of where they fell then waited till night-time and crept back into the shop to pick them up. The next day I would sneak out and buy some delicious yellow pea cake. I was still generally naughty in and around the shop, but Grandmother never found out about this particular deceit. My cousin knew, of course, but often he shared the cake with me.

I was always restless and in the summer months I loved to go swimming. No matter how hard Grandmother tried to prevent me from going down to the river, all I had to do was wait till everyone was having their midday nap. The temperature along the Yangtze regularly reached 40°C and it was hard to resist falling asleep in such heat. Grandmother used to put her bamboo rocking chair by the doorway and sit in it in an attempt to stop me going out. Sometimes I picked up the big rush-leaf fan and sat on a little stool at her feet and fanned her, pretending that I wasn't interested in going out at all. When she had fallen asleep I would cover her face with the fan and then step over her and run down to the river, like a fish in desperate need of water, to join the other boys.

I taught myself to do the 'doggy paddle'. Then an older boy taught me how to float, which I found extremely pleasurable. One day, before I knew it, I had floated a couple of miles downstream. I even went beyond the old dragon cave where the water got rough and flowed much faster and where, I found out later, many people had drowned. I remained unperturbed, however, and continued to float freely with my eyes closed. I didn't realise that I was in any danger, so I felt no fear. Luckily for me a fisherman spotted me right in the middle of the river, although he mistook me for a dead body at first. He pulled me into his boat and took me to the shore and then sent me home. When Grandmother heard the fisherman's description of what had happened, it set her shaking violently and she cried: 'You! My little descendant. I don't know what we would do if anything happened to you. You really want me to pay with my old life.'

After that I was locked in a room. The maid brought me food, but I refused to eat it. I also refused to come out for the next three days. I used the room as a toilet and the smell was unbearable to me, but I still didn't give up. Eventually Grandmother, with the rest of the family at her heels, came to talk to me and promised that she would never lock me in again. So once more I got my way.

After that incident I became untouchable, in that no one in the household dared to try and control me. There was, however, one person in the family of whom all the children, including me, were afraid and that was my Second Uncle. At that time Second Uncle was the chief of police, which made him the second most powerful person in the county, and most people were fearful of him. Second Uncle came home once a year for the Spring Festival, which is the Chinese New Year.

It was true that I admired him in his uniform as the chief of police, which included two handguns, one on each side. However, when the time came for each one of us to report to him about our behaviour for the whole of the preceding year, I would be the one to suffer most. My stubbornness prevented me from admitting any wrongdoing, let alone apologising for it. Second Uncle would eventually tire of beating me with the bamboo stick and would then shout, in fact almost snarl, at me to get out of his sight. Then Grandmother would always come to save me from the long bench, where I would have to sit to ponder my sins. I could see that her heart ached at seeing me in pain from the beating, but at the same time she blamed me for being too hard headed to apologise. Later on, whenever Second Uncle was at home, I made sure to put lots of rice paper inside my trousers to protect my bottom against my 'long bench beating'.

One afternoon, soon after my seventh birthday, I was down by the riverbank as usual when I saw a boy from the neighbourhood running full tilt toward me. He excitedly told me that there was a soldier from the County Defence Force in our house. In this quiet little town a soldier's visit was big news and it indicated an important event or even a calamity. I almost flew in my hurry to get home to find out what had happened. When I got there I had to squeeze through the gathered crowd to enter the hallway. Once Grandmother saw me, a grateful smile lit her face, but her eyes were also brimming with tears. She grabbed me in her arms then turned me around to face the soldier, who was smiling at me.

'You must be Xianli then!' he said. He gave me his hand and continued: 'Your father has sent me to take you to him.'

I just stared at him, trying to take it all in and understand what he was talking about. Then Grandmother said through her tears: 'Your father is the regimental commander of the County Force now. He wants you to go to school in the city.'

It was very hard for me to accept this sudden news.

After all the loss of status, power and fortune that the family had suffered, and the pain that the death of my grandfather had caused her, I recognised that pride had returned to Grandmother's eyes.

Then it all happened so quickly. Grandmother packed my bag whilst the soldier kept telling her that there was no need for me to take many things. Grandmother urged me to be a good boy for my father, told me to study hard and wished me a prosperous future which would make her and our ancestors proud. The family, other relatives and all the neighbours came to see me off. Suddenly I had become the focus of attention in the town, and the crowd that had gathered in front of the house kept swelling in number. Everyone was wishing me good luck and a safe journey. A lot of my playmates showed envy in their eyes.

I didn't feel sad to be leaving because I was so excited and already looking forward to something new. I was very nervous about meeting my father though, because I didn't remember him and had no idea what he might be like. I was also a little worried as to what he might think of me because, under the care of my grandmother and my other relatives, I knew that I had become a spoiled, mischievous little boy.

As I journeyed I practised, in my heart, saying the word *Baba* (Dad), a word that I had never used before. I also wondered whether he would smile when he heard me say it.

Reunited with Father

The County Defence Force was stationed in an old temple on the western side of Yunyang Town. I passed through the ancient temple gateway into a huge paved square. I was told to cross this and go up some stairs to the first worship hall. I paused at the bottom of the steps for a moment with my head down and, for the first time since leaving Grandmother, wondered whether I should have refused to leave my home. With a sigh I planted my foot on the first step and looked up. I caught my breath at the sight of a figure standing at the top of the stairs. He was blocking the rays of light streaming through the huge window on the other side of the hall, but for a moment it looked as if he was the source of the light. Then I made out his smart, grey uniform. He had a leather belt across his chest attached to a holster at his waist containing a handgun. He looked magnificent. The soldier nodded his head and then I knew that this was the man I had come to meet. It was my father! This first image of him is one I can never forget. It is like a portrait hanging in my mind.

I leapt up the stairs, shouting uncontrollably: 'Baba, Baba!' His smile turned into a wide grin as I hurled myself at his legs.

He seized me in his arms and only said: 'Did you miss me?'

From that day I started to learn all about my father. Grandmother and my aunts had tried to describe him to me, but they had only known him before he became a soldier and I saw someone completely different. Many incidents occurred which could describe his character. The first one I remember vividly happened not long after I got there.

One day there was a sudden mixture of loud sounds just outside the temple gates. There was beating of drums and gongs, fireworks were going off and people were marching. I ran out to see what the commotion was about and I saw a procession headed by two men carrying large yellow flags. There were four wooden palanquins, each being carried by four stocky men. The first was a sedan chair completely enclosed by red curtains. On the second one there was a dead pig lying on its back and red ribbons had been tied around each foot. The third one was piled high with silk and other textiles. On the last one were many boxes of various sizes and red envelopes. I guessed that the red envelopes contained silver coins. When the beating of the drums and gongs stopped one of the curtains on the sedan chair was swept aside and a man stepped out. He was wearing a long, black silk gown and a red skull cap. The top of his walking stick was carved into a dragon's head. He had a long moustache and gold-rimmed spectacles were perched on the end of his nose. From his dress and demeanour he certainly looked important. In fact he was the former regimental commander and my father had taken over his position. He addressed the guard:

'Please tell Commander Lin that Commander Xue has come to congratulate him on his new position.'

When Father heard this he sneered and told the guard to ask Commander Xue to wait at the gate. Then he ordered six soldiers to fetch wooden poles and to accompany him outside. Without a word they pushed Commander Xue to the ground and started to beat him. Commander Xue screamed for help, but nobody from the gathered crowd stepped forward to help him or object to his treatment. In fact within the hour the crowd had doubled in size and some people had set off fireworks to celebrate Father's action. These people praised Father and said:

'This will put a stop to that devil Commander Xue, who won't dare to carry on imprisoning innocent people, stealing our land, raping our women, murdering the witnesses and selling opium.'

On the other hand, the high-powered officials and the rich said: 'Such an unreasonable man, this Lin. If he doesn't like Commander Xue then he should leave. How dare he beat up the person who came to congratulate him and to bring him so many gifts.'

Father heard both sides of what was being said and didn't try to defend himself but said to the crowd:

'When I first came here I received a delegation of local people who presented me with a signed petition of complaint about Commander Xue. It listed many criminal acts carried out under his orders, including the murder of six innocent people. I wanted to make an example of him to warn other tyrants that such behaviour won't be tolerated and they won't be able to get away with it in future. I also wanted to send a message to the people to reassure them that not all officials are corrupt and ruled by money. This was only a small lesson for Commander Xue. It is nothing in comparison to what he did to others: the people without any power or influence.'

The other incident which set Father apart from others was when a band of brigands under the leadership of 'Iron Feet Bear' reached the outskirts of Yunyang. They had been murdering and looting around the borders of Sichuan, Hubei and Hunan Provinces for some time and were a formidable force numbering about a thousand. The citizens of Yunyang were panicked because they knew that there were little more than a hundred soldiers in Father's regiment and felt that they were no match for the brigands. Father called an emergency meeting with the city officials with some suggestions for them. It was decided that the Chamber of Commerce would procure ten pigs, one hundred kilos of rice, five hundred kilos of salt, chicken and duck eggs and two thousand silver coins. All this would be offered to Iron Feet Bear by a delegation in return for leaving the town untouched. At the same time Father would stage a military practice, including the firing of guns and cannons, from the highest point in the town. When Iron Feet Bear saw so much food and money presented to him, as well as hearing what appeared to be a strong military presence in the background, he left the town in peace and moved on to Hunan Province.

Father's reputation spread and he earned much respect from the population of Yunyang. Even many of the town officials began to see him in a different light. Still, though, Father lived in such tumultuous times and there were many things he wasn't able to control.

The worship hall of the temple was used as the conference hall for the regiment. Off to one side of the hall were the main offices and two further rooms were used as the living quarters for Father and his batman. Down two sides of the square were the living quarters for the rest of the soldiers. When I came to live with Father I shared a room with his batman, who was the soldier who had come to fetch me from Grandmother's house in Yunan. His family name was Wang and I wanted to call him 'Brother Wang' out of politeness and respect as he was a lot older than me. However, he said that this wasn't appropriate because I was the regimental commander's son and he was only a butcher's son. He told me that it was his duty to serve his commander and now me, 'the young master', and that he couldn't be my brother because we were in different classes. Almost all the soldiers called me 'Little Master' or 'Young Master' and I believed I deserved their respect seeing as I was in a different category to them. My ego was fed well!

One day Uncle Chen Yuping came to visit while Father was out. Uncle Chen Yuping was Father's best friend and was one of the two young men whom Father had met on the pagoda hill in Yunan. He and Father had left Yunan together and made their way to Wanxian County (now Wanzhou District) in search of a new life. In fact they both ended up joining the military force of the powerful warlord, Yang Sen, who had his base there. They also trained at Yang Sen's military academy and were greatly influenced by two of the lecturers there: Zhu De and Chen Yi. Zhu De and Chen Yi belonged to the Communist Party and were already famous for being talented military strategists.

While waiting for Father to return, Uncle Chen Yuping asked me to make him some tea. I immediately called the batman to make it. A little later Uncle Chen Yuping asked me to go and buy him some cigarettes, but I became angry and said: 'No! I am the young master. I do not do such things. You can call the batman to do it for you.'

Father was told about my behaviour when he returned and he was furious. He later told me off, saying that I was spoiled and arrogant and how he was deeply ashamed of me and my attitudes. I was very scared as it was the first time that Father had been so angry with me. I learned my lesson and realised that respect had to be earned and was not my right.

I started at the primary school, which was located in the eastern part of the town, and, seeing as the regiment's base was in the west, I had a very long walk to get there. Father was worried that I would get lost and sent his batman to accompany me there and back each day. At first I was glad of this as life in Yunyang was more complex than it had been in Yunan. The roads were wider and more numerous and busy with carts, rickshaws, barrows and bicycles. There were market and food stalls everywhere you looked and there were more people than I thought was possible. Everything was confusing to me, but gradually I got to know my way around and my father's batman was able to return to his normal duties. However, whilst walking through the town on my own I was distracted by anything and everything and I was often late for school. I would be punished for this by having to stand up throughout the lessons and having to clean the classroom at the end of the day. Because of this Father insisted that I should leave earlier in the mornings, but this meant that I wasn't given much for breakfast by the regimental cook, who didn't like having his routine interrupted. He always put too much oil in the rice he gave me and I had diarrhoea over and over again. I became very thin.

Seventh Aunt, who had married into the Tang family in Yunyang, was worried about me and bluntly said to Father:

'I want to talk to you about your son. Since he was born you have never taken care of him and it is obvious that you still don't have a clue about how to look after him. Is there a single part of you that looks like a father? Just look at him – he's skinnier than a chicken foot! Listen, even if you don't care about him, I do. This child is never going to thrive living with you. Tomorrow he's moving to my home and I will give him the family he needs.'

I know that in his heart of hearts my father loved me, but

Seventh Aunt was correct: he didn't know how to take care of a child and anyway he was also too busy. He gratefully accepted his sister's offer to take me in.

Seventh Aunt was married to the youngest son from the richest Tang family in the region and his name was Xingpu. The Tang family owned more than ten salt wells and a hundred of the better salt pools. Xingpu had four older brothers who were all either landowners or salt merchants, but he was intellectual and had graduated from the Politics and Law Academy in Chengdu. He then became the Minister of Finance in Yunyang. He had a portly figure and was given the nickname of Luohan, meaning 'Laughing Buddha', by the local people. The name only fitted his outward appearance however, because behind closed doors he was an entirely different character.

Seventh Aunt treated me like her own child and she also asked her children to be kind to me because I never had a mother to take care of me. She was a very proud person and didn't want anyone, especially anyone in the Tang family, to say that I was living free under the Tang family roof. At the beginning of each month she would give me five or ten yuan in private and tell me to give it back to her at the dinner table saying that my father had given it to me to cover the cost of my food.

I remember my first summer there when my aunt gave me two yuan and told me to give it back to her in front of her husband. She told me to say to her that my grandmother had sent it so that I could have a white linen vest to wear during the summer months just like my cousins. The next day she put a brand new vest on me which she had already prepared for me. Seventh Aunt often said to me that if I wanted to be successful in life, then it was something that only I could make happen for myself. She hoped that I would study hard for a prosperous future and then the Tang family would never be able to look down on me or make her lose face. Her words sank deep into me and 'be ambitious' became my motto in life.

It was noticeable that once I moved to Seventh Aunt's home I wasn't late for or absent from school any more. I behaved well and worked very hard in the classroom and did all the homework diligently. Consequently the teacher often praised me and I made rapid progress in everything. One term, the teacher displayed at least ten pieces of my writing on the noticeboard as examples of excellence.

I finished my six-year school course within four years despite the fact that during this time my father lost his position as regimental commander in the County Force. I remained in the Tang household, but Seventh Aunt was often blamed for bringing me into their family and we both felt the disgrace of the loss of my father's prestigious career. Whilst I had done so well at school, my four cousins who were at school with me were still either in the fourth year or even in the first year. Teachers and relatives praised my success and Seventh Uncle gave me five yuan as a reward, which made Seventh Aunt very proud. She pulled me aside and said:

'Aunty believed in you and was right about you. Even though your father has lost his official position the boy from our Lin family is unbeaten. Your father and the rest of us will be able to depend on you in the future. You will be a credit to our Lin family. Remember – one only has oneself to rely on in life.'

Unfortunately, the better I did in school the more jealous my cousins became. One day Third Cousin tripped me up as I was walking past him and hissed at me: 'See you, you smug creep! You've got nothing to be proud of – your father is no longer a commander. If it wasn't for our Tang family giving you a bowl of rice every day you would be a starving beggar on the street and you couldn't even dream of going to school.'

To my discredit I retaliated immediately. I jumped up from the ground and punched him in the face and made his nose bleed. Once I had hold of him I wouldn't let go and pushed him to the ground and rained punches on him. He was smaller than me and no match. He screamed for help and begged me to stop. I certainly brought trouble on myself and was particularly sorry for Aunty's sake as it put her in a difficult position once more. She was very upset with me and I was forced to apologise to him, but in my heart I was convinced that I was justified and swore that I would get back at him.

Soon after that fight, the house that Seventh Uncle was having built was nearing completion. The new house was on the way to the park and by the main road. With its four floors it was the tallest, largest and most majestic red-brick building in the town. Even though the decoration wasn't finished and there was still lots of rubbish to be cleared away from many of the rooms, everyone was eager to move in. I don't know why, but Seventh Aunt put me in the same bedroom on the third floor with my third cousin: the boy I wanted to pay back. We were still not talking to each other and our beds were as far away from each other as possible in opposite corners of the room. One night my cousin fell asleep whilst reading and when he turned over he knocked over the burning candle by his bedside. I stared at the flame as it danced on the floor and an evil idea came to me. I crept out of bed and over to a corner of the room where a lot of wood shavings had been swept and picked up a handful. I then very carefully dropped them over the candle flame. I convinced myself that I needed to go to the latrine and went downstairs. When I returned to the bedroom I found it filled with thick, suffocating smoke. I started to choke immediately and felt sickened that I had gone too far. I was panic stricken. I dragged my cousin out of the room and down the stairs shouting to everybody that the house was on fire.

Luckily the blaze was put out in time and, apart from a large blackened hole in the wooden floor, nothing else was damaged. When people came to clean and repair the site they found remnants of candle wax and then Seventh Uncle asked me what had happened. I calmly told him that when I left the room the candle was lit and by my cousin's bedside, but when I came back I discovered the fire. Then Seventh Uncle went to question Third Cousin who could only cry and say nothing more than: 'I don't know. I fell asleep. I don't know what happened.'

Everyone came to the conclusion that my cousin had been careless not to blow out his candle in good time and he was severely told off. Only I knew the truth. I also knew that if I never said a word, even if Third Cousin jumped into the Yellow and Yangtze Rivers, he could never clean his reputation. Whereas I, from being an arsonist, had become the discoverer of the fire and had rescued the family from disaster. At the time I was pleased with this outcome, but, as you might conclude from this confession of mine, my conscience has not been clear!

A large party was held for Seventh Uncle's fortieth birthday. Not only family and friends were invited, but it was also an opportunity to impress the businessmen and officials of Yunyang. Equally it was an opportunity for people to curry favour with Seventh Uncle by showering him with lavish gifts. On the first day of the party over seventy banquet tables groaned under the weight of food on them. Over the next two days, thirty tables were laid out. Afterwards we heard the housekeeper say that, apart from the value of the presents, the total cash received came to over a thousand yuan. It was an enormous sum in those days and enough to buy over ten thousand kilos of rice or one thousand grams of gold.

Father and Seventh Uncle had never liked each other, but as in-laws they were considered to be close relatives. Whenever Father visited he made himself at home, even to the point of asking the servants for whatever he needed. It was obvious that Seventh Uncle didn't like this, but he had always managed to stay quiet about it. You could see their mutual dislike always simmering just below the surface. At the party Father was disgusted by the ostentation, the mountains of presents and by every guest trying to ingratiate themselves with Seventh Uncle. He sent me to fetch a large piece of red paper, a brush and some ink from the housekeeper and then he wrote down a ragged verse:

For brother-in-law Luohan Tang's fortieth birthday

Yunyang town, town Yunyang
Contains many strange things
West side has a Buddha's temple
East side has Luohan's temple
Buddha's temple remains hushed
Luohan's temple always bright
Buddha's temple asks for future life
Luohan's temple asks for present life and presents.

From brother-in-law Zhuxi

Father then hung the verse in the entrance hall for all to see. When Seventh Uncle saw it he was with the governor and couldn't say anything to Father, but his anger was evident. The governor laughed at it and told Father that it was: 'Interesting, very interesting!'

Soon after this party, rumours that Seventh Uncle was having an affair started going around. Many people refused to believe it as they only saw his public persona and he had been heard to say on many occasions: 'For public figures and educated people immorality is the worst of all vices. One should never indulge in activities damaging to one's own self or to others.'

Seventh Aunt was seen as a typical example of a genial, able and virtuous wife and mother as well as a dutiful daughter-in-law to the Tang family. All in all they were seen as having a perfect marriage. The rumours, however, were soon proved to be true.

Then Seventh Aunt fell gravely ill and couldn't even get out of bed. Although the best doctors were called, the family was told that nothing could be done for her. She soon died. She was only thirty-five years old. I was devastated by her death. She had been as close to me as any mother could have been. I often think about her kindness and the care and love she gave me. A few years later I came to know that my aunt's death was due to her husband's ill treatment of her. He had never wanted to marry her, but instead of opposing or refusing the arranged marriage, he obeyed his family's wishes. He then vented his anger on her. She was never allowed to turn her back on him and had to leave his presence by walking backwards. We could all see this of course, but behind the bedroom door he did his worst. He regularly beat and abused her and forbade her from ever crying out. The abuse got worse after he took a mistress. When Seventh Aunt had a miscarriage, he raped her and she became infected. Seventh Uncle wouldn't allow a doctor to be called until it was too late for any effective treatment.

Father hated his brother-in-law even more after his sister's death, but he couldn't walk out on the family tie because of the four children who were left without a mother. For the time being, I was also still living there. He was worried that my cousins would end up with an unsuitable stepmother, such as the mistress, so he took it upon himself to find an educated and kind woman as a second wife for Seventh Uncle. With the help of Grandmother and Eighth Aunt, Father decided on Eighth Aunt's youngest sister-in-law in the Zhang family from Yunan. The Zhang family and Seventh Uncle agreed and soon an engagement banquet sealed the matter. They just had to wait for the one-year mourning period for Seventh Aunt to be over before they could hold the wedding.

Matters, however, did not turn out as Father hoped. Seventh Uncle not only continued with his affair, but he brought his mistress to the house and hid her in the attic. Every night he would wait until everybody was in bed and then he would creep up to the top floor to visit her. The Tang children had always been lively and happy whilst their mother was alive, but now the house seemed shrouded in misery and insecurity and it was made worse with the appearance of this mysterious woman.

One day I bumped into the maid who had been engaged just to look after the mistress. She was carrying a bowl of rice and was in a great hurry and somewhat flustered. She said to me: 'Young master, can you help me and take this rice to the attic – I need to go back to the kitchen to fetch the soup. She's waiting. Knock on the hatch three times.'

I didn't need to be asked twice as my curiosity about the mistress was overflowing. I dashed up the stairs and knocked three times. The wooden hatch was lifted and I climbed into the attic in an instant. When the woman saw me instead of the maid she shouted in panic as she knew that nobody was meant to see her. With a couple of glances to the left and right I took in the state of the room. It was dirty and untidy. The bed was unmade and an ashtray was overflowing with cigarette ends, one of which still had smoke curling up from it. Then I looked at the woman and got a shock as she was truly frightful. She was unwashed and her hair looked like a bird's nest. Her skin was pallid and her eyes looked like two black holes. She was

36

extremely thin and she tried to grab me with her skinny arms, but I managed to evade her clutches. In the struggle the bowl of rice was kicked down the stairs and smashed. I ran down after it screaming. Seventh Uncle was furious that I had seen his mistress and the unfortunate maid was severely beaten for asking me to go up there.

I reported to Father what I had seen and he poured his anger into a hurriedly written verse, which I had to deliver to Seventh Uncle:

Miss String Bean

Rouge on face layer after layer
Rings on fingers one after another
In the house exercises maid over and over
Upstairs smokes opium with pleasure
Unwashed features like dirty monkey
Body of beastly witch
Or perhaps ghost from hell
But still flirting with human male
Let's ask who is she – this
Miss String Bean
The 'Mrs' Luohan?

Father also wrote a letter:

Brother Luohan,

You have gone too far. We found you a good maiden whom you have now rejected. What an insult to her and her family. Instead you hide an opium fiend in your house. You must have lost your mind – how can you carry on being so foolish? You will be scorned by the whole town and it is bound to end badly for you.

Your brother-in-law, Zhuxi

As Seventh Uncle read the letter and verse I witnessed his complexion change from red to white and he started to shake. He tore the letter into shreds and threw the pieces into the air.

'Your old man is a lunatic – he's the one who's lost his mind. When he was regimental commander I didn't benefit or make any kind of profit from his position. He doesn't know where the earth ends and the sky begins. All he ever does is offend people and I've even been his scapegoat on many occasions. Now that he's lost his position I still give him anything he wants – money and food. Aren't I still giving you a home – his son who had no mother to care for him? Haven't I done enough for him yet? Still he taunts me. Let me tell you something – don't learn from your father otherwise you'll end up a lunatic just like him. All you'll learn is that endless suffering is awaiting you.'

A few days later Father visited and, as soon as Seventh Uncle caught sight of him, his anger flared up afresh and he started shouting for all the household to hear:

'What have you come here for this time, you ungrateful creature? This is none of your business. You have no right to criticise me. If you're not careful you'll ruin me and then see where that leaves you and your son. Aren't I already providing you with enough? Mind your own business. Look what a mess you've made of your own life – fix that instead of interfering with mine.'

Father managed to remain calm: 'It was only one letter. If you think you're justified in what you're doing then call your mistress down here now so that I can meet her. Perhaps she's a suitable woman to be the mother of your children after all. Prove me wrong. If not I can always ask her to light an opium pipe for you.'

Seventh Uncle could have had Father and me thrown out of his house there and then, but he knew that he had to be careful of Father. Although all women held a lower status than men, a woman from the middle or upper classes, like my aunt, always kept the status of the family they were born into. Therefore her relatives could take the husband to court if they thought she had been mistreated or murdered and the court would take the case seriously. No doubt Father felt guilty that he hadn't protected his sister from her cruel husband, but he hadn't realised the full extent of her abuse until it was too late. Now he felt it was his duty to at least try and protect her children.

The outcome of all this, however, fell very short of what Father was hoping for. Seventh Uncle fell ill and stayed in bed for a month. After that he seemed to give up caring about his reputation and let his 'Miss String Bean' move downstairs and they lived openly in the house together. Of course the wedding with the girl from the Zhang family was never mentioned again.

Father had been suspended from his position of regimental commander of the County Force primarily because the rich and powerful of Yunyang were frightened of him. Father had always been open in his desire to stamp out corruption and he was seen as a threat and troublemaker by many. He was certainly 'leftist' in his views, but to try and put a stop to him he was accused of being a Communist.

Pending investigation, he was given temporary accommodation at the Yunyang Bureau of Industry living quarters. The Bureau was situated on the edge of a small square at the highest point of the town. On the other side of the square was the King Temple. There was a small garden attached to the quarters which was surrounded by trees and overlooked the Yangtze River. I would go and visit him there as often as I could after school.

One summer's evening we were sitting in the peaceful garden enjoying a cool breeze and watching how the sunset patterned the sky with pink. Father seemed to be in a particularly happy mood and had bought some sweets for me. He kept smiling at me and then said: 'How time flies. You are already ten years old.' Then he quickly grew sad: 'You came into this world just as your mother was leaving it. Some things just don't make any sense.'

I reached for his hand and felt it trembling: 'Baba, please don't be sad. Just wait until I grow up: I'll take care of you then – and Grandmother too. I will carry out all my filial duties – you'll see. I want to be just like you. The way you served Grandfather is the way I will serve you.'

Father sipped his tea and stared at the darkening sky.

'Actually, I don't want just a dutiful son, I want a comrade – a loyal comrade. Life is already so different. Before, there seemed to be no choice other than to stay within the family and fulfil all the traditional filial duties. Anyway, my father worked hard his whole life to earn what we had and I wanted to look after him. For you, though, the future will be different.'

'Baba, if you wanted to look after Grandfather, why didn't you want to stay to look after Grandmother and' – I hardly dared to say it – 'me? Didn't you want me?' This question had been in my heart for a long time. So many times other children had told me that I may as well have been an orphan seeing as my mother was dead and my father had abandoned me.

'How could I not want you? You are my son, my only son. I left you because it was the only thing I could have done at the time. I knew your grandmother would look after you well and there were still dutiful people in the household to look after your grandmother. Perhaps I should have stayed, but I needed to work out my own future. I certainly didn't want to end up like my two older brothers. I couldn't see a useful life for myself in Yunan – I couldn't see any opportunities there at all. I sent for you as soon as I thought I was able to support you. Now I want to teach you about my ambitions and goals so that, together, we can march down the same path as revolutionary comrades.'

At school the teachers often talked about the national tragedy caused by invasions from foreigners and about the country's crisis from internal warfare. Much mention was made about national heroes who had left their little homes to save the big home: China, our country. However, I had never heard them mention the word 'comrade' and Father could see my confusion.

'Being a comrade is to have a common goal. Being a loyal comrade is to follow the common goal from the first fight to the end. Being a comrade is a higher goal than fulfilling filial duty because filial duty is only directed towards the family, but a comrade devotes himself to his country.'

Father then pulled two books out from behind his chair and solemnly said:

'You are ten years old now and capable of understanding a lot of things about life. I want to pass on to you these two books. They have been my constant companions since I was at the military academy and now I want you to have them. Read them earnestly. You might not understand them now, but you will do in the future and, when you understand, I'm sure you'll want to follow their teachings. With understanding you will come to realise that knowledge is more precious than gold.'

The books were Sun Yat-sen's *Completions* and a one-volume edition of *New Youth* magazine. Being at the military academy had been a turning point in Father's life and made him into a committed revolutionary and a Sun Yat-sen loyalist. I followed Father's advice and read the books many times. I also made notes in the margins in addition to all of Father's. I kept them with me until Father and I left Yunyang and Yunan for good in 1935. Before I left I hid the books, along with other treasures from my childhood, in the attic of Grandmother's house.

The accusations against Father could not be proven or fabricated any further, but he was never reinstated as regimental commander. He fully expected another appointment to be given to him in due course seeing as he was still receiving a salary with accommodation. However, he had to wait more than two years before being given another job.

Grandmother wanted us to go back home for the Spring Festival. Father was only biding his time with nothing in particular to do, so we gladly went back to Yunan to spend the New Year holiday. On the day Father and I arrived home, the families of Big Uncle, Second Uncle and Eighth Aunt were all gathered there to greet us. At dinner all my Father's favourite dishes appeared on the table. Second Uncle's wife had cooked everything herself. In the centre of the table was a large fish which my first cousin had caught. He had spent half the day standing at the edge of the near-frozen river to get it. Grandmother said that this was the first time that all the family had sat around the table together since my father had left home. It was an extremely joyful occasion.

Finally the county governor sent a message to Father calling him back to Yunyang to start a new job. He had been appointed as the deputy head of the National Civilisation Association, which was later renamed as the Citizens' Education Centre. This new department had been set up as a result of Chiang Kai-shek launching the New Life Movement throughout the whole country. This was based on the four Confucian principles of *Li* (propriety), *Yi* (right conduct), *Lian* (honesty) and *Qi* (integrity and honour) in order to regenerate moral and traditional values within the population.

News of the New Life Movement was on the front page of all the newspapers with headlines such as: 'Hit out at Gambling', 'Bring Down the Opium Trade', 'Clean Up the City', 'Be Healthy', 'Be Prompt' and 'Avoid Wine and Women of Ill Repute'. Posters were also put up everywhere with the same messages on them. The movement was designed to touch every aspect of daily life.

The Yunyang officials felt that the New Life Movement was just a passing wind and therefore setting up a new department to implement it wasn't given much importance. Also, because of its very nature, none of them felt that there was any profit in it for themselves and that's why Father was nominated for the job. Of course, it was right up his street, encompassing all his personal values, so he took it very seriously indeed. However, he found that he would be the 'deputy head' of an empty shell. He had no power, no money and no staff. So he went to the governor with two conditions before accepting the job. Firstly, he wanted the governor to arrange a meeting with all the bureaus, major local businesses and the headmasters of all the schools and the academy to garner their support for the movement. Secondly, he insisted that there should be no interference with his work. The governor readily agreed to Father's conditions because initially he had thought that Father wouldn't accept this lowly job after having been a high-powered commander.

Father began his job by talking to the principal of my school. A couple of days later a group of us pupils were jogging on the street and singing anti-Japanese and 'save the nation' songs. We were soon joined by groups from other schools. Basketball teams were created from amongst students, teachers and the general public alike and games arranged every Sunday in the square in front of the Confucius Temple. These proved to be very popular with everybody. There was an abandoned tennis court which we cleaned up and a tennis club was formed which ran every afternoon. This quickly became my favourite sport and I was soon chosen for the team. All this must have seemed easy to Father when taking into account what he achieved next.

He then turned his attention to Yunyang's main street. It was a road over two miles long intersecting the town from west to east and it was paved with flagstones. It served as the main market for the town and there were stalls along its whole length. There were piles of rubbish everywhere you looked left to mount up. People spat just anywhere and dirty water was thrown into the middle of the road. Swarms of flies hovered over the decomposing food waste and rats competed with people for space on the permanently muddy ground. Father led some primary school pupils and their teachers in putting up slogans reading: 'Don't Spit', 'Be Neat', 'Kill Flies and Rats – They Spread Disease'. Then they started sweeping the road and removing the rubbish. A lot of people willingly joined in with the clean-up. Father went to the town chamber of commerce and persuaded them to fund the production of more than a hundred spittoons for the market. They were sprinkled inside with lime and placed at intervals along the street. He also employed some cleaners to empty the spittoons every ten days.

Once the market was clean, Father then turned his attention to other parts of the town. One Sunday he led a group of students in sweeping the streets leading up to the Yamen (town hall). It was midsummer so hot and dry and, as they swept in wide arcs with their long bamboo brooms, much of the dust became airborne. Some of us followed carrying buckets of water, which we sprinkled around in an effort to dampen the dust down. We were all bare backed. As we reached the gates to the Yamen we encountered the governor coming out with his two wives. Father blocked their way, determined to speak with him. The two wives, with their over-painted faces, held handkerchiefs over their noses and looked disgusted by the scene in front of them. The governor looked embarrassed and he said awkwardly: 'Good job! Well done Commander Lin.'

Father replied with a derisive laugh: 'As you know, I am no longer a commander, but I won't let myself go to wrack and ruin. I am making myself useful and doing some of the smaller things which nobody else wants to do.'

'Your efforts are obvious for all to see. You have changed the look of the whole town. I am going to encourage all the officials to learn from your example.'

'Well, perhaps you can also encourage them to give some practical help – and whilst we're talking, perhaps your own department would like to help too...'

The governor and his wives were desperate to leave, so he cut Father short and as he moved on kept saying over and over: 'Of course, of course! Yes! Of course we all support you.'

At least the governor subsequently arranged with the Finance Department to fund the manufacture of many dustbins and the employment of five more street cleaners. In addition, each Saturday afternoon, all the many different government departments had to organise their own neighbourhood clean-up as part of their duties. Truly the town environment changed for the better – the people even seemed happier and more polite to one another.

Father's final major task in this job was to attempt to stamp out the widespread use of opium. Indeed, many members of our own family were addicted to opium: Big Uncle, his wife and only son, Second Uncle and his mistress, Seventh Aunt's husband and his mistress and also Eighth Aunt's husband.

There was a woman known as Zhang Five who had become

a powerful figure in Yunyang's underworld of vice. She was the fifth child from a very prosperous family which eventually fell on hard times. Zhang Five was very beautiful and had no option but to become a rich man's mistress. Later on she opened a 'teahouse', which in fact was a front for a brothel and a gambling and opium den. Zhang Five was clever and devious and her business became very successful. She never priced what was on offer in her teahouse, but suggested that her clients paid what they felt the services were worth. Every pleasure in the house was available to all the clients, even if they left without spending any money. However, if somebody didn't pay up, then she would make sure they paid tenfold later on in one way or another. She was adept in the art of blackmail and her thugs could be employed by anyone to sort out personal vendettas. There were many people who became entangled in her web and they were very afraid of her, but there were an equal number of people who benefited from her and gave her their backing. Father could not believe how much vice and crime emanated from her teahouse, nor how there wasn't anyone in Yunyang who dared to challenge her.

Father went to the governor with a demand that Zhang Five's 'teahouse' be closed down under the rules of the New Life Movement. The governor just shook his head and smiled.

'My brother,' he said, 'I understand how you feel. I also agree with you in principle. From my heart, I admire your righteousness and resolute spirit. This is indeed what General Chiang Kai-shek would want us to do, but brother, these things are easy to say but not easy to do. We could try to arrest her, but you know as well as I do that she doesn't act on her own. There is a string of powerful men behind her, let alone all the bullies who have a foothold there. For example your brother-in-law, Luohan Tang, is her honoured guest – although he shows his smiling face to the world, his belly is full of sinful liquid. My brother, as officials we can only try to keep the peace and that is good enough. Don't think that you can change everything. If I manage to keep my own position for a couple more years, then I will be lucky. Look at you, you have done so many good things but still they ousted you from your seat – why? Because you are a person with integrity, but you do things on impulse without caring about the consequences further down the line. You don't know who you are dealing with. Learn from your mistakes and shut your eyes this time – let this go.'

The governor sounded sincere, but Father left dissatisfied and immediately went to see Second Uncle who was still the chief of police. When Second Uncle heard that Father wanted him to arrest Zhang Five he laughed with derision and bitterness:

'My little brother, you are really trying to make life difficult for me, aren't you? You know I smoke opium and I sometimes go to her house. How do you think, even in *your* fevered imagination, that I could possibly arrest her? I am not a clean man like you – I would be in her clutches in an instant. They don't call her "Bitch-Tigress" and "Poison Witch" for nothing, you know. Those who oppose her always come to a bad end. Even though Yunyang is a small place, the waters here run deeper than you know. This is something you can't control – turn your head – look the other way. In fact, I don't think that you have a suitable character to stay here – why don't you find another town which needs your talents?'

Father was incensed and once more wished he had the power he used to have in his former job as Regiment Commander. However, there is a saying, 'Use simple methods to treat complicated matters', and Father came up with a plan. One Sunday, he led a couple of teachers and thirty students on a march in the street. They carried banners and shouted out the slogan 'Support General Chiang Kai-shek's New Life Movement'.

When the group reached Zhang Five's establishment they quickly ran inside, causing a commotion and shouting loudly: 'Catch them all – don't let anyone get away.'

In fact they made no attempt to capture anyone, but the customers were terrified and fled the premises like headless chickens. Within minutes the whole place was empty except for the frightened serving girls. Zhang Five appeared in a panic, wondering what had caused her customers to flee, but when she saw only students she relaxed and ordered them: 'Get out! How dare you come into my house? Who told you to come here?'

Father stepped in front of the group and said: 'It was me.'

Zhang Five quickly masked her face with a sweet smile:

'Oh! It's Commander Lin, isn't it? Welcome! How come you don't know me? Your brother-in-law Tang is my noble guest! If I have offended you somehow, then I would like to ask for your forgiveness now in person.'

She approached Father and whispered: 'And for your brother's sake, don't do this to me.'

Then she turned to the girls who were cowering behind her: 'Come girls, come on! Get ready to entertain and serve our most precious guest.'

Father was disgusted and barked at her in military-style: 'Stop your dirty practice. You clearly understand that everything you do here is wrong and I am here to put a stop to it. Pick up your opium equipment and the gambling kits and you and your girls come with me now.'

With the help of the teachers, students and the growing crowd, Father marched them to the Yamen and called the governor: 'Here are the criminal, the witnesses and the evidence. Put Zhang Five in prison.'

The governor had no choice and had her put in prison. Both

Zhang Five and Father were waiting for her rich and power-ful backers to come forward to save her. A month went by and nobody showed up. It seemed that all her protectors had melted away. Nobody even stepped forward to take care of her whilst she was in prison and she soon died there.

After that Father acquired the nickname 'Lunatic Lin'.

Once again, Father was only appreciated by the ordinary people. The rich and powerful were more nervous of him than ever. Once again he found himself being accused of being a Communist. In those days the accusation of being a Communist was called 'giving someone a red hat' and so Father found himself with his second 'red hat'. After that he needed to be careful not to stir up more trouble for himself, so he opted for the quiet life to let things settle down. It was understood that he wouldn't continue with the New Life Movement job, but rather than him being sacked it just fizzled out. However, he was still provided with accommodation and enough money for necessities, so he spent his days reading and meeting with friends, both old and new. It was a time for debate and new ideas.

A Special Prisoner

By midwinter of 1933 the Nationalists and Communists had broken their treaty and were back to fighting each other again.

One day Father was summoned to Governor Li's office for an emergency meeting. Governor Li was pacing up and down. He immediately confided in Father about how worried he was as to how he could best protect Yunyang Town, because he had been informed that the Communist Red Army Fourth Section had fought their way into Sichuan like an army of red ants. They had already occupied the north of Sichuan and were continuing to take other areas. The head of the warlords, Liu Xiang, had already launched 200,000 troops to fight the Red Army coming into his eastern region of Sichuan. The order had been sent to all local governors that their own forces needed to be prepared for a defensive fight.

Governor Li had decided to set up a special defence headquarters and he wanted Father to help him with this task. Even those people who hated Father knew that he was the right man for the job. Governor Li wanted to appoint Father as the chief commander presiding over five other military officers, who had all worked for Father in the past.

Father was a Nationalist at that time, but during his time in the Military Academy he had been very impressed by two of his lecturers, Zhu De and Chen Yi, who were Communists. Since then he had made quite a few friends who were also Communists and he thought highly of them too. At this stage then, he was uncomfortable about being sent to fight against the Communists and he firmly refused the proffered position. He told the governor that even General Chiang Kai-shek's eight million troops had failed to conquer them, so who was he and what could he do against them?

One of Father's friends, Zhao Wei, who was already a committed Communist, came to see him with the proposition that Father should accept the new post. He said to him:

'You should have a clear understanding about this. This fight against the Red Army is really a power struggle between Chiang Kai-shek and the warlords and your duty, as you've been told, was to defend Yunyang. What would happen if you found that you were not able to sustain a defence? You would have to run – you would have to withdraw your troops. How and when to withdraw would be crucial and we could tell you this nearer the time. Think about it, if you don't go to the front line then someone else will and they may not have the citizens' best interests at heart and might leave them to suffer. You should take this post and we will be here to help you.'

Father listened and ruminated on it and finally decided to accept the position. He went to see Governor Li to lay out before him his suggestions and plans:

'The Communist Red Army is a well-trained and tough army. Against them our small County Force would be defeated just as easily as dashing eggs on stone, so what we need to do is quickly increase our numbers with a volunteer army. I will start recruitment and I may also be able to arrange some local contribution of guns and ammunition to bolster what the government need to provide. Most importantly you will have to cover the military expenses. I know that you are normally obliged to pay a tax of 30,000 yuan to Liu Xiang, but you, as the local governor, could tell him that you need this money to organise the defence force.'

Governor Li was thrilled about Father's suggestions, as he had been getting increasingly distressed and anxious about how to deal with the situation, and he said:

'Good idea, excellent. I knew you were the right man for this job – the older the ginger, the spicier it is, eh? I will do whatever you say. You appoint the captain of the volunteer army and gather the forces together, and you will be the chief commander who takes care of everything.'

The defence army headquarters was swiftly set up in Narrow Gate, a smaller town near Yunyang. Soon they had gathered together about eight hundred young men from the region to form the volunteer army.

Father concentrated his efforts on the new force and often had meetings with Zhao Wei to hear his reports, but Father didn't know that there was secret planning going on behind his back. Zhao Wei and his committee were plotting to take Father's defence troops to join forces with the Red Army and then to overthrow the Nationalists' control of Yunyang. They managed to keep their real intentions secret from Father. They also knew that the newly recruited volunteers were, in the main, sympathetic to the Communists and would gladly go along with their plan. The Red Army leaders, however, suddenly changed their minds and left Sichuan and went north. With the Red Army gone, life went on as before for the time being. However, the Sichuan underground Communists didn't want to give up what they had so carefully planned and prepared for. They decided to carry out their own independent uprising to 'liberate' Yunyang and the neighbouring region.

At the beginning of November 1934 they set up the 'Yunyang Uprising Headquarters' and in January 1935 started an armed revolt in the region. However, their plans were leaked and also there was a lack of cooperation within their group. Warlord Liu Xiang's force clamped down on them and in a very short space of time the revolt was completely quashed. Hundreds of people were arrested or killed and the rest of them fled, including Zhao Wei and his committee. Father was advised to leave too, but he said no:

'I am a man who has never gambled, never used a brothel or smoked opium. I am not corrupt – I have never bribed anyone or embezzled anything. I have never murdered anyone. In my whole life I haven't done anything which weighs on my conscience, so what would I be hiding from and why should I flee?'

'But they say that you know those Communists well.'

'That's where they are wrong – the Communists didn't trust me or take me into their confidence. It's too bad really as, in my opinion, they were over-enthusiastic and without experience. More importantly, they didn't have anyone who understands military strategy and had no real commander. This is what is called a "scholar's rebellion", a theory on paper – it never succeeds.'

Soon after the uprising, Warlord Liu Xiang set up a Special Committee for Clearing Out Communists and its main function was to arrest and execute Communists, radicals, anyone who had joined the uprising and anyone who was even slightly suspected of having a connection with it. Their slogan was: 'Better to mistakenly kill a hundred rather than let one go.' This special committee said that they had received some letters disclosing that Father was either a Communist, or a radical suspected of being a Communist. Furthermore, he was accused of being the one behind the curtain pulling the strings. This was enough reason for them to arrest Father and send him to prison. It was a big scandal in the city that Father had been put in jail. Those who hated him, though, were in high spirits and said: 'This should teach Lunatic Lin a few lessons.'

Others, however, felt it was an injustice. Lots of people, including students and teachers, wrote to the government to protest, saying that Father was a good man. Many people sent food and other daily necessities to Father in prison.

Often people say 'it never rains but it pours'. Around this time Second Uncle arrested a criminal, who was not only a pimp but was also notorious for violence and theft. In order to get revenge on Second Uncle he collected and disclosed information about how Second Uncle was embezzling government money to support his opium addiction. Second Uncle was then swiftly sacked from his job. In normal circumstances, as chief of police, Second Uncle would easily have been able to get Father out of jail within a couple of days, but this time there was nothing he could do to help. He told Father that the only person who could help him now was their brother-in-law, Luohan Tang. Father told him that the only thing that Luohan Tang would give him was a string of insults. This proved to be the case when I accompanied Second Uncle to talk to him.

He immediately became angry and said: 'When has my young brother-in-law ever considered me – he is a lunatic and dares to provoke anyone and everyone. He opposes me in everything and constantly embarrasses me in public. This time he has stirred up a fire only to burn himself with it – well, let him taste life in jail for a while – he deserves it.'

Second Uncle had to prevent me from leaping at Luohan Tang in my own anger before we left.

Father only stayed in one of the cells of the main prison for ten days before he was moved to a wing especially for political prisoners. This gave him certain privileges and much better conditions and I could visit whenever I liked. But what he saw and experienced in the main cells deeply shocked him. Each cell was vastly overcrowded. There were two or three wooden spittoons in each cell, which doubled up for use by everyone as slop buckets. Each morning someone had the unenviable task of carrying these spittoons, overflowing with urine, to the latrine pit at the back of the prison compound to empty them. The cell walls were thick with dirt and smeared with traces of blood from the remains of all of the bedbugs and mosquitoes which had been swatted against them. The prisoners smoked the cheapest tobacco, the smell of which, mixed with the stench of lack of sanitation, was enough to suffocate you and make you retch. Prisoners were never given the opportunity to wash themselves nor have their hair cut. With their long, filthy, matted hair they resembled those ghoulish figures portrayed on opera stages. The red lumps resulting from the bites of the bedbugs, mosquitoes and lice quickly became infected and suppurating when scratched with long, dirty fingernails. Some of the prisoners were so bad that you could not see a patch of clear skin on their bodies and there was no medical treatment for them at all. The whole night long there was a continuous sound of moaning, groaning, sighing and shouting from those in the throes of a nightmare. It was a living hell. Worst of all, the prison director regularly embezzled some of their food supplies. The amount of food was already inadequate, of very poor quality, and there were only two meals a day. Breakfast consisted of extremely thin rice porridge made with mouldy and gritty rice accompanied by half-rotten pickled vegetables. The extreme heat of summer made the already horrible environment much worse, with infectious diseases often killing five or six people each month. One year cholera wiped out more than half of the prisoners.

When Father had been the regimental commander of Yunyang County Force he had been responsible for sending many people to jail, but he had never been aware that conditions for the prisoners were so appalling. What Father could not bring himself to face most of all was the fact that many prisoners' cases were still to be decided and they would ultimately be found not guilty, but they still had to endure these terrible conditions. Even those who were guilty and convicted, however, were still human beings and deserved better treatment. Father told me that he was unable to sleep for days on end with wondering whether he could do something to help. Then one day he asked me to deliver a letter straight into the hands of the governor's secretary. Before I left he read it to me. Firstly Father accurately reported the conditions in the jail and then went on to say:

'You all know as well as I do what kind of person I am. I am not worried about my own future here – the truth about my case will come to light soon enough. Right now I am worrying about the other prisoners, because they are in such terrible conditions and living in the worst surroundings I have ever seen. There are people here whose cases haven't been decided yet and, if the conditions do not change, they may die before judgement is made on them. You, the Yamen, are the officers whose responsibility it is to look after the people as if you were their parents. I am pleading with you now: show some kindness, do something good for once, let them survive and give them a chance to start a new life.'

Then Father made a few practical suggestions as to how to clean the dirty surroundings and change the bad habits of both the prisoners and the jailers. He outlined a plan of how the prison could be run and made largely self-sufficient by relying on the prisoners' own efforts. He also pointed out that he didn't think that there could be any objection to such a system and that it would only be beneficial for everyone.

At the end of the letter Father put a couple of quotations

from the works of General Chiang Kai-shek and mentioned that the New Life Movement was still in operation. He said that some time before he had been responsible for the movement in Yunyang and, seeing as how no one had told him that he had been sacked from that job, he felt that it was still his duty and he was still willing to carry on with the work of the movement inside the prison.

There ensued an unprecedented programme, put into action under Father's leadership, entitled 'Prisoner Self-Save'. The name of 'Lunatic Lin' was spread even further afield.

The prison director, who had occupied his position for three years, had never entered the main prison cells, not even once. Now he had to follow the governor's order to allow Father some authority within the prison, but at the same time keep a close eye on him too, and so he had no choice but to venture into the cells himself to give the mobilisation order. He stood on a long bench to make himself seen and heard by the two hundred or more prisoners:

'You all need to listen to Commander Lin. Do what he says.' Then he quickly covered his mouth and nose and ran out.

Father stepped to the front and said: 'I am no longer the commander, but one of you, a prisoner. All I want to say is: please don't write yourselves off by thinking that your situation is hopeless and so act recklessly. Anyone who has not been given a death sentence still has hope of walking out of here alive. What I will lead you in doing is to make changes to your personal habits, improve your living environment and transform the sanitation conditions. You all need to stay healthy to be able to reunite with your families. When each of you gets out of here, try to be a good person for the rest of your life – don't commit any further crimes.'

To encourage the prisoners' own driving force, Father left it up to them to select a few leaders from amongst themselves and to persuade their own families to contribute some buckets and carrying poles. Then he selected ten young, well-behaved, strong prisoners to go down to the river to fetch water. Father went with them. They all, including Father, wore prison uniform and were accompanied by four prison guards. At first the prison director said no to Father going as well, but Father smiled at him and said: 'I think I am the person who can control them best.'

The prison director was anxious in case things should go wrong, but when he thought about it he realised that Father was unlikely to run away and even the governor had given orders to let him do what he wanted. So he agreed and Father went with them. Never before had the local people seen a team of prisoners walk across the street carrying buckets and, full of curiosity, they followed their every step. In the end, a job which should have taken less than an hour took half a day to finish. Next day the prison director decided that the team should leave at the crack of dawn to go down to the river and so they managed to collect enough water before there were people on the street to hinder them. They found the largest woks they could to boil the water in and, once it had boiled, poured it all over the bamboo bed-boards to seek out those well-fed bedbugs hiding in the crevices. Then they burned the straw mattresses. The bedbugs inside them, which were as big as ladybirds, exploded like firecrackers in the flames. The prisoners threw boiling water all over the uneven surfaces of the walls and floor, dislodging even more bedbugs. The water flowed out of the cell into the yard like a stream, carrying the bloated corpses of the bedbugs with it. It was such a horrible scene that I shudder at its memory even today.

The drains were blocked too and Father used a drill rod to push through the blockage to let all the water out and he even poured boiling water between the stones of the pavement. This job took two days to complete. Next they moved on to getting rid of the body lice.

A week was spent boiling the prisoners' clothes and bedding. Luckily it was in the middle of the hot summer and they didn't have to worry that they had nothing to wear for a couple of days. They used over a hundred buckets of water for this and the prisoners' families provided the wood used for boiling the water.

A more difficult job was to get over two hundred people's long, matted, filthy hair and beards shaved. Five of the prisoners who had been barbers volunteered. At first Father was worried about using knives in case things went wrong, so instead they borrowed several pairs of scissors from their families. However, it wasn't possible to do a close shave with scissors and also it was a very slow process, so Father requested some proper barbers' tools. Two guards watched over the barbers whilst they worked to help keep order and to speed up the process, but still it took five days to shave all the prisoners. Father looked at the pile of hair mounting up; he wanted to sell it, but no one wanted it because the potential buyers were afraid of transmitting the lice, so Father had no choice but to burn it.

Next was to get their nails cut and to persuade them to wash themselves. This was easier said than done. Almost all of the prisoners didn't want their nails cut as they said that long fingernails were useful for scratching their itching bodies. To get them to wash themselves was the hardest of all as they literally hadn't washed for years and a thick, crusty layer of dirt, pus and blood had formed and was stuck firmly all over their skin. In order to clean that outer layer off they needed to soak in warm water until it softened so it could then be peeled off gently. This process caused a lot of pain and it especially hurt those who were badly infected, so most of the prisoners refused to have a wash. Father first tried to convince the prisoners to undergo this torture willingly, but his persuasive tongue was useless on this occasion and he was unable to make them see the benefits. Instead he had to resort to ordering them to wash and to help each other to do so. It took about eighteen days for everyone to finish.

After about one month the transformation of the surroundings and the prisoners themselves was remarkable. The prisoners started to call Father the 'Buddha Yeye'. Father was happy to see the achievements, but his plan had barely started yet as he wanted to make the jail into a good example for jails everywhere. He wrote to the governor and prison director setting out his overall plan. The prison director, being a witness to the new look of his prison, backed up all of Father's suggestions.

Father then asked the prisoners' families to contribute vegetables and flowering plants to start a garden. The prison director bought some bricks and let the prisoners construct flowerbeds with them. Among other things, they planted grape vines, wisteria, jasmine, roses and peonies. A long stone bench was provided to complete the useful and restful garden. Some slogans were written on the wall, such as: 'give up the vices, return to the virtues', 'repent and be saved', 'give up bad habits' and 'implement a new life'.

Father also suggested that the prisoners needed a doctor to visit them once a week. He further suggested that some of the families would be able to pay for medication, but for those who couldn't, the government should fund it. The governor saw the huge improvement in the prison, so he didn't hesitate to take Father's advice. Father found someone to make additional spittoons and arranged for them to be kept clean. He took out a subscription to a newspaper on behalf of the jail too and set up a time in each day for those who could read to read the news out loud.

Looking at how the jail changed every day for the better made Father content and he was proud of the results of everybody's efforts. Still not finished though, his thoughts turned to finding a way to further improve the prisoners' diet. This needed money, but for a while Father didn't have any idea how to find any extra. Then one day he saw a prisoner's family member bringing in a couple of pairs of straw sandals and his eyes lit up, because here was the solution: the prisoners would start making straw sandals! Not much initial investment was needed, it was easy to learn to do and they would probably sell well. So Father took ten yuan from his own pocket and sent me out to buy flaxen thread and straw. Very soon sandal production was under way, involving all the prisoners except for the sick and disabled. Each day they produced over two hundred pairs and they sold extremely well to large wholesalers and small businesses. Father even redesigned the sandals and his were better looking and more practical than the traditional ones and, more importantly, they sold for more money. As soon as the money started coming in, meat was bought every second day and tobacco, soap and toothpaste were also purchased. Compared with life in the past, life in the present for those prisoners had turned from hell to near heaven.

The good news about the changes at the prison spread rapidly and soon reached a number of eminent citizens. The governor wanted to show off his achievements to further his career, so he called Father and the prison director to his office and told them that he wanted to invite some politicians, officials and businessmen to visit the prison. The prison director knew he had to prepare well for this visit and as soon as he went back to the jail he ordered another deep clean and more flowers to be planted. He also brought out the stored prison uniforms for everyone to put on for show.

On the day of the visit ten prison guards, smart in uniform, stood to attention on either side of the front gate and welcome banners were flying high. The prison director led in the visitors, who looked as if they were expecting the worst as most of them had handkerchiefs covering their mouths and noses. As they walked into the yard loud applause broke out from amongst the prisoners, who were lined up in front of the cells. Father stepped forward to welcome the wary, but curious, visitors. This was quite embarrassing for many of them because most were familiar with Father, either having been his boss or in some cases having worked for him, and now he was in front of them wearing a prison uniform. The prison director apologised; he had forgotten that Father should have been set apart from the other prisoners.

An elderly, humble-looking gentleman carefully inspected each cell and noted the tidy beds, the white walls, clean floors and the blooming garden. At each revelation he shook his head and muttered to himself: 'Unbelievable! Incredible!' Finally his eyes stopped on Father and he reached to take hold of his hands and said to him: 'My brother, I'm sorry you have had to put up with all of this. You have suffered, but because of you the prisoners now live in relative ease and comfort. Everyone calls you "Lunatic Lin", but tell me where we can find more crazy people like you! You have changed this place from a dungeon to the prototype of a humane prison system. I shall report to the governor and tell him that he must review the evidence of your own case and, if he can't prove anything, then he must let you out immediately.'

True to the old gentleman's word, he went to see the governor and demanded that Father's case should be decided. Indeed, there was not enough evidence to prove that Father was a Communist and he was informed he would be released shortly. The news was received in the prison with mixed emotions by all of the inmates. On the one hand they were happy that

Father was to gain his freedom, but on the other hand they were so sad that he would no longer be amongst them. The prisoners gathered together some money between them and arranged to buy some meat and fireworks in order to hold a farewell party. On the night of the party there was much fun and laughter, as well as regret. Father made a short speech:

'I only did what my conscience told me was right to do, so please don't thank me. Before I leave you I want to say something to all of you: anyone who is guilty of a crime should admit it, honestly serve your sentence and, when you get out, start a new life and become a decent man. Those of you who have an unjustified case: you should appeal it. There is one more thing: the achievements of the prison did not come easily, so I hope everyone will help to keep it this way, and take care of each other.'

On the day Father came out of prison, much to his surprise, he found many of the prisoners' families waiting for him at the gate. They draped him with large, red silk flowers and Father walked out of the prison to the sound of exploding fireworks and people cheering. There was also a sedan chair waiting for him which had been sent by Luohan Tang with an invitation for Father to rest at his house for a few days. Father accepted.

Luohan Tang, forcing a smile, greeted Father at the gate of his house and said 'Welcome home. You have suffered hard days', and led him inside. 'Don't think about anything – rest, just rest. When you are fully restored we will talk.'

A room had been prepared for Father. A set of new clothes was laid out on the bed and a hot meal was waiting for him on a table. A barber was sent for to cut his hair and shave him. Father slept deeply until noon the following day.

Father gave serious thought as to his future prospects and realised that there was nothing left for him in Yunyang and decided it was time to move on. When he announced his decision to Luohan Tang, it looked as if a heavy burden had been lifted. Then he presented Father with 150 yuan to help us make a fresh start. The governor also gave him 300 yuan, telling him that it was a 'goodwill gesture'.

Father and I went back to Grandmother in Yunan, where Father was going to leave me. Once back there, however, I begged them both to be allowed to leave with Father and go wherever and whenever he decided to go.

It was then that I met my half-sister Liuqing for the first time. She had been brought back by the Lin family after her mother, Big Li, died. Father hadn't seen her since she had been sent away as a small baby. Second Uncle's wife took in Liuqing and brought her up as her own daughter.

At the end of July 1935 Father and I left to start a new life in Wanxian and so began the next phase of my life.

First Love

We left Grandmother's house in the very early morning and caught a ferry from the Tangqi docks in Yunan to take us to the main port in Yunyang, where the large steamships were able to dock. We found one which would take us to our destination: Wanxian.

As we got under way I could hardly believe my eyes because the Yangtze River was immense. In comparison, our Qi River was only a trickling stream. I had never seen such a large expanse of water before. The wooden fishing boats looked like mere fallen leaves bobbing about on the water and the buildings on the far bank seemed as small as matchstick models. Seagulls chased and kept up with the ship, which was itself almost flying in the strong currents. In my excitement I ran from one end of the ship to the other until I was tired. The ship had to slow down considerably as the captain carefully navigated our way through the gorges. Many boats and the lives within them had been lost in the treacherous eddies of this stretch of the river.

Our ship managed the 180 miles from Yunyang safely and we arrived just before dark. We disembarked and made our way over to a large group of sedan chairs, all lined with green satin, which were waiting at the docks. After a noisy haggle over the price, Father engaged one to take us to the house of one of his friends, Lan, from military days. There was no room for me in the sedan as well as the luggage, so I walked behind.

Lan and Father had both served in Warlord Yang Sen's army. Lan had reached the rank of lieutenant colonel. However, Yang Sen had lost the war to become the 'King of Sichuan' to Warlord Liu Xiang and when that happened Lan lost everything. He lost interest in continuing in the military and stayed at home. His wife couldn't bear the loss of name and status and left him. She took everything she could with her, including all their savings, and money became very short for Lan. By the time we arrived at his house he was down to having only five jiao per day for food, which he spent in a small bean-curd restaurant next door. He would arrange mahjong games at his house for groups of his friends and they would pay a one-yuan cover charge. Whenever Lan joined in the game though, he always won as he was an expert player and this would cover his other living expenses.

Lan gladly accepted Father's offer of fifty yuan for us to stay with him until we managed to sort ourselves out. In those days, as long as we spent modestly, it was enough for the three of us for several months.

Before long Father met up with a friend, Huang, who was also from Yunyang. He was the manager of the New Life Movement Citizens' Education Centre in Wanxian. He welcomed Father with the offer of a job at the centre. The salary wasn't much, but it solved our immediate problems and best of all it came with accommodation. So we left the hospitality of Lan and moved to the education centre. In fact, there wasn't much for Father to do because Huang was just trying to help out Father and had hurriedly created a position for him. To fill time, we visited Father's friends, read and went to the opera, which was one of Father's favourite pastimes. We also played a lot of tennis. Life was quite relaxed for a while.

Then Father bumped into two other good friends from their days in Warlord Yang Sen's army. They had come to Wanxian to attend the Ninth District Security Conference. One of them, Shike, was the security captain of Zhongxian (which means 'Loyalty Town'). They were so happy to meet up again after so many years and we went to a teahouse in the Xishang Park to celebrate. The three of them talked animatedly for a long time before Father turned to me and said: 'Here are your two uncles. They are in positions of power and are doing much better than I am. They are going to sort out your schooling for you.'

Without hesitation Uncle Shike cheerfully said to me: 'No problem! I will sort out a school for you in Zhongxian. Come with me tomorrow.'

As simply as that, I packed my suitcase and accompanied Uncle Shike to Zhongxian the next day. Zhongxian lay nearly two hundred miles upriver from Wanxian and was within the mountain range. Later Father travelled further upriver to Chongqing to see his ex-boss, Brigade Commander Lei.

I had been staying a couple of days with Uncle Shike in the security officers' accommodation before he called me into his office:

'I have been speaking with the principal of the academy, Mr Ma. Tomorrow, you can start school. You will start off in the final year and then, next year, you can finish school altogether. The tuition fee, food and accommodation fee, I have paid them already.'

I was very happy to be going to school once again, but I hadn't given the fees any thought at all and replied with some embarrassment: 'As soon as we can, Father and I will pay you back…'

Uncle Shike quickly interrupted me: 'No, no, not at all! It

is my pleasure. I am merely repaying a debt of kindness. Your father has helped me and so many other people in the past. You can be justified in feeling proud of him. This is nothing for me in comparison.'

I had missed the beginning of the school year, but nevertheless I settled in well and soon caught up. I threw myself into every activity wholeheartedly. I tried hard in everything I did, not just for me, but I wanted Uncle Shike to know how much I appreciated his kindness in putting me through school and, of course, I wanted Father to be proud of me. My greatest joy was playing all sports and I was put in the basketball, tennis and athletics teams. Creative writing was one of my best subjects and I wrote many articles and poems.

In one of my poems I poured out all my feelings. It was two hundred lines long and I wrote it all in one go. I can still remember how it began:

Spring's breeze touches wondrous hearts
But my heart is suspended in the depths of winter's night.
Spring's green willow dips its head towards the ground
While in its branches the cuckoo utters its first sound.
Incarcerated in a cold, lifeless ruined house
I impatiently scribble these words.
My only company
My long, skinny shadow on the wall
Dancing in the reflection of spring's emerald glow.
The only sound
The cuckoo's mournful echo.
People say a mother's love is the greatest of them all
I can't, won't let that saying exist
My mother, long since, passed away
How can a mother's love come my way?

The poem finished on a note of determination and enthusiasm

to overcome all the barriers and walk towards a new, bright world. My teacher, Yang, asked me to read it to the class and he also put it on the board for 'written works of excellence'. A lot of students copied it down and most of these were girls. Although we were part of the same school, boys and girls were educated separately so that we didn't have much to do with each other. After my poem appeared on the board, though, I started to receive letters from a lot of the girls.

One Sunday, Teacher Yang invited me to his house for lunch. There were three girls there as well and one of them was his niece, whose name was Guanqing. I had noticed her playing basketball – in fact she was the girls' team captain. She always jumped very high for the ball and each time she scored a basket I would cheer loudly along with the other fans. She had also caught my attention because she was very pretty and when she smiled, which she did a lot, she had dimples. I was so surprised to see her at Teacher Yang's house and to learn that she was his niece. That afternoon we all chatted amongst ourselves, but I would really have liked to talk solely to Guanqing. She was very quiet and whenever I managed to catch her eye she turned her head away in shyness. In the end she ran into the kitchen to help her aunt. As we were all leaving, Guanqing gave me a jar of pickled bean curd and said: 'I noticed that you like to eat this – take it back to school with you.'

I was immediately embarrassed because I realised that my chopsticks had been more or less glued to the dish of pickled bean curd during lunch. It was indeed my favourite and reminded me of Grandmother's own. It dawned on me that my table manners probably hadn't made a very good impression.

About a week later Teacher Yang took me aside and out of the blue he asked me an embarrassing question: 'Xianli, tell me – what do you think of my niece, Guanqing – do you like her?'

Of course I did. In fact she was often on my mind and in my

dreams, but I was startled to be asked this question and was far too shy to admit how much I liked her and said awkwardly: 'She's alright!'

'Well, she got a very good impression of you. Would you like to be friends with her?'

Again, of course I wanted to be friends with her, but I couldn't say anything more than: 'I am still young – maybe it's not good to talk about such things now.'

Teacher Yang was encouraging: 'But, you know, there is no obstacle for you two to be friends.'

After that day, because Teacher Yang gave me some hope, my thoughts were perpetually on Guanqing. In fact I was in love, first love. It was such a sweet feeling but also very disturbing. I could not eat and I could not sleep. I didn't know what to do. I couldn't bring myself to confide in Teacher Yang, nor did I dare to write to Guanqing. It would have been unthinkable to arrange to meet Guanqing in public; nobody dared to do that in Zhongxian as it was a very conventional town, almost feudal. One day I couldn't hold my feelings in any longer and went to see the wife of one of my father's friends; she was a nursery school teacher. I stammered out my story and then she clasped her hands together and simply said: 'Leave it to me, you can see her tomorrow at my place.'

I thought I would have lots to talk about to Guanqing, but when I saw her I was struck dumb; I couldn't even stammer! I just smiled and nodded in response to whatever was said. Father's friend's wife saw that we were both restricted and she excused herself and left us alone. I managed to relax a bit and we started chatting. A while later I couldn't resist the sudden impulse to hold her hand. She then rested her head on my shoulder and that was enough to bump my blood pressure through the top of my head! Later I regretted not having enough courage to put my arm around her and kiss her, just once.

One evening Uncle Shike sent a message to say that a parcel had arrived for me from Chongqing. I presumed that it was from Father who was still there, but I didn't recognise the handwriting on it. When I opened the parcel I found a thick woollen coat, but there was no letter or even a note. A warm coat was exactly what I needed, and wanted, and wondered who could have known this if it wasn't from Father. Uncle Shike had kindly given me an old cotton-padded jacket, which barely kept out the cold, and also his old army coat. The coat, although warm, covered me from head to toe and I was scared people would laugh at me in it so I only used it as a blanket at night.

That night I dreamed my mother came to the foot of my bed. She was choking back her tears:

'My son! It's so cold, but you wear so little. Are you cold? When you were small at least you had your grandmother to take care of you, but now, look at you, you are on your own. Where is your father? How come he is not here to take care of you? Look at this. I have made a coat for you to keep you warm. Get up and try it on. Let me see you in it.'

In my dream, my mother was so young, so pretty and so gentle. I fell into her arms and was enfolded in her love. I looked deep into her eyes and saw love radiating from them. She was smiling at me. I laughed and laughed till my eyes brimmed over with tears of joy. I awoke to an empty room, but the coat was still there. I was restless for the remainder of the night and wrote down a short poem:

In a time of hardship I saw a star
At the moment of darkness a light shone for me

71

A coat covered me with warmth
And brought my sweet mother back to me.

Next day I wrote to Father asking him about the coat. He replied to say that it was a complete surprise to him and that he hadn't sent it nor had he asked anyone to do so either. Later on, he wrote to tell me that he had met a remarkable woman, a heroine, called Chen Lianshi, and it was she who had sent me the coat. I was intrigued by this news and my young imagination quickly formed a picture of this friend of his, the heroine Chen Lianshi. I even thought how wonderful it would be if she became my mother.

Just before the end of the school year I received another letter from Father telling me that he had returned to Wanxian. He also told me that he had enrolled me on an officer training course there and that he had managed to do this through his friend who was running it. He said that after the course I would be able to take on a teaching job in any school. He wanted me to get there as soon as possible. I knew that this was an excellent opportunity for me and when I told Uncle Shike, Teacher Yang and all my friends about it, they were certainly very glad for me. Uncle Shike gave me some money and Teacher Yang and his wife insisted that I have a meal with them before I left. They invited Guanqing too. I told Guanqing that when she had finished school she should come to Wanxian to study at the teacher training college there and, after that, we could work together as teachers in the same school. For the whole of that day Guanqing was very quiet. I noticed her stealing glances at me and she looked downcast. When nobody else was around she quickly put an envelope into my hand and told me to read it later.

As soon as I stepped out of Teacher Yang's house I opened her letter. I took out two white, embroidered silk handker-

72

chiefs. One of them had a pair of mandarin ducks on it, which was a well-recognised symbol of two lovers. The other one had the words 'blooming flowers and full moon', which traditionally meant perfect conjugal bliss. There was also a photograph of her in sportswear, holding a basketball, looking full of vitality. Most importantly, she had written a note:

I hate that we only got to know each other so late, but hope that the beautiful dream will still come true.

Please forgive me, but tomorrow I will not be there to see you off.

Guanqing

I was so happy about how everything was turning out that I did not notice there was a sadness in the air, which Guanqing seemed to have sensed already. She had a foreboding about the future that I did not feel. I was too overwhelmed by the things happening in the present, by the thought of seeing my father again, and by what good things the future seemed to hold for me.

By this time I had amassed a collection of letters from many other girls too. Some of them simply complimented me, some of them wanted to be my sister, some of them said I was their idea of Prince Charming and others were more direct and wanted to marry me and had enclosed photographs of themselves! Uncle Shike, especially, teased me about all these letters and at my leaving party he made me hang them up on a string from one end of the room to the other. Then he blindfolded me and told me to pick out one to decide which girl was going to be my future bride. Burning with embarrassment, I grabbed a whole handful of letters. Everyone guffawed and slapped their thighs in merriment and told me that I was too greedy with girls. I fled from Uncle Shike's house, took a deep breath and prayed that my future was with Guanqing. From that joke I realised that most people still didn't know that I was in love with her.

Zhongxian: a small, even insignificant, remote town in the mountains and one small stop in my life, but it left me with a host of memories.

Getting to Know Shibo

After arriving at Wanxian docks I went in search of the address Father had given me and I found the house without any problem. I was surprised to be greeted at the door by a woman and she told me her name was Chen Xianming. Father had never mentioned her in his letters and so I was shocked to find out that she was living with him. I suppose she wasn't bad looking, but she was unkempt. Her hair was messy, her clothes were crumpled and her complexion was pallid. The house was dirty and untidy with cigarette ends and sunflower seed shells all over the floor. All in all she reminded me of 'Miss String Bean' in that filthy attic of Uncle Luohan Tang's. She even had the same kind of shrill voice as Miss String Bean. I did not like her at all and I couldn't understand how Father could put up with this kind of woman. It didn't make any sense to me. I didn't know where she came from, where Father had met her, or even whether they were married or not. I didn't ask and Father didn't tell me and it remained a source of embarrassment between us for the rest of his life. From the first moment I met Chen Xianming to the last time I saw her, I never changed my opinion of her.

Apart from the living arrangements, which I detested, I spent an enjoyable summer with Father playing as much tennis as possible in Xishang Park. Tennis was my passion and secretly it was my dream to become a top-seeded player in the future, but obviously it was never to be.

Then it was time to start the three-week course which my father had enrolled me on. It was an intensive, military-style course run by the Nationalist government. The participants were mainly middle-aged head teachers from secondary and primary schools, whereas I was only seventeen. I was the only one who didn't have a job or experience of any kind and, to be honest, I shouldn't have been there at all. It was plain to see that I had a special relationship with someone who could pull strings. On completion of the course most of the participants would end up as Guomingdan intelligence officers.

From dawn to dusk there were military exercises and crack-down drills which seemed pointless to me and I was soon bored with it all. I would often feign ill health to get out of them so that I could read in my room or simply have a lie in. Every afternoon there were compulsory political lectures and study sessions on subjects such as 'Collectivism: the Three Principles for the People' by Dr Sun Yat-sen; 'One Leader: General Chiang Kai-shek' and 'One Party: the Nationalists'. By this time I was already influenced by people around me who were either already Communist or on the road to becoming Communist and also by my own reading of radical articles, so I found these study sessions to be utter rubbish. Of course I couldn't admit any of this whilst on the course.

When the course finished it was obvious that I was never going to become a Nationalist intelligence officer and so I was sent back to Yunan, my home town, to be a teacher in the Southern Primary School.

Although there were over ten thousand workers and their families in this salt mining and industrial town, there were only two primary schools in the area. There was one on each side of the Tangqi River and they were both very overcrowded. The Education Department regulation stipulated that there should be a maximum of forty children in each class, but in fact there were usually sixty or more. Schools were never given enough funding and so struggled to employ an adequate number of teachers. I was still lucky to be taken on, however, because I was so young and hadn't done the normal teacher training course. Later, I found out that the head teacher had even taken a pay cut to fund my salary, which started off at twelve yuan per month for a part-time post, although right from the start I was working more than full time.

I was to teach the third-year pupils PE and maths and there was another, middle-aged, teacher for the other subjects. The building for the third year was more than a mile away from the main school; there were over two hundred steps up to it and it had few facilities. The other assigned teacher was often absent through ill health and no other teacher was willing to trek up to the building to take his place, so it was up to me to teach all the subjects, including music. This meant that I had 130 children for each class on many occasions. I took teaching very seriously and devised many strategies for keeping control during the lessons, but when we went out to play I made sure that everybody, including me, had fun! All in all it was a very happy time.

As soon as I settled in at the school I wrote to Guangqing in Zhongxian and to my delight she replied quickly. In our many letters to each other we made plans for a future together.

At the end of February 1937, after the Spring Festival, I was offered a job at the Northern Primary School teaching PE for twenty-four yuan a month plus accommodation, so my hard work across the river had paid off. It was a different regime at this school. We had morning assemblies where we had to stand to attention, sing the national anthem and ceremoniously raise the flag. Then the news was read to us, often featuring the Japanese invasion and the ruthless acts of violence perpetrated on our citizens by the Japanese. For the morning exercise I would have to lead the pupils on a jog through the streets shouting out anti-Japanese slogans. There were many other activities organised by the teachers, some of whom were Communists, inspired by a large-scale campaign called the 'Ninth of December' by the Patriotic Students Movement. This movement and its anti-Japanese campaign had been started in Beijing by the Communist Party and was very active throughout the whole country. I joined in wholeheartedly and put forward ideas for many of the activities. I felt total dedication to my life and work at the school. However, in addition, I often felt that I had so many ideas, thoughts and emotions that I needed to express that the only way was to write them all down.

I had always enjoyed the common form of folk poetry called 'ragged verse', no doubt influenced by Father, and I wrote one about the salt-well workers. When I was a boy I had always wondered why they looked so wizened and I knew they didn't live into old age. I remembered how each salt well had a derrick over it with a series of pulleys and thick ropes attached. On each pulley a large bucket was tied to each end of the rope and the rope would pass round the waist of the worker to help him pull up the full bucket. As the full bucket came up the empty one would go down. As the worker pulled he shouted out a number to the overseer, who wrote it down, and each worker would be paid according to how many full buckets he pulled up. The salt water would then be tipped into a channel, made from split bamboo, to take it to the giant woks for evaporation by heat. The vapours given off from the well, steam and burning coal were all poisonous and the heat was terrific. Consequently the workers didn't wear many, or any, clothes, and

78

worked for ten hours per day completely unprotected. They rarely lived longer than forty years.

The Song of the Pulley Workers

Ninety-six, ninety-seven,
A whole day's hauling
Only worth two bamboo tubes of rice
Rope-blistered hands
Rope-deformed back.
Four seasons through the year
Nothing covering naked body.
Hours longer than before
Salary less than their worth
Holding the same money as before
But can't buy same amount of rice.
Wife, kids, crying from hunger at house
What can I do?
Unable to buy two tubes of rice.
Bastards! This is not the job I want to do.
Whoever can feed my mouth
I am willing to follow,
To be a gangster, to be a robber
I am willing.

With encouragement from my room-mate, I sent it in to the *Wangzhou Daily*, which was the largest newspaper in Wanxian at the time, and they published it. The editor even encouraged me to send in more of my writing, which I did. I wrote about all sorts of subjects, such as school life, anti-Japanese feelings, people being exploited and how the rich were getting richer and the poor were getting poorer. Writing articles and poems became a part of my everyday life and my pen was like a horse galloping away with my thoughts. To my delight, most of my writing was published in the newspaper. I even wrote an open letter to my Seventh Uncle, Luohan Tang, disowning him and exposing everything that I had seen going on in his house when I was living there as a boy. I called him two faced and corrupt, and listed his many vices. It was all true except that I changed both our names. I used 'Lin Qing' rather than my childhood name. After it was published I sent a copy of it to Seventh Uncle. It caused a scandal in Yunan and Yunyang as it wasn't hard to work out who it was really about and many people went to him to challenge him about it.

I received a letter from Father telling me that Chen Lianshi had been arrested in Wanxian and that he wanted me to join him there as soon as the school holiday began. This news came as a great blow to me as I already held Chen Lianshi deep in my heart. I could never forget her kindness when she had sent me a warm winter coat when I was studying in Zhongxian over a year ago.

I couldn't wait for the school holiday to start to find out why Chen Lianshi had been arrested, so I asked for early leave from the head teacher and rushed to Wanxian.

Meanwhile, Father had taken over the running of a small hotel near the port. Chen Xianming, my 'stepmother', was running it with him. When I arrived she tried to welcome me with a smile, but I ignored her overtures and just asked: 'Where's my father?'

Her smile was immediately replaced with a sneer: 'Huh! Where else would he be at this time of the morning? Serving his heroine – as usual – at the prison.'

I didn't answer her, but just asked the receptionist to give me a key to one of the rooms and went there to wait for Father.

Father was surprised to see me sooner than expected, but

was very happy nevertheless. We didn't waste any time and, after having something to eat, we went to visit Chen Lianshi in the prison. Father stopped to buy two cartons of cigarettes for her and I brought along some cake which I had carried from Yunan with me.

It suddenly occurred to me that I didn't know how to address her, this heroine of my heart, when I met her for the first time. Sticking to tradition I should have called her 'Aunty' followed by her family name. *Lian* means 'Link' and *Shi* means 'Literary' or 'Poem'. Father said that he had already thought about it and that I should call her 'Shibo' and told me why:

'She is an exceptional woman – full of spirit – and has all the qualities of a truly courageous man. So "Shibo" is a much better name for her than any of those traditionally given to women-folk.'

Bo is a respectful title for a man who is older than one's own father. So 'Shibo' was a name coined especially for me to address her by and, as soon as I met this remarkable woman, I understood why this was an appropriate name for her. I called her this until the end of her days.

Whilst we were walking to the prison, Father told me about the events leading up to Shibo's arrest.

The Communist Party headquarters in Shanghai had wanted to send her to Russia to study military strategy and management. They had selected her in preference to hundreds of male contenders because she had demonstrated outstanding leadership of the guerrilla force in the Huaying Mountains. The mission to Russia had been decided on and arranged several months before the death of her husband, Liao Yubi, who had been executed by the Guomingdan. However, seeing as Shibo was also on the Guomingdan's 'wanted list' she went into hiding. A liaison had been sent to escort her on the first part of her journey, but it took him several months to track her down.

When he eventually found her he only gave her three days to sort out her affairs, such as handing over leadership of the guerrilla force and making arrangements for her two children. She arranged for the children to be sent to Chongqing to be looked after by a good friend of hers, Sister Zen, and their living expenses and schooling were to be taken care of by the Party. Then she set off for Shanghai guided by the liaison. For safety, neither of them knew anything about the plan beyond getting to Shanghai.

Liao Yubi in 1925

The first part of the journey from the Huaying Mountains took them to Yuechi, which happened to be Shibo's home town, from where they had to catch a boat to Wanxian. From Wanxian the plan was to take a steamship to Shanghai with changes at Yichang and Wuhan. Whilst in Yuechi the liaison told Shibo to be careful not to talk to anyone there in case she was recognised. On the boat, though, a woman approached her who had known her in the days when Shibo had been a school teacher in Yuechi, so Shibo couldn't avoid talking to her. In fact, Shibo had taught this woman's daughter. However, she felt sure that the woman knew nothing more about her so felt confident in taking her on as a travelling companion. Indeed it seemed a better cover than being seen with the liaison. Shibo also had the feeling that she was being watched while on board the boat, but wasn't sure whether this was the case or was just the result of her feeling nervous.

When they reached Wanxian it was already dusk and so they had to overnight there. The liaison chose the hotel for all of them and Shibo was to share a room with her travelling companion. Shibo remained in her room while the liaison went to buy the steamship tickets for the following day and the woman went into the town to visit friends.

Life is full of coincidences. The hotel chosen happened to be the one that Father was running. Father had been out when the three of them had checked in, but when he returned and saw the name Chen Lianshi on the register his heart leapt. He took the stairs two at a time and pounded on Shibo's door in great excitement:

'Shijie, Shijie, is that you?' [*Jie* means 'Sister'.]

Shibo opened the door very cautiously and was greatly relieved to see Father grinning from ear to ear. Neither of them could believe that they had encountered one another again on the off chance like this. Father especially was overjoyed and grabbed hold of her hands and wouldn't let go, thinking that she might just vanish. He then busied himself trying to make her as comfortable as possible. He fetched buckets of hot water so that she could wash and get warm. He brought her tea, food and cigarettes. Then they hurriedly and quietly explained what had happened to them since they last saw each other.

Less than an hour later Father and Shibo heard shouting in the hall downstairs and Father went to see what it was about. He found some military police there checking the hotel register. In those days the military police were not interested in tracking down criminals, but rather they were searching for 'non-conformists', which was just another term for Communists. They wanted to question Shibo and made their way directly to her room. The experienced Shibo, as ever, was prepared for anything and stayed calm. They searched her bags and found nothing suspicious. However, when they searched the other woman's luggage they found a package stuffed inside one of her tiny silk, embroidered shoes. They opened the package and found ten opium pills. Of course Shibo had known nothing about the package, but no matter how she explained herself and how much Father guaranteed her innocence against his own life, it was of no use. Finding the opium pills gave them justification to arrest her. Once at the military police station she was questioned by a senior officer, who happened to be the father of one of her ex-pupils, and he was able to confirm her identity as a teacher. This could have been the end of it, but clearly the military police had targeted Shibo and she was quickly transferred to the Yamen. Father said that the liaison had waited around for three days, but when there was no sign that Shibo was going to be released, he left the town. The woman from Yuechi never returned to the hotel at all. Three months later and Shibo hadn't even been questioned, let alone had a case hearing.

I asked Father whether he had any thoughts on how the military police had found her in the hotel so quickly. I also asked him outright whether Chen Xianming may have alerted them to her arrival. He said he thought not, especially as Shibo herself had had the feeling that she was being watched on the boat despite all her precautions. In my heart, though, I felt that Chen Xianming had betrayed her out of jealousy. Father never hid his admiration for Shibo and once Chen Xianming was confronted by her in person and saw that she was an elegant, beautiful, well-mannered and well-educated person, her jealousy had probably boiled over. What's more, she witnessed Father's almost outrageous affection and warmth towards Shibo, something that she herself had never experienced from him or even knew that he was capable of.

When we arrived at the Yamen we turned left to get to the women's prison. Father approached one of the cells and coughed. A face quickly appeared at the small opening in the cell door. This was my first glimpse of Shibo and I saw that she was indeed a very striking women. Her hair was jet black, shiny and neatly combed. Her lively and vivid eyes were set under unusually thick eyebrows. She caught sight of me and smiled: such a smile! I was smitten by her immediately. I couldn't hold in my fervour any longer and shouted out: 'Shibo.'

'You must be Xianli. When did you arrive?'

Her smile broadened into a laugh as I tripped up in my excitement and haste to get nearer to her. I was unable to get any more words out and so I just shoved our packages at my idol through the opening. She took them and opened a packet of cigarettes, took one out and handed it to Father before taking one for herself. Then she asked the prison guard for some matches. Father sat on the floor by the cell door and they started to chat. I watched her every movement and there was no hint of her being intimidated by being in prison; it was more like seeing her in her own house receiving guests. She was calm, unhurried and showed no sign of being dispirited.

I didn't know it then, but my whole life was going to be

linked with Shibo and her family. Once I had met her in person I certainly didn't want to go back to Yunan to teach any more. I wanted to stay around and look after her and my father.

For some time I had been harbouring an ambition to work full time for the *Wangzhou Daily*. I was already a regular contributor to the paper. So when I found out that they were looking to employ a proofreader, I applied with great anticipation. The job only paid eight yuan per month, which was only about one-third of what I was getting as a teacher, but I didn't mind so long as I could stay in Wanxian. I got the job using my editor as a reference and they also offered me a position as an intern reporter, which thrilled me even more.

Generally I spent my monthly salary on buying whatever Shibo needed, including cigarettes. She was a very heavy smoker and often got through two packets a day. Father had never smoked before, but he started just to keep Shibo company. Every time we visited we took her something. We cooked food, often special dishes, for her. This made Chen Xianming very angry indeed and one day her anger spilled over into a very vicious attack. She tried to poison the food which Father was just about to take to Shibo. Luckily I saw her do it and without a word I went over to her and slapped her very hard several times on her face. After that we normally picked up some food for Shibo from stalls on the way to the prison, just in case.

The other prisoners in there were a mixed bunch. There were prostitutes, thieves, opium addicts, opium traders and murderers. However, Shibo's knowledge, integrity and manners set her apart and she was well respected by the others. Everyone called her Master, Teacher or Big Sister Chen. Shibo had become the mother figure and all the women came to her with their accounts of how life had brought them down. She listened to each and every one of them. Many of the women

86

had become prostitutes, just to survive, for a variety of reasons. Most of them had been born into extreme poverty and many had become poverty stricken. Then there were many girls who had been raped and, because of society's prejudices, were subsequently ineligible for marriage. Some didn't care though, and thought that prostitution was a relatively easy way to earn money. However, they had all led bitter lives. Shibo counselled them, telling them that it was possible to start a new life after they got out of prison. She also persuaded one of the rich women, Crazy Hao, to spend some money for a good cause and buy penicillin to treat the women who had a sexually transmitted disease. In those days penicillin was imported from Western countries and was extremely expensive, so not widely in use.

Father was a soft-hearted man and listening to all the prostitutes' stories gave him food for thought. Whereas formerly he would have dismissed these women as being merely immoral and called their way of life their 'choice', he started to wonder about the reasons behind it all. After interviewing some prostitutes on the streets of Wanxian he wrote a poem about them entitled 'Street Chickens'. This was a name commonly given to prostitutes.

Street Chickens

By the door standing, on the street strolling.
Cold rain, bitter wind, dark night falling.
Fearful of police and soldiers
Savagely they shout – get out, get out!
Scared, shaking and panicking.
Hope against hope, a guest tonight tomorrow fed
Who knows? Eight nights now, no one asked.
A wretched life, who to tell?
No one cares.

87

Put glycerine on face, comb through hair
What's the use?
Surrounded by squalor.
In front come hooligans
Behind arrive wastrels
One might give two, three bronze coins
Others give nothing for a whole night of hours.
Begging in a whisper, dare not shout out.
Grieving!
Who knows our misery?
Who thinks we need pity?
Have to go short of food in the bowl
Have to sell the warm shawl.
Must buy powder, must buy rouge
Paint for eyebrows, colour for lips.
Lean on the door, auction my smile
In men's arms pretend a romance.
Laughing!
Laugh at those 'noble gentlemen'
Who spit on us, but seek us out.
They don't think we're human.
Can they not see
Mother burdened with tears, son groaning in pain
All wailing with hunger and cold?
They don't even look.
What is the sense of feeling shame?
Where to look for a better life?
Reality shows
Starvation the only real feeling there is!

Father was constantly trying to get Shibo released, but to no
avail. He had heard that she was a skilled artist so he bought
her some brushes, ink, colours and rice paper and encouraged
her to start painting again, at first just to pass the time. Her

skill was evident, even in the paintings she wasn't happy with. Crazy Hao paid the prison warden to get the altar from the prayer room moved into the cell under the window, so that she wouldn't have to kneel on the uneven floor in the dim light. Shibo crumpled up and threw away a lot of her paintings, but every one of them was picked up by someone or other and she would be asked to sign them. Finally she was happy with one of them and hung it up on the cell wall. It was a painting representing the four seasons with peonies, wisteria, chrysanthemums and plum blossom. Father thought the painting was stunning and wanted to take it to his good friend Liu Menghan to invite him to compose a poem to go with it. Menghan was a highly skilled calligrapher, famous throughout the country, who earned his living by also composing poetry and doing seal cutting. He was very eccentric, however, and never made much money because, if he didn't like someone, he wouldn't sell anything to them no matter how much money was offered. Also, on principle, he refused to allow any high-ranking official to get hold of his work. On the other hand, if he took a liking to a person then he would give away his work for free! When Menghan saw Shibo's painting he studied it closely and then held it up reverentially: 'Such talent. She is a remarkable woman indeed. It is incredible to be able to wield both the brush and the sword!'

Father had known Menghan for many years and had rarely heard him compliment anyone, but now he couldn't say enough to praise her. Father then brought all Shibo's paintings to Menghan so that he could compose a poem for each one. The two talented people combined their gifts to produce one piece of artwork.

One of Shibo's paintings

Father continued to think of ways to get Shibo out of prison. He had heard that the chief judge, who was responsible for the Wanxian prison, had longed to possess a piece of calligraphy by Menghan, but had never managed to get hold of one. Father thought that it might encourage the judge to review Shibo's case if he was given the 'Four Seasons' painting and poem. From the judge's point of view, what could be better than to have Menghan's calligraphy on a painting done by an artist whom Menghan admired so much? It would be a coup for him. Menghan agreed to allow the chief judge to have a piece of his work in order to help Shibo. The news of this artistic partnership spread and people were soon clamouring to buy their work. If Father thought anyone might have some influence on Shibo's case, then he gave them one of the works.

Soon many important people visited Wanxian women's prison to ask for Shibo's paintings. Unfortunately, the chief judge especially saw this as a business opportunity and he regularly visited and controlled access to Shibo.

Chen Taitai, one of the rich women, had been sentenced to three years because her husband had been accused of murder, for which he was sentenced to ten years. He had formerly been a division commander in Warlord Liu Xiang's army, but he didn't want to fight the Red Army. Obviously he couldn't refuse outright, so he pretended to fall ill and stayed at home until he eventually got the sack from the army. After this he became the leader of one of the gangs in the town. Chen Taitai and her husband had left two children on their own at home when they were sentenced and she was desperate to get back to them, so she begged Shibo to write an appeal to the chief judge for her. Shibo agreed to try and help them for the reasons of the children being alone and the fact that Chen hadn't wanted to fight against the Communists. Chen Taitai then also gave a large sum of money to the judge and very soon both she and her husband were released.

After that many women approached Shibo for help and her

paintings became the key to unlock the cell door. However, the key didn't work for Shibo herself.

Father kept going to the chief judge and reminding him that there wasn't any evidence to prove that Shibo had committed a crime, but each time the judge would say: 'Soon, soon. It will be soon. I am watching her case.'

Much later our suspicions were confirmed that the longer the chief judge kept Shibo under his control in prison the fuller his pockets got. During those months he amassed about 1,300 yuan, six pairs of gold earrings, a pair of gold bracelets, two fox-fur coats, countless precious ornaments and bolts of textiles, herbal tonics and of course the artworks done by Shibo and Menghan.

After Shibo's Release

Around this time the Communists and the Nationalists started their second round of cooperation to try and defeat the Japanese. Public opinion on this was at fever pitch and every day our newspaper would reprint articles from influential Communist newspapers and magazines. Then, in all of these publications, we were being told that the Nationalists under Chiang Kai-shek were pulling back from the front-line fight against the Japanese. We were told that the Nationalists were withdrawing almost to the point of being inactive and this angered the nation, especially the youth. Then our newspaper started to receive letters from hundreds of young people wanting to know how to join the Communist Party. Editor Li was very touched by the patriotic nature of these letters and wanted to help. He called us all together one day and suggested that we could set up a foundation to send some of the poorer youths to Yanan, which had been the Communist Party's heartland since the early 1920s. To do this, however, he would have to make two sub-editors redundant and spread their duties around to the rest of us. With the saving in salaries and his own personal contribution, each successful applicant to the foundation was given thirty yuan and sent to Yanan. During the year that

I was working at the *Wangzhou Daily* we must have sent over a hundred young people there. Yanan became a sacred destination for revolutionaries and the *Wangzhou Daily* became the most important newspaper for many a young radical.

My time was divided between evenings at the print factory and my hunt for news for my articles during the day. My job as proofreader started after the editor had approved all the articles. I was responsible for proofreading the local and supplement news, which usually took around five hours, but sometimes I didn't leave the factory until dawn. In those days we only had electricity for three out of ten nights so we had to rely on paraffin lamps. The fumes from the lamp on my desk would cover me in soot; even my spit was black. Each day I managed to write about three articles. If the subject matter wasn't suitable for straight reporting, then I used a different format to make my point, such as a poem or a jotting. I rarely used my real name for these pieces, but used various pseudonyms like Baldy, Black and White or Red and Blue. Baldy was the one I used the most. I was paid less than one yuan for each article, but my motivation was seeing my work in print and not the money.

Although my life was very busy, visiting Shibo in prison was still one of my priorities. Father never stopped trying to get her released. Shibo had been in prison before in 1932 in Yuechi, her home town, and Father knew that a man named Lei Qingchen had rescued her that time. So he followed up the name and found out that this man was the commissioner in Luzhuo County. Father wanted to ask Commissioner Lei to use his influence once again to help her, but Shibo was cautious, knowing that he was a favourite of the Nationalist chief intelligence officer. Although Shibo knew that Lei Qingchen had once held Communist sympathies, and was a distant relative, it had been several years since she had been in contact with him and so she wasn't sure what his views were any more.

She thought that it would be better not to contact him and that way, at least, her true identity wouldn't be revealed and so make matters worse.

However, Father went against her wishes and wrote to Commissioner Lei explaining what had happened to Shibo and asking for his help. Within a couple of days Lei Qingchen had sent a telegraph to the Wanxian Commissioner, who in turn went to the chief judge and told him that he must release Shibo. After that there was no delay. The judge came to inform Shibo that she would be released as long as she could find a local person as her guarantor. This person had to have a business premises in Wanxian in order to qualify. This was what they called a 'shop guarantor'.

I jumped up and down and cheered at this news, but realised that it was up to me to find the shop guarantor, as Father had recently gone to Zhongxian to start a new job there. His new position was as chief commander of the Zhongxian Defence Force. I was at a bit of a loss at first and wondered who I could ask to get some ideas. Then I thought of Wu Changwen. Wu had been sent to Wanxian by the Party to stay with his sister in order to recuperate. He had had a dramatic escape from a siege at Honghu Lake District and as a result had become very ill.

When I caught up with Wu I poured out to him that I needed to find a shop guarantor urgently so that Shibo could get out of prison. He put up his hand to stop me: 'Calm down. By the look of you I thought the sky must be falling. This is easy – don't worry – let's go and talk to my sister.'

I was so relieved. I had forgotten that Wu's sister owned a sewing and embroidery business with proper premises. She agreed without hesitation to be the shop guarantor herself and the next day we sorted out all the paperwork. Finally, after fifteen months, Shibo was released from Wanxian jail.

Shibo's release from prison, 1937

Chen Taitai and her husband arranged a house for Shibo to stay in as repayment for having been instrumental in getting them both out of prison. The house was lavishly decorated and they had provided everything that she could possibly need with no expense spared. The wardrobe even contained clothes for all four seasons, including a fox-fur coat. They also employed a woman who could be trusted as a maid. Shibo invited me to stay there with her, for which I was very grateful as I had been sharing a bedsit with one of my colleagues from the newspaper. I used the only bed during the daytime and my colleague used it at night. That night I telegraphed Father the good news about Shibo's release and where he could find us.

The Chens organised a celebratory banquet for the next day and two chefs arrived to prepare the food. The Chens invited their friends, local celebrities and some of the people whom Shibo had helped get released from prison. There were many toasts to Shibo during the dinner and then Mr Chen got to his feet, held his cup high and addressed her most seriously:

'Sister Chen, today is a very special day and we are all honoured to have you here. My brothers and I wanted to use this cheerful occasion to make one request of you. We hope you will be agreeable. We have all experienced what kind of person you are and we know a little bit about your past. We believe that you are truly exceptional, and are a heroine, and that it is indeed our good fortune to know you. We brothers have talked things through and we want to ask you to accept us as your sworn brothers. We do not want you to risk anything for us, but we are agreed, Sister Chen, that we want you to be our helmsman. I want to give my chair to you. From now on we can share joys and sorrows and stick together through thick and thin. We hope, Sister Chen, that you won't disappoint us.'

Then he went down on one knee, held his cup high and bowed his head to Shibo. All the other men lined up in front of her and followed suit.

This was unexpected and Shibo looked as astonished as I was. She agreed to join the gang, however, but insisted that she could not accept the first chair (ie position of seniority). Mr Chen seemed to understand and gave her the third chair. Then, to my amazement, one of the men brought in a cockerel and swiftly slit its throat. He passed it over each of our cups to allow the drops of blood to mingle with the potent rice wine. Mr Chen assured Shibo that nothing was required of the gang members except to get together occasionally. Then Shibo turned to me and said:

'Xianli, this is an opportunity for you too. You should join. It may give you help and benefits in the future.'

Mr Chen didn't hesitate in giving me the fifth chair in their gang so I raised my cup to drink with all of them.

Later I questioned Shibo as to whether it was a good idea to be in this gang. She told me that during the chaos and turmoil of war, people often formed gangs as a support system to get them through the hard times. She thought that Mr Chen was basically a good person who followed his ideals as far as possible. He had been sacked from his army position because he didn't want to fight the Red Army, but staying in his position could have given him a higher status in society and a better life. As for the other brothers of the gang, she thought they were good fellows too and it couldn't do any harm to be sworn brothers with any of them.

Three days later Father turned up on the doorstep in great excitement. I led him upstairs to the sitting room and he stood in front of Shibo with both hands cupped in front of his chest and he kept repeating: 'Congratulations! Thank heavens you don't have to spend another year in that dire jail.'

'This is all due to your hard work.'

'You know, a few days ago I dreamed that you were free and then I received the telegraph from Xianli to prove it! I already had to make a trip to Wanxian for a meeting next week, so all I had to do was bring it forward.'

I was enjoying seeing them so happy together and then Shibo suggested that we should celebrate by having a meal at a nearby restaurant. We decided to make it an early New Year celebration as well, as Shibo pointed out that we couldn't know when Father might be able to visit again.

Several weeks later, Shibo was receiving a stream of visitors from all walks of life almost every day. She had also done a lot of painting, stating that 'her heart had settled into peace now that she was out of prison'. She seemed very happy, but gradually I became aware that she was only content during the daytime when she was fully occupied. In the evening, however, it was evident that she had a great deal on her mind and then I realised that she wasn't sleeping very much. I would hear long, heavy sighs from her. I asked her what was wrong and why she felt so heavy hearted. She would only say that she had important things to sort out and needed to take a trip to Yichang. Shibo asked Mr Chen to make the travel arrangements for her and so he hired a boat for her and a man to accompany her all the way there.

A month later Shibo returned and I could see that she was feeling even worse than before she left. She then told me the reason behind her trip to Yichang. She was trying to re-establish her link with the Communist Party, with a view to either continuing on her way to Russia or receiving a new mission from them. When she arrived in Yichang, however, she was met by the full force of the Japanese bombardment of the area. She found that the location for her prearranged meeting with her Party contact had been blown to smithereens. She stayed in the area in the hope of still making contact with the Party, somehow, until it was no longer possible, because the Japanese advanced to occupy Wuhan and then Yichang itself. At that point the city disintegrated into chaos. After several days of direct bombing, dead bodies were being left where they fell in the streets and disease started to spread. Everybody who was able fled from Yichang and Shibo had no choice but to do the same. Yichang was destroyed. She arrived back in Wanxian with empty hands and her dream of going to Russia to study was crushed once again, but this time for ever.

On the third day after Shibo's return from Yichang, the maid announced that there was a military officer to see her. He was tall and distinguished looking. He was wearing a yellow wool uniform, on the shoulder of which was a badge showing the rank of major general. Shibo was certainly surprised to see him and said: 'Good heavens! What kind of wind blew you here?'

This man was Lei Zhonghuo, the celebrated Major General Lei. Lei had been an officer in Warlord Yang Sen's army for many years, but he had also been following his own ideologies and had undermined Yang Sen's objectives on many occasions. For instance he had been regularly supporting Shibo and her husband Yubi's guerrilla force in the Huaying Mountains in their struggles against the warlords. He arranged for the purchase and transfer of weapons between Chongqing and the Huaying Mountains and he was key in the setting up of Shibo's tailoring shop in Chongqing. The profit from this business was used to fund the guerrilla force, manufacture all their clothing and set up a spy network. Lei had been one of their major patrons. Although he had always managed to keep his true allegiances secret, Yang Sen had now sidelined him and had left him without a regiment.

He sat down, took a deep breath and started to talk: 'Lianshi, I have been looking for you so hard! If I hadn't met Commander Xiao, I still wouldn't know that you had been in Wanxian jail for well over a year.'

I brought tea to him and addressed him as 'Uncle Lei'. He scrutinised me and asked: 'Is your son really so big now? It doesn't seem possible.'

Shibo smiled. 'Where could I get such good luck from? This is Lin Zhuxi's son. Such a capable young man. He is already a journalist.'

'Aah! So you are Xianli. I heard you are a very good tennis player!'

He turned back to Shibo in a hurry to get to the point of his visit:

'Yang Sen wants to send me to the front-line fight against the Japanese, but he told me that I had to recruit my own force – he wouldn't give me even one man. Well, I'm not afraid of having untrained troops and I felt sure that I could easily get a sizeable number of volunteers. So I unfurled my flag and started recruiting in the eastern region and, guess what, your old right-hand men, Chen and Li, turned up. After we spoke, they went out and found others and now I have three thousand men altogether, including most of your old fighters.'

Lei couldn't contain his excitement and sprung up from his chair and started pacing up and down the room, the soles of his shiny army boots clacking on the floorboards.

'Lianshi, this time we are not killing our own people – it is a fight against the Japanese invaders. You see – we should all be happy.'

He pulled his chair nearer Shibo's and sat down again.

'Lianshi, I have a request for you. Please – do not refuse me.'

'Please say it.'

'I want to invite you to join me at the front line. Let's fight the Japanese together!' Lei didn't give Shibo any chance to reply and carried straight on, even more impassioned:

'Lianshi, you must know by now how much I admire you. When I was helping you buy guns and set up the tailoring shop, I could see for myself just how capable and courageous you are and how knowledgeable you are about *so* many things, including military strategy. Of course, I heard all the stories about your reputation in battle and your skill with guns, but I thought that perhaps they were exaggerated somewhat. But now! Now, after talking to Chen and Li and some of the others from the Huaying Mountains – those brothers of yours – they told me so much more, so many stories about what you did.

Now, Lianshi – from the bottom of my heart – I am over-flowing with admiration for you. We want – we *need* – you to come with us. So many of your fighters have joined my force. I will give you a regiment. Chen and Li have a battalion each. They will be under your command. What do you say?'

Shibo stayed quiet for some time and then said: 'Major General Lei – such important matters. Can you give me time to think before I give you my answer?'

'Very well, I will ask Chen, Li and some others to come to see you this afternoon so you can all discuss this between you.' He left in a great hurry.

Shibo couldn't rest at all after Lei left. She smoked one cig-arette after another until the room disappeared behind a cloud of blue smoke.

Later that afternoon Chen led a group of men to the house. I witnessed big, strong men kneel down before Shibo and cry their hearts out. They told her that after their Big Brother Liao (Shibo's husband Yubi) had been executed and she had gone into hiding, their people had been massacred by the war-lord. Many other people in the Huaying Mountains who were completely innocent had been cruelly slaughtered too. After a while, I couldn't endure listening to any more of the stories of extreme brutality and went out for a long walk. At dusk I returned to the house and helped the maid prepare food for the men before they left.

When I went back upstairs to see Shibo she said to me: 'Xianli, this time I really will leave Sichuan to go and fight the Japanese.'

'Have you decided for sure?'

Shibo looked at me steadily and nodded her head: 'But I have to wait until they are prepared and then I will go and join them.'

Lei heard from Chen about Shibo's decision and he came

to the house very early the following morning. Shibo very earnestly warned him:

'You know, Yubi and I fought Yang Sen – that rat-goblin – for years. Please be very vigilant. It is possible that he may not really trust you. Do not let him trick you.'

'I have no illusions about Yang Sen and I have already made up my mind. It is very likely that all he wants us for is to carry on his feud with Warlord Liu Xiang. Liu Xiang wears the crown of Sichuan now and Yang Sen is still smarting from that defeat. If he has no intention of fighting the foreigners, then I will take my men to Chen Yi or Zhu De and join the Red Army – I can't believe that they wouldn't want us to help them.'

Shibo nodded her head: 'That's good – clever rabbits always have three holes to bolt to. If you're dealing with scum like Yang Sen then you have to be cleverer than he is, otherwise you may be the one to suffer.'

Lei went to the stairs and called to his batman to come up. The batman came up carrying a bamboo basket and put it on the table. Then he lifted the cover and took out one of the tightly packaged, brown-paper parcels. He opened it up carefully to show Shibo and Lei pointed to the contents:

'Lianshi, here is 1.4 kilos of the very best crude opium. It's worth about 1500 silver yuan. Get someone to sell it for you. This is an advance payment for you to buy the things you need. After that, just wait till I have arrived at my base and then I will send you some more money.'

Before he left, Lei took Shibo's hands in his: 'Lianshi, sort out everything as soon as you possibly can. When I am ready, you *have* to come immediately.'

Once Lei had left, Shibo remained restless and said to me: 'This time I will be fighting for the sake of the whole country. The coming battles won't be like those cat-and-mouse skirmishes against the warlords – the Japanese have aeroplanes with bombs. It will be a modern war. Look how in only a few months they have managed to occupy half of China – none of us can afford to underestimate the Japanese.'

The next day I accompanied Shibo to the Life Bookshop in the high street and she bought many books on military strategy and politics. There were so many books in fact that I couldn't carry them all and we had to hail a rickshaw to take us home. Then I went to the *Wangzhou Daily* offices and borrowed lots of articles for her to study. In the following days she read all day long and well into the nights. She concentrated in detail on accounts of specific battles, then she analysed them and discussed them with me. She was full of enthusiasm.

As for the crude opium, Shibo asked Mr Chen to sell it for her. She sent some money to Sister Zen and her two children in Chongqing and included in her letter a plea to Sister Zen *never* to send her children back to their home town, Yuechi. There were two reasons for this request, which were: firstly, because she knew that her sister-in-law would ill-treat them and keep them like slaves. Secondly, she was afraid that their presence there would be reported to her enemies who would then kill the children in order to 'clean the root'.

Shibo was as prepared as she could be.

I received a letter from Second Uncle to say that it was Grandmother's sixtieth birthday and he wanted Father and me to go home for the important celebration.

Father asked both Menghan and Shibo to honour his mother with a piece of artwork for her birthday. He also invited both of them to come with us.

The invitation seemed to make Shibo feel a bit awkward and after two days she said to me: 'Xianli, I will do a very good

104

painting for your Grandmother and I hope it will make her happy. And although I would like to attend the birthday celebrations, there are two things I am not sure of – I wonder if you can think of a solution for me.'

'Shibo, if there is anything you have difficulty with, please just let me know.'

'The first problem you already know about – I am waiting for your Uncle Lei's letter calling me to join him and his troops. What if – and this is a big thing – what if he cannot find me? You know he needs me to leave as soon as he gives the word. The second problem is…' she paused, slightly embarrassed: 'The second problem is – in what name can I attend your grandmother's celebration? I am not from your family – not even a distant relative – nor am I your fellow countrywoman – so in what capacity can you and your father introduce me?

'The first one is easy – we won't be at Grandmother's for very long, less than a week in fact. We can always leave contact information with the maid should the letter arrive from Uncle Lei before we're back. However, I am sure that he is nowhere near ready yet – he has over three thousand people to sort out. The second problem is not so easy – and I don't know what to say!'

I was a young man so my experience was limited, but I realised that Shibo did have to be careful. She was used to doing many things not normally expected of a woman. Many of these freedoms, though, had been afforded to her because she was married and this gave her protection. Now that she was a widow, she had to be mindful of her reputation. Following an unrelated man back to his home, where life carried on in the traditional ways, was risky. After much deliberation, Shibo decided to accept the invitation so as not to disappoint my father, her good friend.

Shibo then set aside all else to concentrate on painting. In the end she did four paintings on silk, each one representing a different season. She mixed the colours herself and in order to get a dense black, she used the soot from the bottom of the wok and mixed it with ink. She painted butterflies, bees and birds amongst the flowers, to depict movement, and then added magpies which we called 'the birds of happiness' to represent Grandmother's birthday. The wings on the insects and birds shone with iridescence and were so skilfully done that they looked as if they had just flown into the paintings. When they were finished Shibo hung them on the wall and took a step back to inspect them:

'Xianli, I think these are my best paintings to date. I am happy with them.'

Then I helped her to take them to Menghan so that he could add his calligraphy to them. As soon as we entered his frame shop we saw that he had done four scrolls, mounted on silkscreens, and they were magnificent. I thought about how much effort these two skilled masters had made for my Grandmother. It would be an honour for our family and Grandmother's good fortune to be presented with these expert works of art.

After leaving Menghan, Shibo wanted to buy more presents for Grandmother. She kept asking me what she would like, but all I knew was that Grandmother lived very frugally and I had no idea as to her likes or dislikes, so I was of no use to her at all! Nevertheless, among other things, we came away with a velvet hat, a leather jerkin, four metres of black velvet and some ginseng tonic. I kept telling Shibo that it was more than enough, but she didn't stop until she had spent about one hundred yuan. She also bought a present each for everyone in the family. By the time Father arrived from Zhongxian, all the presents had been wrapped and the only thing left for him to do was to place the calligraphy and paintings inside a decorated wooden box, which had been specially made for them.

The next morning, the three of us went down to the docks and hitched a ride on a textile cargo boat which was going to Yunyang. I stood in the stern to help the boatman steer, while Father and Shibo sat together. I didn't mean to listen to Father and Shibo as they talked, but a wayward breeze blew their conversation to my ears...

'You see, I am neither related to you nor connected to you by being a fellow countrywoman, so how on earth are you going to explain to them who I am and why I am accompanying you to your elderly mother's festivities? You must surely see my problem.'

'Oh – well – err – well – umm! In what name – with what status? Aah – in the name of being a heroine, of course! My family know all about you and they respect and admire you as much as I do – they can't wait to meet you. You don't need any particular status – don't worry about it.'

'Well, that's you boasting *again* – you're always doing that – you really do praise me too much! But let us remember the Confucius saying: "If names aren't correct, then words won't ring true." I would like – I *need* a proper name and status to be legitimate.'

'Then perhaps you can acknowledge my mother as your godmother – what do you think about that? That would be sufficient, surely.'

'No, not good.'

'Well, what then? Why are you laughing at me like that?'

'I have an idea. What if we became in-laws? I like Xianli so very much – if he became my son-in-law then it would be my daughter, Ninjun's, very good fortune – she couldn't want anyone better than Xianli.'

'Really?'

'Of course, really!'

'I would like that very much, but are you sure you wouldn't regret it later?'

'I could never regret it.'

They laughed merrily together and I smiled to myself thinking that it was a very good trick of Shibo's. It would satisfy everyone and we wouldn't have to go through with it. I hadn't told them about Guanqing yet, but we had made plans for our future together. She would come to Wanxian and go to the education college there. In the meantime I would introduce her to Father and Shibo – as soon as she had finished her final exams at school. I hadn't had a letter from her for two months now, but I supposed it was because she was so busy studying.

We were met at Yunyang port by Eighth Aunt and my eldest cousin. Eighth Aunt had hired two sedan chairs, one for herself and one for Shibo, and three horses for the next part of the journey. It was another thirty miles to Grandmother's house in Yunan. However, Shibo didn't want to be carried in a sedan chair but preferred to ride a horse. Eighth Aunt was horrified and rushed over to her: 'No, no – not possible! A woman on a horse? People will laugh – and what if you fall off and hurt yourself?'

Shibo wouldn't listen and took the reins to my horse and leapt on its bare back, so Eighth Aunt had to dismiss one sedan chair and hire another horse. My cousin led the way and Father and I were at the rear, but Shibo kept urging her horse into a gallop, overtaking my cousin and circling us at the rear. Father was delighted with her antics, but warned her not to tire the horse as it was travelling twice the distance as the others. We cut quite a spectacle and many people stared. It was obvious that they had never seen a woman ride a horse before.

After fifteen miles we left the horses and sedan chair and had to take a small boat to travel up the Tangqi River, against the current, until we reached the rapids. At this point we had to get out and walk and let the boat haulers pull the boat through the shallows. Much to everybody's consternation, Shibo decided to help the haulers and took one of the ropes. Eighth Aunt was almost crying in her efforts to prevent her: 'This is not right. You are our family's honoured guest *and* a woman. We cannot allow you to haul the boat. What will people think?'

'Please do not worry – I know what I am doing – sometimes I used to haul the boats in my home town on the Qu River. I just want to exercise my bones a little!'

Not one of us could stop her, so we all had to help haul it! After we got back on the boat after the rapids, Eighth Aunt took Shibo's hands and said with much amusement: 'Shijie! If I hadn't seen you ride a horse bareback and haul a boat with a rope with my own eyes, then I would never have believed it – not even if I were told a hundred times. It seems that my brother's description and stories about you are true after all – we thought he was just telling tall stories!'

When we arrived at the dock in Yunan it was dusk and all the family, except for Grandmother, was there to greet us. It was wonderful to see them all again. Grandmother was waiting at the gate of the house. She reached for Shibo's hand to greet her first and said: 'You see, I wanted to come down to the riverside to greet you, but they wouldn't let me!'

Soon we were all sitting together after a meal and Shibo gave out the gifts she had bought. She gave Grandmother all hers last. Grandmother was overwhelmed and kept repeating: 'I like, I like. I like very much. You are so polite.'

The ladies surrounded Shibo and inundated her with questions, while Father and I hung up the paintings and calligraphies in the hall ready for the banquet the next day.

Everybody started to arrive at noon on the day of Grandmother's birthday. Our branch of the Lin family was still considered to be important in the region and all the distant relatives who had been invited were happy for the opportunity to meet Father again. He had returned home, not as a fugitive like the last time, nor as a regimental commander, but this time he held a higher position. They described him as 'Liu Xiang's man' and many of them viewed him as a useful contact.

As people filed in they commented on the calligraphy and paintings. They were much admired and many of the ladies tried to touch the butterflies to see if they were real! Two elderly men, who thought they knew a lot about art, asked Father what man had done the paintings as he was obviously a great master and they wanted to look out for his name in the future. Father thought this was hilarious and indicated Shibo and said: 'Gentlemen, let me introduce you. This is Master Chen Lianshi. He is a lecturer at the Chongqing Southwestern Art Academy.'

'Ha! I saw her yesterday – riding a horse,' a man shouted out from the crowd.

'Well, I saw her hauling a boat,' said someone else.

During the meal there were many toasts to Grandmother, but there were also toasts to Father congratulating him on his position and to Shibo as an honoured guest.

After most people had left, Uncle Luohan Tang's second oldest brother arrived. He was the richest man in Yunan, being the owner of the salt factory. He had come to invite Father and me, as guests returned home, and Shibo, as a far-off guest, to his house for a meal on the following day. Father said that he had wanted to take Shibo to the Dripping Temple the next day and asked him whether he would be willing to host a meal at the temple instead. He agreed to it and everybody liked the idea.

The next morning, Eighth Aunt arranged a sedan chair for Shibo as it was almost ten miles to the Dripping Temple, but once again she refused, saying that walking was the best way to admire the scenery.

The Dripping Temple had been built before the Ming Dynasty and was situated halfway up a mountain. The back of the temple was on a cliff edge and the front overlooked the Tangqi River. Pine trees studded the mountainside. We went through the lower gate to the temple and came to the Lawn Pagoda, which was built on two large rocks and straddled a spring. The spring then formed a stream which dropped into a large pond on one side of the lawn before carrying on down the mountainside. This was the reason for the name Dripping Temple. The abbot came to greet us and to lead us up to the main temple. We crossed a small bridge over a lily pond, which was full of fish and turtles. The abbot explained that they had all been brought to the temple by philanthropists who supported the temple, in order to free the creatures' spirits. Some of the turtles were over a hundred years old. At the temple Second Uncle Tang hosted a banquet for us. During the meal, Shibo turned to Second Uncle Tang and respectfully called him:

'Erge [Second Brother], I am told that you are fortunate to hold many salt wells and salt stoves in your hands.'

'I am truly fortunate in the accumulated merits of my ancestors, yes.'

'Yunan has over two thousand years of salt mining history and I understand that you have a particular method of evaporation here to produce the salt crystals.'

'Yes, there are certain ways of doing it.'

'Well, I've come such a long way. It would be such a pity if I didn't get to see the famous Yunan salt wells and the factory whilst I'm here – don't you think?'

'Er, ah!' Second Uncle Tang was struck dumb as were the rest of us. However, I realised that my poem about the pulley workers had probably aroused her curiosity.

111

Since salt mining had started there, no woman had ever been into the area of the salt wells in Yunan. Around the stoves was especially dangerous. The heat of each stove reached several hundred degrees and even the air was searing. Accidents did occasionally happen where one of the workers slipped, or was overcome by the fumes and fell into the woks from where there was no return. The other main reason, of course, was that the men worked naked. Second Uncle Tang didn't want to refuse an honoured guest's request, but he was at a loss to know how he could allow it. Father and he stepped aside to discuss it and finally Second Uncle Tang said to Shibo:

'Alright – if Shijie is determined to see the salt wells then I will think of something to make it possible. However, we really think that you cannot go to the stoves as it is far too hazardous. If you all meet me at the big well tomorrow morning at ten o'clock I will be waiting for you.'

When Grandmother heard about the following day's plan, she got very upset:

'Since the creator separated the heaven from the earth no woman has ever been to the salt wells. It would offend public decency and corrupt public morals. You must not do this – not under any circumstances. You are the honoured guest of our Lin family and I cannot allow you to visit that place.'

Father had to calm her down by telling her that, after all, we wouldn't take Shibo anywhere near the salt wells and that we would merely be going to Second Uncle Tang's house for a meal. Grandmother was greatly relieved and said: 'This is acceptable.'

The next morning we were all surprised to see that Shibo was dressed in a grey trouser suit and had tucked her hair into a cap. She also wore a pair of very dark sunglasses so you couldn't see her eyes. She could, more or less, have passed for a modern young man.

When we arrived at the main well, Second Uncle Tang and his steward were waiting for us. The well had been completely enclosed by corn stalks and the opening into the area was covered by a black cloth curtain. Just being near the well was enough to set us sneezing and to make our eyes water, as the alkaline fumes were so strong. We could hear the pulley workers shouting out the numbers of full buckets they were hauling and the splash of the brine being poured into the bamboo channels. The steward pulled aside the curtain so that we could see the well itself and I was astonished to see that the labourers were wearing blue shorts and had white cotton towels around their necks. The area had also been cleaned up in comparison to when I had seen it last, but the fumes were far worse than I remembered. The men stopped working for a moment to have a look at us, but all eyes rested on Shibo. She really stood out from the rest of us and it may have been better had she not tried to disguise herself, because she looked like a foreigner and that was just as unusual as having a woman visit. Shibo stepped forward to speak to one of the workers, but Father pulled her back quickly. Unfortunately, Shibo commented to Father about the appalling working conditions too loudly and the labourers realised that she was not only dressed in a curious fashion but was, in fact, a woman. They all surged forward and Second Uncle Tang ushered us out through the curtain in a panic. We were followed all the way home by a noisy crowd.

When we were safely inside, Shibo removed her cap and sunglasses and said: 'Look at you all – has a woman going to the salt wells really scared you that much? I don't think it seemed to be much of a problem. I was very careful not to say anything that I shouldn't have so as not to make trouble for Second Brother.'

'Shijie – you have no idea! You don't realise how much trouble Second Brother went to so that you could see just one salt well today. He arranged for the shorts and towels that you saw the labourers wearing to be made overnight, just so that they would appear decent in front of you. He had to give them orders to wear them, otherwise they would be sent home without pay. He also ordered them not to talk to or question us – their language is obscene by the way – or even look at us. They did a huge clean-up too. And another thing – Second Brother didn't know that you were going to dress up as a man today!'

'Ah! Yes, this is my fault – I forgot to tell you that I sometimes dress up as a man when going to certain places in order to avoid trouble. Please give my apologies to Second Brother.'

'I would also like to point out that there is no point in dressing up as a man if you are going to sound like a woman when you talk!' said Father.

A few days after we arrived back in Wanxian, Shibo received the anxiously awaited letter from Lei, but he wasn't calling her to go yet. He obviously wrote the letter in high spirits. He said that the troops had been gathered together successfully and were busy training, but they were still waiting for the uniforms and equipment. He also said how impatient he was to get to the front line and start fighting the Japanese. He enclosed a bank draft for 1500 yuan. He asked Shibo to use five hundred of it to buy some medicines for the troops, especially something for diarrhoea, and that the rest of the money was for Shibo for her own final preparations.

In the very early hours next morning, Shibo knocked on my door. She apologised for waking me, but said that she needed to talk. I had never seen her look so weary and anxious before and it made me worried. I made her some tea and lit her cigarette before I dared to ask what was troubling her.

114

'My child. Am I really able to take on the title of regimental commander?'

'Shibo – you have fought so many battles before. You have led your people – you have even done this on your own. What can you be afraid of now by joining up with Uncle Lei's bigger troop?'

'I not only fought – I was even sent to the execution ground and survived – so who and what am I afraid of? Nobody and nothing. But then I was in the mountains leading my enemies around in circles – one shot here, another there. Anyway, most of the warlord's soldiers were addicted to opium and were soon incapacitated by their cravings, which almost made it easy for me. I had a little over a hundred people under my command then – we used home-made guns and cannons. We hid the gunpowder amongst the rocks. Now – now it is all going to be so different: I will have more than a thousand troops to command. And now… those Japanese come from a different world; now they drop bombs from aircraft. I saw it in Yichan – the bombs dropped from the sky like raindrops and left the earth looking like a honeycomb. There was no place to hide.'

'Shibo, if you feel unsure about it there is still time to write to Uncle Lei.'

'What are you thinking Xianli? Do you think I am a coward?' She spoke sharply, but tapped me on my forehead gently: 'What I am afraid of this time is that my luck will run out and I may not return from this war – it is far bigger than any of us – and if I die, then who is going to look after my children – Ninjun and Yabin? I think I have to ask you and your father to take care of them in my place.'

I didn't say a word, because the thought of losing Shibo made me feel like I was falling through space. She inhaled deeply on her cigarette and sighed equally deeply:

'This country may be on the brink of disaster. If I don't fight now for my country, then I will feel that I had wronged it and wronged my husband too, who died for the cause. If I do go to the front line, though, I will be feeling so guilty about my children. They have never known a day's peace. Yubi and I were constantly on the move and we often had to leave them hidden, because we knew our enemies were not only after us, they were trying to kill them too. You know, we even had to hide our names – they have never been able to call me "Mum"; it is safer if they call me *Boniang*.' ['Aunty' – specifically the wife of the eldest paternal uncle.]

Shibo fell into silence and we both stared at the candle flame as it gently danced. I was unable to put my thoughts in order. I felt so safe there next to her within the pool of kindly yellow light, but beyond it the darkness seemed threatening. As if from a long way away, Shibo spoke again quietly:

'Xianli, do you think you could be a brother to Ninjun and Yabin and could you see them as your own sister and brother? Do you think you could take good care of them?'

Then Shibo looked unbearably sad when she said: 'Tell them – when I'm gone – that it was never because I didn't love them or I meant to abandon them. Tell them that the choices were impossible ones to make. To be a mother meant turning my back on the needs of our country, but to be a freedom fighter meant not being there to fulfil the needs of my children. The truth is, I am just a woman and cannot split myself in two.'

I found myself kneeling in front of Shibo and crying my heart out.

Later we went out together to buy the medicines as requested by Uncle Lei and then posted them to him. When we got back to the house Shibo told the maid that she didn't want to see any visitors at all from then onwards. Then she shut herself away to read newspapers and books on military strategy, whilst waiting for news from Uncle Lei.

By June many devastating pieces of news were appearing in the newspapers each day. One day the reports said that the Japanese were concentrating their bombardment along the banks of the Yangtze River. Another day they said that they had already occupied Anhui Province. Day after day passed and still there was no news from Uncle Lei. Shibo was getting very agitated and I tried to divert her attention by suggesting that we went to the cinema to watch an anti-Japanese film which was currently showing. Just as we were about to go out the door Uncle Lei came running up and we were both taken aback:

'My heavens – you are back! What happened? You left us with a long, horrible wait.'

Uncle Lei didn't say anything. When we went back upstairs to the living room he sank heavily into a chair and put his head in his hands. He sighed: 'Lianshi – we lost – I – lost everything.' His voice was rasping and we could barely hear him. Then tears spurted out from under his eyelids like a river bursting its banks. Shibo placed a towel in his rigid hands.

'A man like you does not cry easily. Take your time to tell us what happened.'

'I led our men as far as Anqin and was on time to meet Warlord Yang Sen – he was very happy to see that we had over three thousand volunteers. Then he told us to wait there for uniforms and arms and we trained hard in the meantime. I wrote to you at this stage and was still full of hope that it wouldn't be long before we were a properly equipped force ready for action, but we waited and waited. Then we heard that the Japanese were occupying Anhui Province and still we were left unprepared and waiting. Finally Yang Sen arrived to say that the Japanese ground forces were fighting their way rapidly to Anqin and that his troops had suffered heavy casualties. Then he told me that he wanted to take my men to replenish the ranks in other regiments. I was furious with him as this didn't make any tactical sense – we were a proper unit and the men were all loyal to Chen and Li under my command. If we had been armed we could have moved there and then to the front line as a force to be reckoned with. I shouted at Yang Sen that I was not his recruitment agent. I refused to split them up. But before we even had time to decide what to do next, the Japanese unleashed a three-thousand-strong ground force attack, backed up with artillery and an air bombardment, on Yang Sen's twenty mile-long defence line. Yang Sen's troops were wiped out and then the bombardment reached us. What could we do without any weapons except for knives and sticks the volunteers brought with them? Not much, that's what. The Japanese encircled Anqin and took the city in two days – they even had gunships on the river bombarding us. I can tell you – not many of us survived and those who did were lucky to escape out of the town.'

Uncle Lei paused for a long time, sighing all the while, and he still hadn't looked at Shibo until he said:

'I felt so – so humiliated. Three thousand men – wiped out – and many of them were your brothers, Lianshi. I did not have the courage to come here to see you – I did not know how to explain the loss – the waste – the senseless waste of so many lives. Instead, I went in search of Zhu De – I wanted to offer myself to fight in his force against the Japanese. When I found him in Yanan, he had already been made the chief commander of the Communist forces. Zhu De persuaded me that I would be more useful coming back to Sichuan to reorganise here for the reason that Chiang Kai-shek is in the middle of moving his Nationalist Headquarters to Chongqing. He said that local knowledge and contacts are invaluable and so I would be able to make a bigger difference from Sichuan. Lianshi – only after Zhu De talked to me was I ready to come back here. He is right – we need to re-establish ourselves here – and even if we find that Chiang Kai-shek really doesn't have any intention of fighting the Japanese, then we still have the option of going to Yanan to join Zhu De and the rest of the Communists.'

Uncle Lei had brought a magazine with him, *The New North-West*, to show us. Published in it was Mao Zedong's article 'On Protracted War' (May 1938), which had been presented at the Yanan Association for the Study of the War of Resistance against Japan. The next day I took it to work with me to show everyone and we decided to publish it in the *Wangzhou Daily*. It created a furore throughout south-east Sichuan because people were looking for answers for what was happening throughout the country.

Lost Love

Shibo was not in good spirits. Her dream of going to Russia had gone for good. All the lengthy and detailed preparations for going to the front line to fight the Japanese had been for nothing. Her efforts to re-establish her link with the Communist Party had also failed. I felt powerless to help her so I wrote to Father asking him to come to Wanxian in the hope that he might be able to make a difference. He wrote back saying that he was unable to leave his soldiers in the middle of their training, but that perhaps Shibo and I could go to Zhongxian instead. I jumped at the idea, because it was, of course, where Guanqing was.

Mr Chen managed to hire a boat for us to set off very early the following morning. I could hardly contain my excitement, but I was also worried because I hadn't had a letter from Guanqing for so long. In our letters to each other we never held back our thoughts and emotions, so I couldn't understand this break in our correspondence. I had very deep feelings for her.

The mist cleared before we reached the Yangtze Gorges with the sharply peaked mountains rising immediately from the shores of the river. It was a stunning view. Shibo pointed out the highest peak in the distance.

'Look, look at the Qing Liangyu peak. Beyond it is the famous Treasure Stone Village. The heroine Qing Liangyu lived there in the Ming Dynasty. Have you heard of her?'

'Yes, Grandmother mentioned her sometimes when she used to tell us about our Lin family ancestors. She said that Qing Liangyu had been a leader in this region and that after her death the local people named the mountain after her. They still believe that she stands guard up there.'

'That's right. What else do you know about the history of Sichuan?'

'Grandmother told us that our ancestors came to Sichuan to join the Encircle Land Movement. She said that this meant that anyone, by using a trail of straw, could encircle a piece of land of any size and anywhere they liked, after which it officially belonged to them. At that time Sichuan was considered virgin land only just separated from the heavens.'

'Ah! That was the time called "Fuguang" – the filling up of Sichuan by people from Fujian and Guangdong Provinces, a mass migration in the early Qing Dynasty (in the seventeenth century). Now I'll tell you about before that time – why Sichuan became so empty of people:

Zhang Xianzhong was the leader of a peasants' rebellion and he succeeded in becoming the emperor of the Dashuan Dynasty. He wanted to establish his capital in Chengdu in the 'Big Western State' (Daxi). On 16 October 1644 he led his force to occupy Chengdu and he immediately started to brutally kill the populace. He also ate people's body parts. Women were taken to the military camp for his soldiers to rape and then their small, bound feet were cut off. There was soon a mountain of feet and he called this 'The Lotus Peak', then set fire to it. As he watched the feet burning he called it 'candlelight towards heaven'. He kept the boys aged between fifteen and twenty

121

as his fighters. Promotion in his military force was gained according to how many people each soldier killed each day. He sent his men out with the specific order to kill as many as they liked and he called this 'mowing the lawn'. During his affairs-of-state meeting with his ministers each morning, he released his dog, a mastiff, to sniff at those who were previously opposed to him but who had later crossed over to his side. He suspected that they were likely to betray him, seeing as they had betrayed somebody else already. If the dog barked at one of them, then he commanded that the man be taken out and killed and he called this 'heaven killing'. Emperor Zhang Xiangzhong was a peasant himself and illiterate and, therefore, he hated scholars. On false pretences he lured all the scholars from across the land to gather in his capital and, when they were all together, he ordered their slaying. There were thousands of them. There was one amongst them, though, whom the emperor saved because he was very fond of him. He was a young scholar, widely thought of as a genius. The emperor kept him at his side all the time for a while until one day he said to his men: 'This scholar – I am really fond of him and I don't like to let him out of my sight. If I kill him, I won't have to care so much about him.' So he killed him.

The rivers flowed with the bodies of the dead and the earth of Sichuan was coloured red by their blood. The whole of Sichuan Province was left with less than a hundred families and one town. This town consisted of thirty-two families comprising thirty-one men and thirty-two women. So this is why Sichuan was so deserted – Zhang Xianzhong almost wiped out the entire population.

What a shocking story. Then Shibo said:

'Do you know the saying "When the world is in disorder the chaos started in Sichuan, but when the world is governed Sichuan remains ungovernable"? That is to say that throughout history Sichuan folk have always been rebellious. We've always needed people like the heroine Qing Liangyu to lead us, but not many like her have come forward down the ages. I admire her with all my heart.'

'But Shibo – you are one of them – you could be compared to Qing Liangyu.'

'What – me! Hah – who am I? I'm a failure time and time again – heart set higher than the sky – nothing achieved and no success.' She looked towards the peak of Qing Liangyu and shook her head, grimacing bitterly.

We arrived in Zhongxian at noon and waited at the port, thinking that Father would be there to meet us, but there was no sign of him, so I led Shibo into the town and we checked into a hotel. I wanted Shibo to rest while I went to find Father, but she insisted on coming with me.

Zhongxian is a very hilly town, like most towns in the eastern region of Sichuan. It was only two miles up the hill to Father's headquarters, but it took us over an hour to get there because Shibo stopped to read every word carved on the stone 'loyalty archways' which spanned our path. They had been erected to the memory of all the chaste or virginal women of the town who had died loyally for their husbands or betrothed. Shibo was outraged by the suffering imposed on women and girls by a feudal moral code and said that nothing could justify it.

Father wasn't at the headquarters when we finally got there, but the adjutant received us very politely. He obviously mistook Shibo for my mother because he took us straight into Father's room. It was a small, sparsely furnished, untidy room. The single bed had a straw mat on the base and a thin quilt was pushed carelessly to one side. The table was piled high with newspapers and sheets of writing paper. The adjutant brought us some tea and said to me:

'Look at your father's room – it's nothing like a high-ranking official's living quarters, but it is his choice.' He then apologised to us for not meeting us at the port, saying that they were expecting us to arrive in the afternoon. He was about to send someone to fetch Father, who was busy with field operation training, when we asked whether we could go to him instead to see how the troops were being trained.

The adjutant took us to a clearing in some woodland on a hill nearby where Father was giving a lecture to about two hundred soldiers. After a while the adjutant interrupted him to let him know that we were here. Father packed his things up immediately and asked another officer to take over. He ran over to us like a happy little boy.

'Ah! How come you managed to arrive so early? I wanted to meet you at the port – and why didn't you let the adjutant summon me sooner?'

'You are such an important man now that we couldn't bother you. Anyway, it was a chance to listen to your lecture and learn something!'

'Shijie, you are teasing me again, aren't you? I learned from you – you see how I took my soldiers into the field to follow the Communists' way of training troops: hard training and plain living, so when the real fight comes along they won't be too fragile. I want them to be as good as the Communist army.'

'Shh! My brother, are you blind – can you not see where you are? This is still the Guomingdan's rear – you need to be more careful what you say and what you do.'

'Hah – it doesn't matter – I've already been accused a few times of having a red hat on my head – I don't really care what they do to me any more.'

'Look, we have so much to do yet – I don't like you being so careless. You could jeopardise the safety of all of us.' Shibo shook her head and sighed.

124

We returned to the hotel and then went out for a meal. Father took us to a restaurant and ordered the best marinated bean curd in the town:

'Shijie, you must try this, it's delicious. It's the local delicacy and Xianli's favourite too.'

I nodded and the thoughts of Guanqing filled my head as I remembered how she had given me a jar of home-made marinated bean curd once. I couldn't concentrate on anything else for the remainder of the meal.

The next day I left Father and Shibo to their own devices and went in search of my old friends. More importantly I was going to try and see Guanqing somehow. Each time I wondered why she hadn't written to me for so long, my insides twisted. I decided to go and see Teacher Yang first. I walked through the park and passed the tennis court. It looked sadly neglected and it was obvious nobody had enjoyed a game there for quite a while. It had been one of my favourite places.

I reached Teacher Yang's gate and hesitated as I was so nervous, but I took a deep breath and moved forward to knock on the door. It was Teacher Yang who opened it and his wife quickly appeared behind him. They were both so glad to see me. We sat and chatted about all sorts of things, but I was really waiting for them to mention Guanqing first. I think they were deliberately trying to avoid talking about her, so I had to ask:

'Teacher Yang, tell me, has anything happened to Guanqing?'

'Don't you know? Weren't you keeping in touch with each other by letter?'

'Yes, we were – regularly – but then her letters just stopped. She never told me that anything was wrong – in fact, it was quite the opposite – we had so many plans together. I just don't understand. I've sent several letters to her without receiving a reply.'

Teacher Yang hesitated and he and his wife kept glancing at each other. Then he let out a long sigh:

'Xianli. Guanqing – she's already married.'

'Married!

They were both silent, but nodded their heads. Suddenly my head felt like it had been split open by lightning. Teacher Yang continued:

'It was when she was still preparing for her college entrance exam that her father announced, without any warning, that he had arranged a marriage for her with a young man from a rich landowning family. He not only smokes opium, but he's also a dissolute womaniser. Guanqing refused, in fact swore to heaven that she wouldn't marry him. Her father then locked her in the house. Guanqing stopped eating and drinking and became very ill, but this didn't soften her father's heart. In fact it seemed to make him more determined that the marriage should take place quickly. One morning she was forcibly dressed as a bride, put into a sedan chair and eight men carried her to the groom's family.'

Teacher Yang's wife gently took my hand and told me how the wedding went. It was so hard for me to accept this awful news and I really didn't want to hear the rest of it. My eyes fixed on her moving mouth, but my brain wasn't there any more and only a few words here and there caught my ears:

'Look at you – such a good boy – a good father too – you – Guanqing suited – so well – Teacher Yang and I – high hopes for you both – match made in heaven – all her father's fault – her prospects aren't good – married to a good-for-nothing – so different to you. How could he listen to all that nonsensical scandal?'

I don't remember when or how I walked away from Teacher Yang's house, but I walked around aimlessly for a long time without being able to put my thoughts in order. My heart was aching. I just couldn't understand why Guanqing's father didn't want me to marry her. How could it be that, in his eyes, I was no better than an opium addict? I thought I was a decent enough person. Teacher Yang's wife's words echoed in my head: 'all that nonsensical scandal'. So that was it: I had the horrible realisation that my open letter exposing the corruption and vices of Uncle Luohan Tang had been the catalyst for all this. I was glad at the time that it caused trouble for him, but had no idea that it would have this outcome. Guanqing's father must have thought I was foolish to cut ties with the richest branch of my family and that I had ruined my prospects for the future. Also Father had been in prison, accused of being a Communist, and I was turning out to be a radical. So there was my answer; Guanqing's father probably thought that being associated with me might bring down not only Guanqing, but the rest of his family too.

I carried on wandering around the town, blaming myself. She was married. She was gone. She was beyond my reach. All those promises we made to each other, all those heartfelt declarations of love, had gone like a puff of smoke in the wind. My beautiful Guanqing had been snatched away from me.

I finally went back to the hotel and Father and Shibo were waiting for me to go to dinner. They were animated and looked like they were enjoying themselves immensely. They didn't notice my unhappiness.

After dinner Father rushed off for a meeting. Shibo and I walked with him for a short distance before making our way back to the hotel. I didn't know what Father had said to Shibo, but he had certainly lifted her spirits and she was back to her enthusiastic self. Finally she noticed my absent-mindedness and distress. She looked at me quizzically, then started asking what I had been doing for the whole day. I could not hold in my story any longer. I was hurting so much. I told her everything. Shibo showed me gentle sympathy, but then she said:

'Don't worry – I will take care of this. Look at you – such a good young man. I am sure you will find someone else very soon – a good girl.'

I knew exactly what she meant. She meant her own daughter, Ninjun. Apart from the girl's name I knew nothing about her. I wasn't interested in knowing any other girl. Shibo's kind words didn't make me feel any better at all.

Very early next morning Father came to see us off on our journey back to Wanxian. He presented us with two jars of pickled bean curd. So I left Zhongxian with a heavy, aching heart and I never saw or heard from Guanqing again.

Shibo was still in a good mood when we arrived back from Zhongxian, and tried to lift my spirits. We moved briefly to a beautiful new house and Father often brought his friends over.

One night, when the house was full, Commander Xiao pulled out two new handguns. He put one gun in the palm of his hand to feel the weight of it and then said to Shibo: 'Shijie, we have all heard that your shooting is very good, can you show us?'

We all gathered eagerly around Shibo and watched as she confidently picked up both of the guns: 'In my region, no matter if you are a bandit or a guerrilla, most of us have two guns with us at all times. One gun has only twenty-four bullets and that is not enough in an emergency.'

While she was talking, she had readied both guns to fire in three swift movements: firstly she ejected the magazines by pushing each one against her hips, then we heard the magazines going back into place and lastly she cocked the pistols with her thumbs. It was done so quickly that my eyes could not follow her movements. Then she went over to the bed and covered her forearms and hands, still holding the guns, with the quilt and for a few seconds we could only hear what she was doing. When she pushed back the quilt we saw that one of the guns was lying in pieces on the bed. Then once again she hid her arms from view and we listened to what she was doing. She pushed back the quilt again and there was the gun reassembled.

Everyone was impressed by then, but it wasn't enough and we wanted to see Shibo shoot. We went out to find somewhere quiet in the park; it was evening and there were only a few people still enjoying a walk. Commander Xiao walked ahead by about fifty paces, lit a cigarette and stuck it in the ground. Its glow was so faint in the dusk that I could hardly see it above the grass and had to strain my eyes. We watched as Shibo calmly raised her left arm, the gun in her hand pointing towards the faint glow. In the hush I watched her finger pull on the trigger, followed by a loud bang, a puff of smoke and the smell of gunpowder. The bang startled the birds, who instinctively flew skywards with a loud flutter, and then, as quickly as the shot rang out, the little light disappeared. I ran in search of the cigarette, followed by the others, to see for myself it had gone.

'That was amazing!' Commander Xiao shouted and cheered: 'You truly deserve your reputation.'

I was gasping as I ran back to Shibo and proudly said to her: 'Shibo, the cigarette is gone!'

She smiled: 'This is only fifty paces away. Years ago, my guerrilla brothers had lit incense on a tree branch from a hundred paces away, so today Commander Xiao made it easy for me.'

This was the first time I had seen Shibo use her gun; I was so proud of her. All of a sudden it seemed that the sharpshooter before me must surely be a different person altogether from the woman I was used to seeing painting scenes of beauty on fine rice paper and who gave me history lessons! What a truly talented woman. I was lost for words in my admiration.

We didn't have much time to settle back into life in Wanxian before someone came to the *Wangzhou Daily* office with a message from Commander Xiao telling me to go and see him urgently. Commader Xiao told me that he had received an anonymous letter informing him that the Guomingdan's Special Committee suspected Shibo of being a Communist and was taking action to arrest her without delay. I rushed home to tell Shibo and she said that no wonder, she had seen some men hanging around near the house in the past few days.

Under the cover of darkness the same night, Shibo and I crept out of the house and went down to the port and I saw her off on a small boat that was going to Yuechi. I watched the boat disappear into the darkness and two years of life spent with Shibo came to an abrupt end. Loneliness enveloped me like a cloak.

I Become a Communist

On 1 May 1938 Uncle Menghan invited me to visit him. As soon as he saw me he broke into a grin and poked me with a long, thin finger just like he used to do when I was young and he was teasing me:

'Today is a happy day! Later on we are going to hold your Party membership ceremony.'

I was shocked and could hardly believe what I was hearing. I had only filled in my application to become a member of the Communist Party a few days previously and never dreamed that it could happen so quickly.

Within an hour we were joined by two colleagues who worked with me at the *Wangzhou Daily* who, along with Uncle Menghan, had put forward my application. Under the circumstances at that time we could not have an open or big celebration. There was no Party flag or portraits of Marx or Lenin. We couldn't even hold up portraits of Chairman Mao and Commander-in-Chief Zhu De. The ceremony was relaxed and informal. I, as the applicant, had to introduce myself and describe my family background and explain why I wished to become a member of the Communist Party. Then one of my colleagues, as my guarantor, talked about the challenges of

131

being a member, commented about the way I worked and said that he recognised that I was a radical and forward thinker. Uncle Menghan, representing the Party, talked about the Party principles, the requests which would be made by the Party to me and the need for moral integrity and discretion in order to be a revolutionary. Then we all turned to the north, which is where the Communist Party was based, in Yanan in Shangxi Province, and I swore allegiance. Then to mark the occasion, I changed my name to Xiangbei, which means 'Towards North'. To end with, they both said that they wanted me to study hard, be strict with myself and strive to be worthy of the name of a pioneer of Communism.

That night I was so excited that I didn't get a wink of sleep. It really felt as if I had started a new life. My heart was completely given over to the Party and nothing else seemed important to me any more. My life was no longer mine alone. I felt as if I was connected to a higher power, which would give me never-ending strength to overthrow Chiang Kai-shek's government in order to create a new China where there was democracy and social equality. I had finally found where I belonged and my purpose in life.

The anti-Japanese Save the Nation campaign in the Wanxian area was on the same large scale as everywhere else in the rest of the country. The Party organisation decided to stimulate the patriotic feelings of the masses even further and extend its influence by sending some of its members to the countryside to spread its ideas. As a new Party member I wanted to be part of the spearhead of every mission and was very pleased when I was sent to a country school to teach. Within no time at all I organised many of the Save the Nation activities for the students and set up a school committee to continue them.

Soon I received another mission via Uncle Menghan. I was

asked to select a suitable location and premises in order to set up a new school. Eventually, through one of my students, I found a large property and the Guohua School opened its doors in January 1939. We ended up with 550 pupils and the school had to expand to a nearby monastery. Education was free and we accommodated those pupils who lived too far away to travel each day. There was a general shortage of schools at that time, due to the fact that people had to relocate from the Japanese-occupied areas, so the government was encouraging new schools to be set up. Therefore it was easy to get permission for ours. However, what they didn't know was that our aim was to spread the Communist philosophy. A lot of pupils came to our school from Shanghai and Nanjing. We had nineteen teachers, thirteen of whom were Communist Party members and five were Communist sympathisers. The last teacher had been sent by the Education Department and so was a Nationalist. In addition to the normal curriculum, we included study and debate on current political affairs, philosophy and culture. We especially used material written about the Save the Nation campaign and Chairman Mao's article 'On Protracted War'. Unfortunately, within six months, we had attracted the attention of the Education Department and we were warned by contacts that many of us, students as well as teachers, were on a blacklist and our arrests were imminent. We had no choice but to flee and did so on the night of 18 July 1939. The next day a Nationalist Army Unit arrived to make their arrests. Even though they didn't find any of us from the blacklist, they still closed down the school immediately and kicked everybody off the premises.

The Party then sent me back to Yunyang to help at the Yunyang branch committee. They made me responsible for youth activities and propaganda. Then the Party managed to get me a position at the (Guomingdan's) People's Education Department, which of course didn't know that I had become a Communist. So on behalf of the Education Department, I went round the various schools and picked out those children who enjoyed singing and dancing and organised them into an after-school club. I called this club the 'Kiddie Theatre'. I directed their plays, which were rehearsed after school and performed each Sunday on the streets of Yunyang and the surrounding area. I also wrote articles for the *Wangzhou Daily* praising them.

In the summer I went to Wanxian to report on my work to the Party. I was given the news that the Children's Theatre, which originated in Shanghai, was due to arrive in Yunyang. The Party told me to receive the children and take care of all their needs whilst they were in Sichuan. This Children's Theatre was made up of a group of children who had been found in a refugee camp in Shanghai. Due to the Japanese bombing they had all been orphaned. The Communist Party had picked them out and formed them into a propaganda team to perform on the streets of Shanghai, but when the Japanese occupied the city they had to leave. They travelled through Jianshu and Hubei provinces and performed their street plays wherever they stopped. Their plays were not just anti-Japanese, they also pointed out the Guomingdan's lack of resistance against Japan. So when they reached Wuhan, the capital of Hubei Province, the Guomingdan authorities tried to put a stop to them by incorporating the children into their own forces with a view to dissolving the troupe. However, at that time the Communists and the Guomingdan were allied and this group of children soon came to the attention of Zhou Enlai, who was not only the Communist Central Committee leader, but also a Guomingdan politics minister. Therefore he was able to put them under the care and protection of his department whilst they were in Wuhan. He then sent them on their way and they travelled through another five provinces to carry on with their stirring performances. In the process they walked thousands of miles. Wherever they went the Communist Party took care of their needs.

I felt enthusiastic about my next task and as soon as I got back to Yunyang I went to my branch committee to discuss it. Then I went to the Guomingdan Education Department and Yunyang Headquarters and told the secretary that this Children's Theatre was being sent by the Guomingdan Central Politics Ministry. He sprang into action at this news and gave me the four best rooms in the headquarters for their accommodation, releasing funds for their food and transport and even enough money to build a large stage for their performances.

On 4 July I led my Kiddie Theatre down to the port to welcome them. We waited for over an hour, but then we saw a boat approaching flying a red flag. We erupted into life at the sight of the boat, unfurled our welcome banners, waved our flags and beat the drums. Then the children on shore and on the boat started shouting to each other across the water.

I was glad I had made ample preparations for these children because when they arrived I saw that some of them were only five years old. The oldest were fifteen. I was so impressed by the way they were able to organise themselves, but it was little wonder really – they had already travelled through more than half of China. In fact they were all more experienced than me and it was quite humbling. The team leader who was accompanying them was also named Lin, but I was taller than him so everyone called me 'Big Lin'.

Early the next morning the children were in the yard exercising and rehearsing for their evening performance. The performance itself was rousing and emotive. Most of the sketches denounced Japan's criminal act of aggression, condemning

135

their brutal slaughter of our fellow countrymen and praising the bravery of our own people in their fight against the invaders. The entire population had turned out to watch and their thunderous clapping at the end was deafening and drew the theatre group back for endless curtain calls. The mood of the six thousand-strong audience was sad and angry and long after the end of the performance they hung around talking to each other with tears in their eyes. This show made a big impact in the region and it was followed up by street performances each day. The children also performed in the hospital to express sympathy to those soldiers wounded in fighting the Japanese. They didn't stop there though, because they helped the soldiers by washing and patching their clothes, washing and cutting their hair and cutting their nails. They also wrote letters back to their families for them wherever they were. The soldiers were deeply touched by the kindness of these children.

Having the Children's Theatre with us broadened the horizons of our own Kiddie Theatre and was an eye-opener for all of us. This group of children from Shanghai never compromised their time spent studying. They read the newspapers, each of them always had two books with them to read and they wrote in their diaries each day. They also held regular meetings to check if anyone had any problems. They had woven themselves into a big, friendly and happy family. A few times during their stay Japanese air raids occurred and I was so worried that I had nowhere safe for them to shelter, as Yunyang didn't have any air-raid shelters at all. Much to my surprise, however, they didn't seem to take much notice of the bombing and even went out afterwards to collect the shell casings and shrapnel in order to send them to the iron and steel factory for reuse.

All good things must come to an end and all too soon we were informed that the Children's Theatre had to pack their bags and move on to Chongqing. They had spent a month with us, but already they were a part of the history of the Save the Nation campaign in Yunyang. The children were so impressive and I remember this time with them as being very happy indeed.

It wasn't long after they left that objections about our propaganda campaign started to be raised in the local government. The governor of Yunyang himself called me to his office one day to warn me to leave at once, otherwise I would be arrested. He told me that I was stirring up even more trouble than my father had ever done. I certainly didn't intend to be the 'meat on anyone's chopping block', so I left without delay. I went to Chongqing as it was a happy coincidence that Father had just sent me a letter to tell me he was there undergoing military service training.

Meeting Ninjun

It was almost dusk as the boat approached the port of Chongqing. The last of the sun's rays were glancing off the steep mountains and highlighted the numerous thatched, wooden houses and sheds, which looked so fragile, clinging to the mountain sides. Everywhere along the river embankment I spotted coolies, dressed in rags, each holding a long wooden pole. They were the famous 'pole army' of Chongqing that I had heard about. Although Chongqing is an industrious and thriving city, its terrain is so mountainous that transportation has always been a problem. In many places the streets are just a series of steep steps and people mainly have to get around on foot. Porters were in great demand, especially at the wharves and the station. At the wharf where the passenger boat I was on was about to dock there were lots of pole carriers waiting in what appeared to be an orderly fashion, but even before the boat touched the dock, the coolies started to leap on board. Then they started fighting each other in their desperation to get employed by the passengers. I couldn't help wondering how many of them failed their leap on board and landed in the water, or, even worse, were crushed between the boat and the dock.

I didn't need a pole carrier as I only had one small bag, but I had to clutch it to my chest to stop it being torn away from me. I followed the sign which said 'Up to Chaotianmen' (Heaven Wharf), which was the main wharf in Chongqing, and then on up to the road via three hundred zigzagging, steep steps. Even though I was a healthy young man, carrying very little, I was still breathless by the time I reached the top.

I had left Yunyang in a hurry and didn't have much money on me, so, although I hadn't eaten since I left, I contented myself by drinking a couple of bowls of tea from a street seller before finding accommodation for the night. By the time I checked in at a small inn I was exhausted and slept till noon the next day. I had two bowls of noodles from a street stall before I felt ready to find Father, who was undergoing training at the Guomingdan Military and Politics Department.

Father and I had got used to being apart, but whenever we did meet up it was always a most happy time. Father said he had a surprise for me and then he took me to a hotel, where I was astonished to be greeted by some of my colleagues who had escaped from the Guohua School with me. Best of all, Uncle Menghan was there too and I was so happy to see him safe and sound.

This was my first trip to the big city of Chongqing and I don't know what I really expected, but it didn't impress me at all. The lanes winding their way up through the hilly city were so narrow that if you stood in the middle of some of them you could almost touch the buildings on each side. The whole city felt dirty and claustrophobic to me. It was hard to find an open, flat place anywhere. I knew that summer temperatures could reach 40°C and that in the winter thick fog often enveloped the city, restricting the view to two arms' length away. People's behaviour seemed generally more aggressive than I was used to and the language used tended to be rude, crude and delivered loudly. Verbal arguments quickly turned into physical brawls. I wondered whether it was the geography and climate of the place that formed the character of the people, but certainly the motto of Chongqing seemed to be 'Let my fist do the talking'!

That's why I was more than happy when Father and Uncle Menghan asked me, after only a couple of days, to leave and go to Yuechi to fetch Shibo. During the two years since I had last seen her I had missed her more than I wanted to admit.

The next day I took a boat upriver from Chongqing and as we approached the Huaying Mountain range I stood in the bow to get an uninterrupted view. I had heard so much about the Huaying Mountains and my thoughts turned to Shibo and her husband and the frightful years they had spent leading their guerrilla force in their fight against the warlords. This was the waterway used by Shibo when she used to smuggle arms and ammunition from Chongqing to her people operating in the mountains. I started to imagine which peaks she might have climbed and which caves she might have hidden in. I remembered the story she had told us about the harsh winter of 1926. Their force, which consisted of a couple of hundred people, was besieged in the mountains and they lay hidden in a series of caves without food, medicine or warm clothing. Heavy snowfall added to their hardship. I could almost hear the sound of the bullets ricocheting from precipice to peak.

The boat arrived in Hechuan, where it terminated, so I decided to walk the rest of the way to Shibo's home town rather than having to take a series of small boats up the Qu River, which would have taken just as long, if not longer. I arrived, exhausted, a couple of days later in the late afternoon, but the market was still in progress. The streets were so crowded that it took me a while to find a teahouse. I downed a big bowl of tea to quench my thirst and then I rejoined the busy streets. Such an abundant market like this was a rare sight. I watched one of the butchers dealing efficiently with his impatient customers. He was so skilful in his assessment of the weight of the meat he cut from the carcasses that he hardly had to add or take away any from his scales. Other stalls had rice, noodles, fresh vegetables, chickens, ducks, geese and their eggs, haberdashery, colourful fabrics, household items, tools, baskets, coal; everything and anything, in fact. The heart of the market was in the central square, but stalls branched out in all directions down the side streets. There were long queues of people waiting to transport their purchases by the small boats which were plying up and down the river.

Fascinating as the market was, I needed to find Shibo, so I asked a woman the way to 'Sunny Ground'. She pointed out the direction to me and just as I was walking away, she asked me: 'Who are you looking for in Sunny Ground?'

'Chen Yuping,' I replied, which was Shibo's maiden name.

The woman looked me up and down and then said: 'You mean Chen Sanjie [Third Sister Chen]? I know where she is. She is still at the market. I will take you there.'

The woman beckoned me on and pushed her way quickly through the crowd. I couldn't believe my luck that the first person I asked directions from actually knew Shibo and where she was at that very moment! I had to hurry so that I didn't lose sight of this woman. She stopped in the doorway of a small restaurant and shouted loudly inside: 'Sanjie, you have a guest.'

Shibo appeared and looked really surprised to see me standing there. She patted me on the shoulder.

'Hah! Xianli, can it really be you? Why didn't you let me know you were coming? How is your *baba*? I received a letter from him not so long ago to say that he was in Chongqing for training. I thought of going to see him.'

Then she said to the woman, her friend who had brought me to her:

'This is Xianli – he and his father are my saviours.'

The same woman insisted on cooking me some soup before Shibo took me to her home. It was a fermented rice soup, a speciality of the region, and it was the most delicious soup I had ever tasted. It smelled of honey and tasted of wine and it washed away my tiredness.

Shibo and I left the restaurant and the busy streets behind us and walked across some rough, empty fields. As we passed one of the largest fields, Shibo stopped and gestured towards it:

'This field's soil is very rich and can produce four hundred pounds of rice at harvest time. It used to be under your Uncle Liao's name, but he sold it to fund the arming of our force.'

We carried on past the fields and came to a huge *huangjiao* (*Ficus virens*) tree, which must have been over a hundred years old. A dog started barking nearby and then a skinny boy of about ten years old ran over to Shibo. He had bare feet and was wearing a worn-out cotton-padded jacket and blue trousers. He half-hid behind Shibo and looked up at me. He repeated the name that Shibo told him to call me: Lin Dage (Big Brother Lin). I held out the present I had brought for him and he snatched it from my hand and ran away. This was Yabin, Shibo's son.

Shibo led me into a small yard where there were three mud huts. In a traditional family compound, the elders usually lived on their own on the north side. In this case though, Shibo had to share her mother-in-law's hut along with her two children. Her brother-in-law and his wife and their four children occupied the hut on the south side. The third hut was very small and was mainly used as a store, but it also contained a coffin and a single bed. It was quite normal to see a coffin in a house in the countryside, as it was considered important to prepare a coffin in advance for the elderly folk to give them piece of mind that they would be properly buried after their death. The quality of

142

the coffin said a lot about the status and wealth of the family too, and if there was no coffin you would know that the family was very poor. Then by the side of the small hut was a thatched shed which housed a couple of pigs and the latrine ditch.

The Liao family home

Could this really be Shibo's home? I was a bit shocked at what I saw because this place was a shambles. Shibo was such a clever, educated woman, who came from a rich, scholarly family. She was fine and brave and deeply respected by so many people, but her living conditions were even worse than many peasant farmers'. My heart sank. But then I remembered Father had told me that Shibo had married for love, which was almost unheard of in those times. Liao Yubi had actually been employed as a worker on her family's estate and, consequently, Shibo was disowned by her family.

In the evening Shibo took me out for a walk. It was the end of autumn and there was a real nip in the air. We walked over to the *huangjiao* tree and she pointed out a small flat area near the base which was covered in weeds and said: 'This is where your Uncle Liao is buried.'

It was an unmarked grave. In fact there was no hint that it was a grave at all, because they were afraid that if the enemy knew that he was buried there they would come and dig up the body. After Uncle Liao had been executed, his head had been put on display in a wooden cage on Yuechi's town wall. Three of his followers risked their own lives in order to take down his head and then bury it with the rest of his body. So there was no inscription on a tombstone and the spot would forever be left to the ravages of nature.

I went over to the tree, respectfully bowed my head three times and said in my heart: 'Uncle, rest in peace. Your enemies are my enemies and we will pay them back.'

Shibo stood silently by my side and tears streamed down her cheeks. I helped her to sit down on some stones near the tree and eventually we started talking. I told her all about my life during the past year and how everything had changed once I joined the Party. I said that I thought I had found my calling in life at last. Then I told her that Father had sent me here to fetch her and that there was a new plan waiting for her.

Then Shibo told me what she had been doing since her return to Yuechi. When Shibo had left her home over three years previously to go to Russia, nobody knew where she was or what had happened to her. There had been all kinds of rumours, such as that she had become one of the wronged ghosts as a result of the Japanese bombing, or that she had perhaps remarried and dumped her children at her former husband's home, or that the warlords had finally caught up with her and killed her. So on the day she turned up in Yuechi, everyone was shocked to see her and looked at her as if she were really a returning ghost. Her in-laws told her that whilst she had been away people had come looking for her, but they didn't leave any names or contact details. Shibo had the feeling that the Party had been looking for her.

Shibo had returned home convinced that there was nothing left for her. She had no home of her own, she had lost her connection with the Party and all her former comrades-in-arms had either been killed or had had to go into hiding like her. Gradually, however, one by one, they learned of her return and came looking for her and looking for hope. Along with some of her followers, Shibo started up a wholesale ginger business – the local ginger was of high quality. She bought it in bulk for sale to the wholesale market in Chongqing. First of all though there was need of funding for transportation. Instead of depending on the established boat business, she decided that they should build their own boat, which would make them truly independent. So they started by cutting down a few trees. Once again I was reminded of how clever and resourceful she was.

I suddenly realised that I hadn't yet seen Shibo's daughter, Ninjun, who had been mentioned to me often enough. Shibo let out a long sigh:

'Although you lost your mother when you were only a baby, at least you had your grandmother and aunts to look after you. My two children have lived a bitter and hard life because of the dangers we have had to face and, most of the time, I have been forced to leave them in the care of others. As you know, they have never, even to this day, been able to call me "Mother". When I came back here last year, I found my poor child Yabin looking no better than a beggar on the streets – he has not been looked after well here. He was filthy and still barefoot in the winter. His hands and feet were swollen, red and covered with chilblains. I found Ninjun had been sent to live with my sister as they didn't want her here, seeing as a girl is not considered to be a root of the Liao family. Neither of them were in school. I have just managed to earn enough money to give them an education. Yabin just started primary school in Yuechi and Ninjun, who is a big girl now, is too old to go back to primary level even though she never finished it in Chongqing. She is at Hechuan Secondary School. It is a good school, but she has missed so much that I'm not sure that she can keep up with her studies there.'

I immediately had an idea: 'Does Ninjun like singing and dancing?'

'Oh yes! She loves them. When she was at the Chongqing Primary School she won first prize in the school singing competition.'

'That's excellent – then send her to the Children's Theatre. It's in Chongqing at the moment. It is directly led by our Communist Party. In fact Zhou Enlai particularly cares for it.'

Shibo's smiling face looked like a flower in bloom: 'That would be very nice – if she can get in.'

Now I had an opportunity to show off: 'Leave it to me. I know them well and I don't think there will be any problem.'

'Alright! My boat is waiting to take five hundred kilos of ginger to Chongqing. We could go with it and on the way stop in Hechuan to pick up Ninjun from her school and take her with us.'

Next morning I went to the wholesale market with Shibo. While she went to sort out her boat's departure time, I went to buy a red scarf, a pair of socks and a pair of shoes as my 'first time meeting' present for Ninjun.

The following morning we set off in Shibo's boat, which was laden with the ginger. There were four men in the bow and the navigator was in the stern. We stopped in Hechuan, which was at the confluence of the Jialing and Qu rivers. It was a strategic place for any force wanting to occupy Chongqing and the Huaying Mountain region. I accompanied Shibo to Ninjun's boarding school. There were large pine trees on each side of the school gates looking like guardians. Shibo entered the school and a while later came out hand in hand with a girl. Full of curiosity, I went forward to greet her. Shibo told her: 'This is your Lin Dage.'

Ninjun aged 14

Ninjun inclined her head to one side and looked at me extremely critically, and with a somewhat ironical smile said:

'I know exactly who you are. Mother has sung your praises so often and apparently you are most likeable! I think she wants to adopt you!'

'Your mother loves you more than anyone else,' I replied.

I was unsure whether she was teasing me or whether she resented me.

'She loves me, you say?' She glanced sideways at her mother. 'Hmm! She left us for a couple of years without a word and you call this love?'

I looked carefully at this girl standing before me. She was of medium height with a round face and very striking thick eyebrows, just like her mother's, above big eyes. Her hair was bobbed and in her blue uniform she looked like a smart city girl. There was something a bit odd about her though, as her neck looked a bit thick and stiff. I didn't understand on that first meeting that she was actually suffering from mumps!

Despite everything, Ninjun seemed happy and was certainly high spirited. I think she was very happy to be with her mother so unexpectedly, as she didn't have many opportunities to spend time with her and my appearance added excitement to the occasion. We didn't waste time in getting back to the boat to continue on our way to Chongqing. Ninjun was quite a chatterbox and soon she had told me a lot about herself.

Ninjun's primary boarding school in Chongqing had been organised and paid for by the Communist Party, firstly because her father had earned the status of a martyr and, secondly, because her mother was being sent to Russia by the Party. The Party had promised Shibo that both her children would be cared for by them. However, Shibo's in-laws wouldn't allow Yabin to be taken away, as he was seen as the root of the family, so he was left with his paternal grandmother and they only sent Ninjun to school. Everything went well for about a year, but then one day the headmaster informed Ninjun that her school fees had not been paid and that she would have to leave. By this time Sister Zen, who had been looking after Ninjun during the holidays, had moved away because of the bombing so Ninjun had nowhere to go except to try and make her way back to her grandmother in Yuechi by herself and with no money. She wasn't happy with this option, however, because, even though she loved her grandmother, her aunt was the one who ruled the roost and she had always treated Ninjun and Yabin very badly indeed. So she decided that she would only go there to collect Yabin and then they would run away together and go in search of their mother. She went to Chongqing port and begged one of the boatmen to let her on board and take her to Yuechi. As soon as she got home she straight away collected Yabin and left again. The first night they hid in someone's pig shed. They managed to stay free for three days, scrounging food from wherever they could, but were then discovered and taken home. Their grandmother's love warmed Ninjun a little, but the elderly lady wasn't able to take proper care of her and was no match for her second son's wife. This aunt was a selfish and mean woman, who thought that having to take care of Yabin was enough of a burden and so wouldn't let Ninjun stay for free. She kept Ninjun as a servant. Ninjun had to cook their meals, clean the house, feed the pigs and look after her two younger cousins. If one of them cried, even once, Ninjun would be soundly beaten by her callous aunt. She would taunt Ninjun by often saying:

'Damn your mother – she is not a mother at all, dumping her children on me. Is she dead, or has she remarried?'

The only thing which kept Ninjun going was the thought that her mother would return one day and take her and her little brother away.

Ninjun was starting to feel very sad and tearful by that point and I didn't know how to comfort her, so I changed the subject by asking her what her new school was like. She stopped crying and sighed and told me that as far as her education level was concerned she was only at primary four, but when she made the jump to secondary school they were already teaching geometry, which she couldn't understand at all. This wasn't a happy topic either, so I took out the presents I had bought for her and watched her expression turn from sad to delighted. Her eyes opened wide as she undid the parcel and saw what was inside. She put the scarf round her neck and tried on the shoes. She paced up and down a bit and stamped her feet and looked utterly content with the feel of them. She turned to her mother and complained: 'There are holes in my shoes, but *you* didn't buy me new ones!'

Shibo looked lovingly at her and smiled sadly: 'You know how busy I am. Well, at least your Lin Dage is very thoughtful.'

Ninjun smiled at me very sweetly and thanked me: 'Lin Dage, you are very kind. No wonder my mother likes you so much. I like you too!'

Seeing her happier for a moment released my heart from her sad story and I teased her by saying: 'Hmm. Do you really like me or just the scarf and shoes?'

'I like everything and you!' She clutched the presents to her as if afraid that someone might take them away from her.

We chatted in a relaxed way as the boat sailed slowly on. I told her lots of stories about the Children's Theatre and then asked her:

'If I introduced you to the Children's Theatre, would you like to join them?'

'Me? Where would I get that kind of luck from? Do you mean it? If I could really get into the Children's Theatre, then I will kowtow to you many times over!'

'No! No kowtows. A simple salute would be better!'

'Alright, a salute then, but if I can't get in I will quarrel with you! What do I need to do to get in?'

'For a start you need to be able to sing and dance.'

'That's no problem. I am the principal solo singer of my school choir. I will sing a song for you now, if you like.'

Ninjun stood up straight, put her hands behind her back and started to sing:

Along the Songhua River

My home lies along the Songhua River
It is covered by forest and coal
There are mountains of beans and sorghum
My home lies along the Songhua River
There live my fellow countrymen
And my elderly parents
Eighteenth September, Eighteenth September
From that sad time on
I left my home
Cast aside everything I cherished
Roaming, Roaming!
Which year, which month
Can I go back to my precious home?
When, at what time
Can I get back to my treasures?
My mother, my father
When
Can we be together once more?

This was a famous anti-Japanese song at that time and it had many high notes and was technically difficult to sing, but Ninjun's voice was clear, sweet and full of emotion. When she finished she was a bit embarrassed and said:

'No! That wasn't very good – I have mumps, so it's a bit difficult to sing properly.'

I didn't expect that her singing would be of such a high standard and so absorbing. What's more, if this was Ninjun not feeling very well, then what on earth would she sound like when she felt well? I was very impressed and said:

'That was very good. You passed my singing exam with flying colours. I think we won't test your dancing right now – if you dance right into the river, I couldn't take the consequences!' We all had a good laugh.

We arrived in Chongqing and I settled Shibo and Ninjun at a small inn by the riverside and then went to find Father and took him to see them. Father was so happy to see Shibo again and to meet Ninjun. He held Ninjun's hand and said: 'Just look at my acknowledged daughter – she is so lovely!'

During the next few days Father was busy with his training and Shibo was trying to find a buyer for her ginger, so they left Ninjun for me to amuse. I took her to the hospital to check out her case of mumps and she was given a course of antipyretic injections over two days. Gradually her swollen glands returned to normal. One evening I took her out to see the lights of this mountainous city and she was very happy. Whenever I took her out she always liked to hold my hand and she didn't seem to be shy or think anything of it, but for me it caused great embarrassment so I started to walk either deliberately in front of her or behind her.

As soon as Ninjun had completely recovered from the mumps, I took her to the suburb of Chongqing where the Children's Theatre was based. It was so good to see the children again. When I talked to the leaders about Ninjun's situation they immediately agreed to her joining the troupe.

The news that Ninjun had been accepted by the Children's Theatre made both Shibo and Father very happy. Father suggested that we all go to have our photo taken together to celebrate a good day. We chose the best studio in the city and dressed up for the photo. Father wore his army uniform and I was in my best and most fashionable Sun Yat-sen style deep blue suit. I was positioned behind Father looking enormously proud of myself and I felt as if the world was waiting for me to save it. Shibo had put on a dark blue cheongsam. She was nearly forty years old, but she still looked young and beautiful. Ninjun was wearing a long, red silk cheongsam. This was Ninjun's first experience of having her photo taken and she looked very serious. Although our lives were so bound up with each other's, this was the only photo taken with the four of us together.

After I sent Ninjun to the Children's Theatre, my attention turned to Shibo's ginger business, which was not looking good. Only two weeks before we set off from Yuechi with the cargo, ginger was selling for 3.50 yuan per fifty kilos, but when we arrived in Chongqing the price suddenly went down by half. Shibo's ginger was already starting to go mouldy and she was very worried. She was having to work very hard indeed to find buyers.

I was staying at the same hotel as Uncle Menghan and the two others from the Guohua School. The three of them were still cautious in case they were being watched by the Guomingdan; none of us had jobs and money was tight. Every day we had to think about where to get enough money to pay the hotel bill. For us, as long-term guests, the hotel was safe and cheap. It only cost eighty fen per person per day including some food. Even though life was tough we were in good spirits at just being together, but joy didn't fill our stomachs. Father sold everything he could, but he didn't have many things in the first place. Then, in desperation, Shibo sold a couple of hundred kilos of ginger at a loss in order to support all of us. When those proceeds dwindled Uncle Menghan opened his mouth:

'Don't worry – I have a plan. It not only solves the hotel bills, but I also guarantee that we will all enjoy one first-class meal a week. My engraved seals sell for four yuan each.'

Uncle Menghan had been born into a poor family, but he was lucky as a child to have been tutored by his cousin who had sat the highest imperial examination of the late Qing Dynasty. He had been taught literature, art and especially calligraphy. His skill became legendary in his lifetime, but his fame grew out of his eccentric character and this made his work even more keenly sought after, as well as harder to get hold of. We felt a heavy stone lifted from our shoulders when we heard that he was willing to support us, because we all knew that he wasn't saying this lightly. But then he said that he would only engrave one seal per day and we all felt disappointed, saying that it wouldn't be enough for everybody's needs. He slowly stroked his goatee beard:

'There are only four of us, the hotel fees total 3.20 yuan per day, one of my seals will sell for four yuan, so there will be a profit of 80 fen left. Why is that not enough?'

'That's too tight a margin – what about cigarettes!'

'Rice spirit!'

'And tea!'

'Don't forget – we have to read the papers and magazines!'

'You said – once a week, one good meal!'

'What about if we want to go to the theatre sometimes!'

Everyone clamoured to put forward their ideas of the necessities of life! In the end Uncle Menghan agreed to engrave two seals a day, but no more. He said that his customers would have to bring their own Shoushan stones (a translucent stone found in the Shoushan Mountains in Fujian Province and prized for being the best material for engraving), so that there was no initial cost to him. Two seals only took him forty minutes to finish, but he said that it would be an insult if such a refined and elegant art form were sold to a mass market and he didn't want to see the dignity of the literati swept away in the dust.

Uncle Menghan had a friend who owned a silk textile shop

and asked him if he could use it as a base for his new business. He wrote and put up an advertisement for his seals, which read:

I, your humble servant
Will engrave your seals
One character – one yuan
Pay more – I don't want it
Pay less – I won't do it.
Three days' collection. Bring your own Shoushan stone.

– Liu Menghan

Within two days the shop was inundated by potential customers. People started queuing in the early morning to be the first in, but Uncle Menghan didn't waver from his resolve to carve only two stones per day.

Father was about to finish his training and his next job was going to be in Jianyou County. I planned to go with him, but before I left Chongqing I took time to go to the Children's Theatre to see Ninjun. She had been there for about a month and I was wondering how she was getting on. As soon as Ninjun saw me she flew over to me with her arms open wide and a big smile. Everybody who saw her greeting me started to tease us but then quickly left us alone together. I felt a bit self-conscious at this and was nervous and awkward during our meeting. When Ninjun saw me off at the gate, this chatterbox became quiet and seemed reluctant to let me leave. I also felt some kind of melancholy come over me as I left.

Ninjun had settled down well, but Father was still worried about Shibo. He had promised that he would help her reconnect with her Communist Party cell a long time ago, but this had still not come about and he didn't know how to make it happen. The only person who understood that Father was hiding a deep love for Shibo was Uncle Menghan and he also saw

155

Father's anxiety about her. He patted Father on the shoulder and said to him:

'Don't worry – we will all look after her for you.'

I had only stayed a short while in Chongqing, a city which had irritated me a lot at first, but when I looked back at recent events I felt that I was about to leave a part of my heart there. I already considered Shibo to be part of my family, but now Ninjun was included in that too.

Father Becomes a Communist

Jiangyou County is situated in northwest Sichuan. Jiangyou town itself was established over 1,700 years ago. It was known as a centre for education, culture and economics in the region and was likened to a miniature Chengdu, which is the capital of Sichuan, but its political atmosphere seemed untouched by current events.

After his latest round of military training in Chongqing, Father was given the position of commander-in-chief of the Jiangyou County Military Force. He was also appointed as the deputy director of the military force of the four neighbouring counties. These positions gave him much greater power than he had ever held before and gave him control over a much wider area.

My mission from the Communist Party was to assist Father in stabilising his power base and to establish a branch of the Communist Party in Jiangyou County. As far as outsiders were concerned, however, I was just Commander-in-Chief Lin's son who had come to stay with him.

On the day of my arrival I was taken by surprise to find soldiers lined up on either side of the road and saluting to welcome me. I felt very proud. The batman took my luggage and led me to a room and said: 'Young master – this is your room.'

This time, though, I knew without being told that the respect I was being shown and the title I was being given were only afforded to me because of my father's position. I was nobody if I wasn't his son!

Father was so excited about his new post that he came to my room and sat on the bed and said:

'I am in a much better position now than I was in Yunyang and Zhongxian. There is so much to do and now I really feel that I have a platform to display my abilities. Huh! It's a shame that you are too young, lack experience and have no military knowledge. Pity you can't be of much help.'

Father slapped his thighs, told me to get some rest and walked out!

In early January of 1940 I had a meeting with my new leader, Lao Hou, in a small village about thirty kilometres away from Jiangyou Town. I reported to him about my mission from the Party and he told me all about the current political situation. Then I brought to his attention my father's request about joining the Party. He said that the Party was aware of my father's political leanings and believed that it was important that he became a member in preparation for future plans in the Jiangyou region and promised to expedite his request.

True to Lao Hou's word, Father had a meeting with him the following day at which he wrote his membership application and I happily agreed to be his guarantor. Father and Lao Hou got on very well with each other from the outset. They were both very well read and were a good match for each other. I found out that Lao Hou's nickname was Brainbox (literally, 'Knowledgeable Paper Bin')!

After the Spring Festival, Lao Hou visited us again. The first words he said to Father were: 'The "Above" have approved your application.'

Father had at last become a Communist Party member. We decided to hold his membership ceremony at a quiet Buddhist Temple called the Temple of Ultimate Bliss on the Observe Misty Mountain by the Fu River. I began by telling them how strange it felt for me to be my father's guarantor, as it was like putting the branch where the root should be. In other words, it was the wrong way round, as it was my father who had led me down this path of revolutionary thought. And now, through all his experiences, I understood what he was seeking and learned how to seek it for myself.

The Temple of Ultimate Bliss on the Observe Misty Mountain, Jiangyou

My father said: 'Meeting Chen Lianshi and her husband Liao Yubi was the real turning point for me in considering Communist ideals. I was so impressed by how they were trying to change society for the good of all people. Then I gradually got to know other impressive people who were Communists. My life has been full of turbulence and my beliefs have always been changeable. In my youth I was a dutiful, obedient son within my traditional, autocratic family, but then I left home because I wanted to find my own future. I became a loyal follower of Dr Sun Yat-sen and remained so for many years, but now I have finally found my true north and become a dedicated proletarian Communist.'

Then he stood up and raised his right fist and made a solemn vow of loyalty to the Communist Party.

Lao Hou excitedly grabbed Father's hand and said to him:

'Today I represent the Party and welcome you into it. You have supported the Party for a long time now and have already given us help and you have proved yourself to be our close friend. From now on you are officially a Communist. In recognition of the help you have given the Party on so many occasions, there will be no probationary period.'

Lao Hou presented Father with a stack of articles which had been produced by the Party, and went on to say:

'The relationship between the Communists and the Guomingdan is so tense at the moment and the Guomingdan have made new resolves and policies, namely: "Dissolve Communism", "Prevent Communism" and "Restrict the Communists". The Guomingdan have arrested huge numbers of Communists and all sorts of radicals. Given this situation, the Central Committee requests that we work towards harnessing the existing anti-Japanese feeling within the populace and form an Anti-Japanese United Front, so that we can confront the Guomingdan in a sensible and polite way for the benefit of the whole country.'

Then he emphasised: 'Now the Party requests you to get involved in all aspects of public relations: foster activists; take firm control of the Four Counties Territorial Forces; stand your ground at all times; be ready for action.'

We stayed the night in the temple and the following morning, while Father was reading his articles, Lao Hou took me for a walk on the mountainside. He talked to me earnestly:

'Xiao [Junior] Lin – we have placed you here mainly because of your father and his position. We hope that, through your father's post and his connections, we will be able to build up a firm, reliable base right under the nose of the Guomingdan. Now that your father is a Party member you are not on your own any more – you are a father-and-son army now. Both of you have a big responsibility. Your father is in special circumstances and so *cannot* have any link with any other members. You must remember that any new members you manage to convert must not, under any circumstances, know of your father's allegiance to the Communist Party. You are quite well known to the Guomingdan yourself as a red activist in eastern Sichuan, as was your father for his frankness and outspokenness, and we don't want him to get any more attention from the Guomingdan. Therefore, both of you need to be very careful and lower your profile. We really want you both to have long-term stability here and then we have a much better chance to succeed with our missions in this region. We have to take advantage of this excellent opportunity.'

In order to cover my identity better, I found a job as deputy head teacher of a private school called Huguang School. The head teacher, Mr Hu, was an honest and kind man who was passionate about education and had no political ambitions for himself. I realised that no matter how passionate I was about the anti-Japanese activities and my own political aims, I had to keep a low profile and only teach the core education. Soon I had earned the confidence of Mr Hu and the rest of the staff. In fact, I became a favourite of Mr Hu and he trusted me to manage the whole school.

Lao Hou visited us again. This time he brought news of specific plans for the region. He said that the already tense relationship with the Guomingdan was worsening and that the 'Above' within the Party had decided to secretly form their own armed force in northern Sichuan. The location chosen for it was in Beichuan County, which was mountainous, forested and sparsely populated by ethnic minorities. They were going to start by setting up a farm and, to begin with, they would have to clear and till the land. Then they intended to start quarrying limestone for the building industry. Next they would collect the sap from the rubber trees. This plan was twofold: firstly, they could get a large number of men into the region legitimately and, secondly, all these activities would generate income for the Party. After all this was up and running, they would gradually be able to move weapons and equipment into the region with which to arm the men.

Lao Hou especially requested that Father made sure to hold on to his power base and, when the time came, Father would be made regional commander of the new guerrilla force. He kept emphasising that we had to keep the plan strictly between ourselves, because the Communist Party had promised the Guomingdan that they would not establish any hidden armed forces within the Guomingdan-controlled areas. If this plan should leak out, it would be very embarrassing for the Party and put us all in danger.

Father and I were full of enthusiasm at hearing these plans. Then Father made the suggestion that Shibo would be an excellent person to be involved in all this, saying how much experience she had in setting up new businesses and, indeed, of leading a guerrilla force. Lao Hou immediately agreed, as he already knew about Shibo and her husband, and he gave Father permission to contact her. Straight away Father wrote to her and said that, as soon as we received her reply, I would go to Yuechi to pick her up. This was good news for me because, not only would I see Shibo again, but I would get the chance to stop off in Chongqing and visit Ninjun. She had constantly been on my mind and, although I had been writing to her, I didn't know much about how her life in the Children's Theatre was going.

Unfortunately, once again other events overtook our plans. Father was dismissed from his post as commander-in-chief of the Jiangyou County Military Force. No reasons were given and no case was presented for investigation – he was simply told to leave his post. This was in late 1941, less than two years from the first time he arrived in Jiangyou County.

I knew very well what the problem was, however. Father's best characteristic was also his weakest. He could never behave in the same way as other ranked officials almost always did. His belief system didn't allow him to flatter the undeserving, even if they were in a position of power over him. Nor would he ever bully anyone weaker than himself. He certainly wouldn't take any bribes, or turn a blind eye to others who did. Many officials were in the grip of personal vices, but Father was truly pure in heart and mind. He still joined in with the lowliest tasks, which would never go unnoticed by ordinary people and they would say: 'Just like the sun rising in the west – a chief commander coming out to sweep the street, it has never been seen before in history.' Words like that weren't very pleasing to some officials' ears. Father was even told by the Party to go with the flow and act like the 'real' commanders, but he couldn't allow himself to act a part.

Inevitably, there were accusations that Father was a Communist, but there was still enough evidence to counter these. He was certainly a radical, though, and it was considered dangerous to give someone like him a position of so much power.

Father had to leave Jiangyou without delay after his dismissal and he went to Chengdu. It wasn't long before I received a warning that my name was on the Guomingdan arrest list. I hid for a couple of days locally, before making my way out of Jiangyou under the cover of darkness.

Once again, two years of careful planning and preparation came to an abrupt end, just like bubbles bursting in the air.

I Love Ninjun

I left Jiangyou County at the beginning of 1942 and went to Chengdu; Father was there already. Almost as soon as I arrived, though, Father was offered a job in Mianyang Town by his old army friend Den Beicheng. Mianyang is about 130 kilometres, as the crow flies, north east of Chengdu.

Den Beicheng had been Father's best friend when they were both in Warlord Yang Sen's military force. After Den left the army, he took up the job of director of grain depots in the northern region of Sichuan, covering more than twenty counties. He was responsible for grain production as well as distribution to the military and civilians within that region. When he met Father in Chengdu and found out that he didn't have a job, without hesitation he offered him the position of manager of general affairs at the grain depot headquarters, which were situated in Mianyang County. Once Father had settled into his job, he sent a message telling me to join him there. No sooner had I arrived than Father told me that my new mission was to fetch Shibo from Yuechi and bring her to Mianyang. I was to tell her that the Party had an important matter which concerned her. I was thrilled to have to do this. I immediately borrowed a bicycle, a famous English brand renowned for being strong and reliable for long distances.

My journey would take me through three counties and I cycled two hundred kilometres on the first day. I was in such an elated mood that I was humming tunes all the way. I thought about Shibo and how it had been two years since I last saw her and her family. I planned that after I had seen Shibo safely to Mianyang, I would then go to Chongqing to see Ninjun. I wondered how she was faring in the Children's Theatre. Although we wrote to each other, there was nothing like talking to someone face to face. When I last saw her she had been a very skinny, vivacious chatterbox of fourteen years, but recently I had heard that she was nicknamed 'Chubby Liao'! I had trouble imagining her being plump, but it dawned on me that in two years she had probably changed a great deal. Perhaps now she might be very pretty, perhaps even beautiful like her mother. Two years ago, her singing voice was already beautiful and I wondered how it would sound now after two years of voice training. The more I thought about her, the more I missed her and I felt a flush spread over my face!

As daylight faded I still had about fifteen kilometres to go before I reached Nanchong, which was the last big town before Yuechi and where I would have to stay overnight. I tried to hurry up before I lost all light. The road was so steep in some places that I had to get off the bike and push it. That meant, however, that I could make up time and preserve energy on the downhill stretches by coasting. I was doing this when I suddenly heard somebody ahead of me scream:

'BRAKE! BRAKE!'

With a sickening feeling, I realised that the bend in the road just ahead of me was particularly sharp. I heeded the warning and braked hard to make the turn, but the bicycle and I parted company and I went flying over the handlebars and landed hard on the gritty surface. I lost consciousness, for how long I don't know, but as I came to I heard the voice of an old man: 'He's still breathing.'

I was gasping for air and I felt someone checking me over for broken bones. Luckily I was just winded and shocked. Someone poured some water into my mouth. The same voice again:

'Youngster – you have a strong lifeline. Just take a look at where you nearly ended up.'

My gaze followed the line of his finger – it was pointing downwards. Feeling even sicker, I saw that I was perched on the very edge of a cliff. The old man said:

'This is a steep abyss and there are quite a few trucks and cars down there. Nobody would be able to find even one of your bones if you'd gone over the edge. Thanks to heaven! You were blessed!'

I stood up gingerly and thanked everyone who had helped me. My bike was damaged and had a puncture, so I had to push it. After only a short distance the handlebars fell off and then I had to carry the bits and pieces on my shoulders. By the time I got to Nanchong it was the middle of the night, but I managed to find a small inn to stay at. I was exhausted and terribly hungry, but they didn't have any food available, so all I could do was go to the well and drink plenty of water. The next day I found somebody to repair the bicycle and, whilst waiting, I gulped down two bowls of rice and bean curd from a street stall.

I reached Yuechi just after dark the next evening. I went as fast as I could through the fields although I could barely see the path as there was no moon to light my way. As I neared the family's compound I got a terrible fright when a dog jumped up at me and started barking. I stood stock still and called out for Shibo at the top of my voice. A girl shouted back asking who was there. Before I could answer, the girl had flung her arms around my neck and I was listening to her singsong voice:

'Lin Dage – it's really you! Why didn't you tell us that you were coming?'

I was staggered – it was Ninjun.

Ninjun in 1943

'Shouldn't you be at the Children's Theatre? Why are you at home?'

Ninjun was jumping for joy and grabbed my hand and dragged me towards the house:

'It's a long story – I will tell you later. Come on, my *boniang* doesn't know it's you yet – she'll be so surprised!'

I wasn't expecting to see her and felt embarrassed that she had caught me scared witless at being cornered by the dog! She was never a shy or conventional type of girl and in that respect she hadn't changed, because she kept hugging me affectionately. She had, however, certainly changed into a lovely young woman in the intervening years and because of that fact, her very enthusiastic hugs also embarrassed me. My heart was beating fast and I was sure that my face must have been bright red!

Shibo looked very happy as I stood in front of her: 'Last night I dreamed about you and your father – I miss you both so much.'

The whole family, which included Ninjun's grandmother, her uncle's family and her brother Yabin, came out to greet me. The grandmother held my hand and asked me how my family and things in general were. The uncle's wife started cooking a meal and Shibo asked her to also give me a bowl of noodle soup and two fried eggs in the meantime, as she thought I must be starving by then. I was grateful for that and I'm afraid that I forgot about good manners and devoured the steaming soup within a minute. Yabin was sent out to buy some rice spirit for a celebration.

After supper Shibo took Ninjun and me outside to sit under the *huangjiao* tree, because it was more private for us to talk there.

The last two years hadn't been easy for Shibo. Her ginger and boat transport business had gone bankrupt. Her brother-in-law had taken to smoking opium and was laying waste to what little money there was in the household and his wife was as mean as ever. Money was needed for Yabin to continue his schooling and now Ninjun had come home unexpectedly. She knew that her enemies were still out there and wanted her dead. Shibo, who had once been hailed as a heroine, could see no way out of her current situation and felt that her life was dwindling away in futility.

Although in my eyes Shibo would always be a heroine, I

looked at her life from her point of view for a moment and I felt tears prick my eyelids. I tried to comfort her:

'Shibo, don't worry. The past cannot be changed and it is behind you now. This time it is our Party, as well as Father, who have sent me to fetch you. They want you – a heroine – to reappear again.'

Shibo laughed bitterly: 'Me – a heroine? I am not even a lowly soldier.'

'Don't say that – it isn't true. Did you receive a letter from Father? He wrote to you almost a year ago now.'

'Yes, I did, but when it arrived I was in Chongqing busy with the business and then I travelled through the Huaying Mountains visiting the ex-guerrillas – they were very scattered. By the time I got back here and saw the letter, six months had passed by since he sent it. I wasn't sure whether I should still go – I replied straight away, but nothing came back.'

'Ah, yes! Of course, by the time you replied Father had already left Jiangyou. But do you know what Father called you to Jiangyou for? We were planning to set up a big farm in the north of Sichuan as a cover for setting up a guerrilla base. Then, when the time was right, we were going to unite with Father's territorial forces, which were a few thousand strong. This was all decided from "Above" and they sent a number of activists and members to work on it. If it had worked out, all your former guerrillas would have found a place at the base too.'

Shibo was so excited when she heard these plans:

'What a wonderful idea – I would never have dreamed that one up. Surely it isn't too late to implement it?'

I shook my head sadly. 'It's all too late! Everybody involved was new to the area and didn't have the social contacts to deal with the local authorities, including Father – that's where you would have been invaluable had you been able to join us. The plan created suspicion and all of the Above's main preparation team were broken down by the Guomingdan. I was on their list too. All our people had to leave.'

Shibo ruefully heaved a sigh.

'Huh! It's all my fault – I shouldn't have stayed away for so long. Why is it that all the lousy luck always ends up at my door?'

'No, nothing is your fault. Admittedly the failure of the farm plan was a great loss to us, but there are lots of other things to do.'

Then I told her in detail how Father wanted her to transport the military grain and I emphasised that it was our Party who had sent me to invite her to come and work with us. Her attitude suddenly changed and she was fired up with enthusiasm:

'Let's go! Let's not delay in case we miss another good chance. If this is the Party's decision then I am more than willing to accept whatever they want me to do. This is the chance to re-establish my link to them.'

'Wait a moment – don't rush! Father said that we need to take Yabin with us and now that Ninjun is home, she must come too. We can sort out their schools in Mianyang – that won't be a problem.'

'Alright – agreed, but let's not delay.'

It was the beginning of autumn and the night air was starting to get cool. We chatted briefly about a few other things before Shibo stood up:

'It's so late already and getting chilly. You must be very tired by now – go and get some rest.'

Before I could reply, Ninjun sprang up in protest. She had been sitting very quietly up until that point.

'Boniang, you have been talking for so long and I didn't get a chance to say a single word. *You* go and rest now – I want to have a little talk with Lin Dage – it's my turn!'

What Ninjun requested was what I wanted too, but I was too shy to say so, so I was glad that she had spoken out:

'Shibo, it's alright – I'm not tired at all and I want Ninjun to tell me all about what happened at the Children's Theatre.'

Shibo patted me on the shoulder and regarded us both with motherly love. Undoubtedly she wanted Ninjun and me to be together and she nodded her head, smiled and left us alone.

As soon as Shibo turned around, Ninjun came and sat close to me. She talked about her time in the Children's Theatre and how happy she had been there, mainly because everyone behaved like brothers and sisters to each other. She said that it had been such an energetic, wonderful place. She also said that, for the first time in her life, she had been living without anxiety and, as a result, she had put on weight and that was why she had been given the nickname of 'Chubby Liao'! Then her laughter died:

'But the good things never last. After the "Wannan incident" the Guomingdan took sole control of the Children's Theatre. We all knew that we would be in danger once we were handed over. Very soon the Above sent orders to dismiss all the children from the theatre. There were about thirty of us and the older ones were sent to Yanan; some were sent to the National Music Institute and the National Theatre and some were sent to ordinary schools. That left seven of us who had all come from different regions of Sichuan and we were told to either go home or go to other relatives. I only got here two days ago.'

(The Wannan incident brought to a close the pact of cooperation between the Guomingdan and the Communists to join forces against the Japanese invasion. On 6 January 1941 the Communist New Fourth Regiment was ambushed by an 80,000-strong Guomingdan force in the Wannan region in the south of Anhui Province. Eight days later, out of a total of

9,000, including several high-ranking officers, 7,000 Communists lay dead.)

Ninjun's voice cracked and then she started to sob. I put my arm around her and patted her shoulder:

'Ninjun, don't cry – don't be so sad. We will think of something – you'll see. Perhaps this is a new opportunity right here – what a coincidence that I should arrive now to pick up your mother, don't you think? We have a new mission.'

'The more I think about it the more miserable I feel about my life. Boniang said that she has had a bitter fortune, but my fate has been even worse than hers. For over ten years I have lived like an orphaned nomad. Only once have I found somewhere I could call home and something I could rely on – such a wonderful place – and it has been snatched away from me. I feel all hope has gone – there is nothing in front of my eyes – there is no future for me. You tell me not to feel so sad, but I don't know what to do – I can't see any way out.'

Her tears kept rolling down her cheeks and I wiped them away, telling her not to cry. She suddenly threw herself into my arms and cried even louder. I think I grew up in that instant, because for the first time in my life I felt that it was entirely up to me to protect someone. There was no way I would let this lonely girl face an unstable future on her own. My determination grew and I swore to myself that I would also help Shibo, who was the most trustworthy and respected woman on this earth, to get her life back and banish her hardship. The bond I already felt in my heart for Shibo and her family suddenly deepened even further. I held Ninjun's hand firmly:

'Don't be afraid. You and your mother, my father and I – we are all inseparable now; we will create our own good fortune.'

Ninjun didn't say anything and she calmed down as we sat

quietly together. She was leaning against me and I could smell the fragrance of her hair. Then she said bashfully:

'You know, everyone at the Children's Theatre was always singing your praises. Every time a letter came from you they all teased me.'

'How did they tease you?'

'They would grab your letter from me and run around shouting out: Lin Dage's letter is here, Chubby Liao – buy us sweets and you can have it back!'

My heart felt the sweetness, but I couldn't help teasing her myself:

'Well, if I had known they were teasing you, I would have written less often!'

Ninjun punched my arm and gave me a hard stare:

'Huh! Don't say that. I loved getting your letters! There was a period of time when you didn't write and my eyes were trying to pierce the clouds looking for a letter from you.'

Ninjun had been talking to me all the while in Putonghua (Mandarin). It had been the rule in the Children's Theatre that everyone should speak it rather than in any local dialect, but although her voice sounded very pleasant in Putonghua, I felt it was strange:

'Ninjun, can we just talk in Sichuan dialect?'

'Why?'

'Putonghua sounds too official to me. Sichuan dialect is more natural and would make us feel much closer and more intimate!'

She punched my arm again, even harder, and at the same time changed to Sichuan dialect:

'Intimacy? What intimacy? That is *so* embarrassing!'

So there we were – it was well past midnight and there was silence all around us apart from the rustling of the leaves above our heads. We hugged each other in the dark. This girl in my arms was now my very dear, beloved girl. That was all – there were no words of endearment and no promises were made, but our young hearts knew that we would stay together, and so we did until Ninjun passed away and left us all.

A week later we were on our way to Miangyang. Shibo and Yabin took the bus and I took Ninjun on my bike.

The early autumn colours were vibrant and varied. All around us was ripe for harvest. The tracks of the wind could be seen in the golden paddy fields as it tripped through them bending the rice stems on its way. It also brought the sweet, but pungent, scent of the late-cropping rapeseed to our nostrils. In the corn fields we passed, the upright stalks were heavily laden just waiting to be picked. The sun was bright in a blue sky which heightened the beauty of everything, but most beautiful of all was Ninjun, who was sitting side-saddle on the crossbar of my bike so close to me. She talked and talked and when she tired of talking, she sang. Her singing was sublime after her training by professionals at the Children's Theatre. We were so happy and love made the world look wonderful. I was full of energy and tried my best to keep up with the bus that Shibo was on, but the road was very uneven and there were many interruptions in the music as Ninjun was being tossed around. Even if I had to pedal to the ends of the earth though, it wouldn't have been a problem, just as long as Ninjun was still there. The journey took four days and each evening we met up with Shibo and Yabin to overnight in the towns along the route.

Finally the two families were together again after two years apart. The atmosphere was so good it felt like we had never been apart at all and we just picked up where we had left off.

Father quickly got down to business, though, and told Shibo that the Above had sent us a message that, in the light of his new job, they wanted us to take control of the transportation of grain to the military. He went on to say:

'The Above especially mentioned that they thought that you are the most suitable person for the job and want you to take responsibility for it. You have also heard of the person we need to approach about getting the contract for the business – Den Beicheng – he is the director of the grain depots in northern Sichuan.'

Shibo's eyes widened.

'Den Beicheng! Of course I know of him! In 1932 Yubi and I were re-establishing our guerrilla force in Yu Village – what we didn't know was that Warlord Yang Sen had sent a brigade to besiege us. Fortunately for us Den Beicheng, who was Yang Sen's military staff officer at the time, sent a message to us to warn us about it. Yubi immediately recalled our force back to the mountains and Yang Sen's troops closed in on nothing. Den certainly performed a deed of merit for our revolution. The problem is – perhaps he knows us too well?'

'Don't worry – Den and I are like brothers. He often talks about you and respects you a lot. In fact he says you are the most powerful figure in the northern Huaying Mountains and he wants to meet you. Den is a clever man – he sees perfectly well what is going on in the current political climate. He has very radical ideas and used to have links with the Communist Party. He knows I'm a "red man" and still wants me to work with him – he's even said outright that if I can find him 'the link' to the Party then he would be very happy. I've set up a meeting with him for you already.'

In the meantime, we found a school for Yabin in Mianyang and it was decided that Ninjun should go to the Performing Arts College in Chengdu, where she could carry on with her music and theatre studies. I didn't want to part with her, but she had such a talent and hadn't had a real chance of pursuing her education yet. I used my contacts to get her a place there.

At her meeting with Den Beicheng, Shibo didn't hesitate in saying that forming her own transport company was no problem for her at all and promised to undertake the transportation of grain to all military installations in northern Sichuan on time. She signed the two-year contract with Den Beicheng then and there. Later, Father told her how astounded he was at her confidence in saying that she could set up a transport business so quickly, but she told him that she already had a plan in mind.

The next day, I went with her to the Wenshui Temple, north of Chengdu, where a lot of flatbed-cart owners and workers gathered. Shibo dressed herself in a long, dark velvet gown and large gold earrings to give the appearance of being a rich businesswoman. She walked in an imperious manner to the Wenshui Temple teahouse with me following behind her. We sat down and she ordered tea and started discussing business matters in a loud voice, making sure that she mentioned the transfer of military grain. In no time at all, everyone wanted to be involved and Shibo was inundated by applicants. She needed forty men who owned their own carts and a manager to oversee them. Within a week we had drawn up contracts with each worker and the Liangchang Transport Firm was born.

The next two years were arduous ones for Shibo and they took a heavy toll on her health. She developed a severe stomach illness. On many occasions, she defended the grain consignments from the hands of thieves and ruffians herself and, in doing so, she faced danger and death. At the outset, Shibo had not only wanted to undertake the contract, but she wanted to make a financial profit for the Party and to gather more recruits. In the end there wasn't any profit, but – as she said herself – she had made the effort for her country and she had made many more friends and increased her knowledge and experience of life itself. She had been responsible for feeding over two hundred men and their families. More importantly to her, she hadn't let down Den Beicheng or my father.

Shibo had just completed the transfer of the last grain consignment under the terms of her first contract with Den Beicheng. It had been an arduous journey for her and I told her to rest in the hotel while I went to Den Beicheng's house to tell him that she was ready to sign another contract with him, if he was willing. On my way there, I was stopped by a middle-aged man, wearing a long gown, who said he had something that he wanted to talk to me about. He politely asked me my name and then said:

'You like reading the *Xinhua Daily*, don't you? And you like writing antisocial poems.'

'Of course I read the *Xinhua Daily* – the whole of China reads it. I also read all the other newspapers too – what's wrong with that?'

'But the *Xinhua Daily* is a Communist paper – you're a Leftist, aren't you? I'm only trying to save young men like you from being influenced by their ideas, that's all. Come with me now.'

As I was telling him that I had no intention of going anywhere with him, I noticed two more men closing in on me and I knew that I was in for trouble. They pushed and pulled me to the police station and I was taken to an empty office and locked in for the whole night. Meanwhile, Shibo went to Den Beicheng's house to look for me, but they told her I had never been there. Through one of her contacts she managed to find out that a young man, calling himself Lin Yeping, had been arrested as a suspected Communist and was locked up in the police station. I was kept there for forty days and, remarkably, I was only questioned twice during the whole time. Yabin brought me food every day, but he wasn't allowed near me; he passed messages to me, hidden in the rice, from Shibo and my father telling me that they were doing everything they could to get me out. Ninjun came all the way from Chengdu to see me. She was worried sick and persuaded the guard to let her into the room. Although it was the most frightening experience to be locked up and not know whether I would ever be free again, at the same time having Ninjun visit me was the sweetest of moments. She declared her love for me and whispered in my ear that no matter how long it took, she would wait for me and that we would then never be apart. My tears wet her cheek. It gradually became apparent that my arrest had been a case of mistaken identity and coincidence. I had published an article under the name of Lin Yeping and the Guomingdan were actually searching for someone named Pi Yeping, who, like me, came from the Yunyang area. Luckily for me, the Guomingdan were unable to pin anything on me, although they were certainly very suspicious that I was a Communist. It put everyone connected to me under the spotlight and was a dangerous situation for all of us. In the end Father used his influence with one of the Guomingdan commanders to get me released. They arranged for a doctor to visit to 'examine' me. The doctor was very stern and methodical. He used his stethoscope to listen to my heart and chest and pressed here and there. All the while he kept repeating in a loud voice: 'This is serious, very serious. You have a very severe illness.'

Then he walked out without another word. Two days later I was released and one of the officers took me to a hotel. He patted me on the shoulder and said: 'Well, take good care of your health. You must stay here because you may be called in for questioning again at any time.'

I was free after forty days' incarceration, but I couldn't risk being picked up again and questioned, so that night I left for Chengdu. Father followed soon afterwards, because word got out that he had used his position to get me released. We feared for Shibo's safety after this and managed to persuade her to leave too and come and stay with us in Chengdu.

Ninjun had also got herself into trouble whilst at the Performing Arts College in Chengdu, because she had become politically active during the two years she was there. She helped to organise, and took part in, a protest march against the Guomingdan and her name ended up on their blacklist. One day she had to jump over the college wall to escape being arrested. She managed to find us in Chengdu and once again our two families were gathered together.

In 1943, Father found a job, through one of his friends, as the manager of the People's Park of Chengdu. Meanwhile, Shibo turned down two job offers: the first one was for the position of magistrate in the county court, and the other one was as a Guomingdan city commissioner. Shibo laughed at the thought of both of these jobs, declaring that she had fought against the Guomingdan for over half of her life and so how could she possibly work for them? She politely refused both jobs, but the offers showed just how much she was respected.

Shibo and Father thought it was time to sort out a marriage between Ninjun and myself. All parents want the biggest and best wedding for their children, but we had to make do. First of all, we were laying low as we were on the Guomingdan wanted list and anyway we never had much money to spare. However, Shibo still found enough to buy some red velvet and have a long gown made out of it for Ninjun and she bought me a new Sun Yat-sen style suit. Father spent everything he had to buy Ninjun a gold ring. We had a simple ceremony followed by having our photograph taken. One of Father's good friends took us to the best photographer in Chengdu as a wedding present. Then we took a walk in the park. Ninjun looked stunning in her gown and I didn't look bad either! Everyone who saw us said that we looked like a well-suited couple. Later the four of us shared a meal in a restaurant. This was how we celebrated one of the biggest events in our lives – in a simple fashion, but we were content with it.

Shibo found a small house for Ninjun and I and she came to live with us, but we were all dependent on Father's meagre wage. Although life was hard, we were so happy just to be together. Then without warning our happiness was interrupted. We came home late one afternoon and found one of our neighbours waiting for us in an agitated state. He told us that someone had visited several times to check our residency. He had asked where we came from, what were we doing and why hadn't we registered at the police station. A wide-scale check was being carried out to uncover Communists and our neighbour had been instructed to tell us that we were required to go and register at the police station first thing the following morning.

Shibo closed the door after the neighbour left and at once said to me:

'Quickly, go and ask your father to find somewhere for you both to shelter for a while – you *have* to leave tonight.'

There was no time to dwell on my feelings of regret and disappointment and I ran as fast as I could to the People's Park to inform Father. He hurriedly wrote a letter to one of his good friends from army days who lived in Penzhou County, which was about sixty kilometres north of Chengdu. He told me that we could trust him and that we should go to him and ask for his help. By the time I got back to the house, I found that Ninjun and Shibo had already packed everything. We waited for nightfall before leaving the house. Shibo went to stay with relatives.

White Cloud Temple School

Ninjun and I gathered together our meagre luggage and very quietly left the house in Chengdu, our first home together. The only way for us to get to Penzhou was on foot, but Ninjun was by now a few months pregnant, so I was worried. It was January and the night air was very cold. We had only covered a couple of kilometres before heavy rain beset us. I pulled out the large, oiled umbrella from our luggage and held it over Ninjun. Ahead of us I saw a man pushing a one-wheeled wooden cart and I sprinted to catch up with him. We negotiated a price for him to carry Ninjun on it. However, an hour or so later, he said that he didn't want to go any further, so we had no choice after that except to keep trudging on. As daybreak neared we were relieved to find an early-opening food stall where we could get something to eat. We were exhausted, cold and hungry and we devoured some hot porridge made out of sweet potato and rice. We were young, however, and it wasn't long before we felt ready to get on our way again. In typical style, Ninjun started singing her favourite song, 'Yellow River Love'. Her beautiful voice heralded the dawn and I joined in too. Singing helped to throw off the tiredness we felt and carried us on for another ten kilometres to the town of Penzhou. We arrived there in the early morning, but we still had several more kilometres to go before we reached Zhou's house in the smaller town of Guankou.

I had misgivings about going to Zhou's house. I had never even heard about this friend of Father's and I hadn't had time to ask him anything about Zhou at all. I felt very uncertain about the fact that Ninjun and I were about to land on his doorstep completely unannounced. What would happen if they didn't like us or they weren't able to have us to stay? Then where could we go? If I had been on my own it wouldn't have been a problem, but I had to find accommodation for Ninjun and our child she was carrying in her womb. I was deeply worried. Ninjun didn't think there would be any problem, however, and she told me with confidence to leave it all to her and let her do the talking. She made me feel better, as I had already seen her deal with many difficult situations in the same way her mother always managed. They shared a quick-witted, brave and resourceful nature. Ninjun knew how to communicate well with people and her manners were exemplary.

Guankou was in the coal-producing region of Penzhou County and many flatbed carts were passing us on the road on their way to pick up coal. When I asked for directions to Zhou's house, many people stopped and they all knew of him. They told us that he was the town head. Then, seeing how tired we were and Ninjun's condition, one of them offered to take us on his cart direct to Zhou's house.

We stood at their door, dripping wet, and knocked. When the master and mistress of the house were called, Ninjun sweetly addressed them:

'Uncle Zhou, Aunty Zhou.'

I immediately handed over Father's letter of introduction and Zhou ripped it open. His eyes quickly searched for the signature at the bottom. With a sharp intake of breath he summoned the maids and told them to prepare a room for us as quickly as possible. Zhou's wife took Ninjun to her room and went through her wardrobe to find something that might fit her and I was given some of Zhou's clothes too. We washed and changed and on returning to the hall we found two bowls of soup topped by four poached eggs waiting for us on the table. We were grateful for such a good meal.

After we had eaten, Zhou took out Father's letter and said to us: 'It's no problem, no problem at all. Your father and I are not ordinary friends, you know, we are friends in adversity and true blood brothers. Your father is a dignified man, who is widely read, knowledgeable about history and understands military tactics. He is frank and brave and he always stands up for his friends if they are suffering hardship. We greatly respect him. Therefore you are as welcome here as if it were your own home. Whether you stay one year, or three, or five – it's no problem. As long as we have food, we will share it with you. As for a job, we can talk about that later. As long as you are in my area of control, you have freedom to do whatever you want.'

Zhou then went on to tell us why he held Father in such high esteem. They had both been in Warlord Yang Sen's troop and Zhou had been the regimental commander when they lost one of the key battles against Warlord Liu Xiang. Zhou was then accused of having sold information to Liu Xiang to give him the advantage. The penalty for this was execution. Unfortunately there was nothing to prove that Zhou hadn't betrayed Yang Sen and his life was on the line. Father, however, made a stand on behalf of Zhou, investigated the accusations and subsequently spoke in Zhou's defence. He said that the charges against Zhou had been fabricated and he was so sure about this that he was willing to lay his own life on the line for Zhou's life. In the end Zhou was acquitted, but he felt so bitter towards

Yang Sen that he decided to retire and return to his home town. Once back home, he had been elected as the town head by the local people and he had been happy there ever since.

Ninjun was determined that we shouldn't take the Zhous' generous hospitality for granted, so she got up very early for the next few mornings, cleaned the house thoroughly and cooked the breakfast. When the maids finally stopped her, she then went to the nursery and undertook to teach the Zhous' three children how to sing and dance. She also amused them by telling them stories.

Aunty Zhou mused to her husband: 'If I had a daughter like Ninjun, I would be very happy.'

'Well, in that case then, I would like to acknowledge you as my godmother,' Ninjun said.

Aunty Zhou clapped her hands and laughed happily:

'That would be *my* good fortune – if you don't mind our country-folk ways, then be my goddaughter.'

From then on, Ninjun called the Zhous Godfather and God-mother and the children gladly accepted her as their big sister.

Aunty Zhou was in her thirties and had been well educated. She was well mannered and her skin was fine and pale. Her family home was in Chengdu, where her father and grand-father were scholars. Zhou, however, never had much of an education, but he was an intelligent, sensible man with a keen moral code. It was a very happy home.

Uncle Zhou asked me what kind of job I would like to do and I told him that I had already done quite a bit of teaching and really liked it, but he let out a long sigh:

'These days we only have one school in the town which only takes children who live close by. There used to be a school five kilometres away from here, but this year we neither have teachers nor pupils so it has been closed down. The children from remote areas find it difficult to get to school and they're too poor anyway. Most peasants prefer to keep their children at home to help with the work on the land and look after the animals. Those children will never get an education and it goes on generation after generation like this. All they know is how to work in the fields and there is never any turning point in their lives.'

I tried to persuade Uncle Zhou to let Ninjun and I revive the school. We were very keen to be useful in some way. He kept shaking his head:

'No, no, that school is in a temple halfway up the mountain and it lives up to its name, White Cloud Temple – there are no facilities there. Could you take the hardship? No, I have thought about it and when the spring comes, you and Ninjun will go to teach in the Town Hall School.'

'But look Uncle Zhou, we came here wishing to do something. You obviously worry about those children unable to go to school, so let us sort it out – it would be a fine thing to make education available to all children, especially the poor ones – we will think up a way of making it possible. I am determined to reopen the school – it could be the perfect thing for us to do.'

Uncle Zhou changed his mind and the next day he called a meeting in the town hall with the elders from over ten villages. He told them about the plan to reopen the White Cloud Temple School. He spoke just as if he was giving military orders:

'Listen – all of you – if the parents refuse to send their children to school, they will be punished. If the family can't afford to pay the fee, the town council will pay.'

In the following days Ninjun and I visited over fifty families in the wider area to encourage them to send their children to school. Ninety per cent of them were living in very poor conditions. The able-bodied men from twenty families had been press-ganged into the Guomingdan army and most of them had been killed at the front. Only two men came back, but they had severe injuries and no money for treatment. In other families some of the men worked as coal miners and the others pulled flatbed carts to transport the coal. The women generally stayed at home caring for the family. Whenever we delivered the news that their children could go to school for free there were tears of joy, and we usually heard the words:

'Of course we want our children to learn to read and write – it would be good for them in the future – but we don't have the money to pay the fees.'

After visiting so many families we knew that the demand was there, and we knew we could get funding, therefore we felt that it was really worthwhile to reopen the school. We started our preparations to move to the White Cloud Temple. For the first time Aunty Zhou quarrelled with her husband. She jabbed her finger at him:

'You are sending them to that ghastly place with Ninjun in her condition. How will you be able to face Lin Dage? That place is so hilly and Ninjun is already too heavily pregnant to manage it. What if she falls or something goes wrong with the baby – how will you square your conscience then?'

Aunty Zhou had lost her temper and it frightened all of us. In the end Uncle Zhou promised that next term he would make sure that we would teach at the Town Hall School instead. In tears, Aunty Zhou finally agreed to let us go and immediately started to gather lots of things together for Ninjun to take. She wanted Ninjun to promise to come home to give birth, saying that she *had* to have mother and baby safely in her care.

The White Cloud Temple was almost deserted. The only person there was an elderly Buddhist nun, who lived on charity. We asked her if she would cook for us for two yuan per month and she gladly agreed. There were a few rooms down one side of the hall and we took one of them as our room. I heaped up some straw on the floor in front of the altar for our bed and spread the quilt on top. Then I tidied two of the other rooms which we would use as classrooms. I made some simple desks and benches by nailing together some wooden planks which I had carried up the mountainside. Below the temple there was a square, flat area with a raised plot suitable for flowers and shrubs. There were already two camellias there which were covered in buds ready to burst. I dug up some wild flowers and transplanted them into the plot in anticipation of a fine display in the spring, which I hoped would please Ninjun.

The weather was still very cold and Ninjun's belly seemed to grow larger every day, but she came with me everywhere. I felt guilty and felt that I had let her down by bringing her to live in such spartan conditions and I didn't know what to say to her. She didn't seem to mind and never complained, but it crossed my mind that she might just be too tired to voice any hard feelings. But, as we settled down at night, she would often say things like:

'This reminds me of life with the Children's Theatre – we often had to sleep on the ground – but this is different because I am with my loved one.'

I was glad to know that she felt like that because it was the same for me – as long as we were together, nothing seemed to matter.

A few days before the reopening, Uncle Zhou gave me forty yuan, saying that it was funds for the school. I knew that he had taken it from his own wallet. I went to town and bought books, paper, brushes and ink. Then I prepared a large banner to hang on the front of the temple saying: 'Congratulations – White Cloud Temple School Opening – Welcome to the Pupils'.

On the day, to our surprise, about thirty pupils turned up. They were all wearing patched, but clean, clothes. Also present were officers from the town hall, village elders and parents. Uncle Zhou introduced Ninjun and I as having come from Chengdu and made some complimentary remarks about our lives before coming to the White Cloud Temple School. Then I addressed the pupils with a few words of encouragement and urged them to study hard and appreciate the opportunity they had been given. Ninjun sang a couple of songs magnificently, which earned applause from the gathering. All in all, it looked as if we had made a good first impression. Then I gave out the books and paper to the pupils, emphasising to them that they had been bought through the kindness of their town head, Mr Zhou. The pupils and their families cheered and once again Uncle Zhou had won the local people's hearts and their respect.

News about the free schooling spread and, bit by bit, the number of pupils grew until we had over forty. We divided the children into two groups and we both taught for two hours in the mornings and two hours in the afternoons. Ninjun taught maths, singing and art and I taught reading, writing and sports.

I planted some vegetables, which was especially necessary for Ninjun's health, and two months later we were eating our own fresh produce. Our joint wages added up to forty-eight yuan per month and we made sure that we saved some money to pay for a wet nurse just in case Ninjun couldn't feed the baby when the time came. Aunty Zhou was still urging Ninjun to go back to her house to give birth, but the mother of one of our pupils had willingly offered to help us. Her name was Mrs Yang and unfortunately her child had just died so she still had milk, but more importantly she was the midwife in the area. We felt confident in knowing this and we continued to make preparations to have the baby there. We made sure we had things like alcohol, thread and clean cloth. All we had to do then was wait for the baby to arrive.

We lacked sufficient medical knowledge, however, and had

miscalculated the birth date – we were mistaken by one month. One night Ninjun woke with pain in her abdomen and the pain kept getting worse, but we didn't realise at first that it was the pain of contractions. By the time we understood what was happening I felt it was too late to go and fetch the midwife, as she lived two kilometres away, and I didn't want to leave Ninjun on her own for long. So I ran to the nun for help instead. I couldn't believe it when she told me that a woman giving birth in a temple was taboo and nor could I believe it when she turned her back on me, put her hands together and started praying to bless the temple, rather than give us any help. So I started running to go and fetch the midwife, but then I heard Ninjun suddenly scream so I went back to her instead.

By then she was in such pain and she was writhing around, shouting and screaming, but I didn't know what to do. I was in such a panic. I don't know how long it went on for, but finally Ninjun stopped screaming and the baby was born. I was so confused and frightened because there was so much blood – I had blood all over me. I hurriedly wrapped the baby up in the quilt and placed it next to Ninjun. I ran back to the nun and begged her to cook a poached-egg soup for her. Then I ran to the nearest home of one of our pupils and asked him to go and fetch the midwife, Mrs Yang, as quickly as possible. When she arrived and took charge, I let myself take a deep breath and then I remembered that I didn't know whether it was a boy or girl and asked her to tell me. She laughed as she held the baby up: 'Congratulations – it is a girl – a little miss worth thousands in gold!'

'Good, good!' I laughed and so did Ninjun.

Aunty Zhou sent us two large chickens, two hundred eggs and twenty silver yuan with a message to say that she was longing to see her goddaughter's daughter. I wrote a letter to Father and one to Shibo telling them the good news and I asked Father to give his granddaughter a name. A week later he sent a cheerful reply and suggested naming the baby Binhua, which means 'The Flower which Blooms in the Winter'. The name suggested a strong character and a resolute, capable individual and we all liked it.

Mrs Yang stayed with us for two days in the temple and then decided to take Binhua with her back to her own home, because it was more convenient for her and so that Ninjun could get some rest. But the very next day she ran back to us in terror saying that Binhua was sick. Ninjun grabbed my hand and pulled me outside and we hurried to the wet nurse's house. Binhua was lying on the bed, shaking and short of breath. Her whole body was so hot that it felt as if she was on fire and her condition terrified us. Ninjun held Binhua in her arms and burst out crying. Mrs Yang and I were also crying, but none of us knew what the illness was or what to do. The country doctor had already been called and he soon arrived. He checked her pulse and opened her mouth to inspect her tongue.

'This is the beginning of umbilical tetanus – it is lucky you found it so early. I can cure this – I have treated many babies for this.'

When we heard the words 'umbilical tetanus' our faces went white, because we knew that nine out of ten babies died from it. We thought about taking Binhua back to Chengdu for hospital treatment, but it was the middle of winter and a long way away. We saw how confident the doctor was about his ability to treat her, so we decided to stay put. The doctor came each day and used his home-made herbal ointment on Binhua's navel and in less than ten days Baby Binhua was well again. The child was like me: she had a strong will to live.

Ninjun with Binhua in 1945

The Spring Festival to celebrate Chinese New Year was coming up and our school started a month's holiday. We tidied up and took Binhua back to Uncle Zhou and his family for her first New Year and we were warmly welcomed.

Uncle Zhou told me that he had made arrangements for us to teach in the Town Hall School in the future and that I would be made head teacher. For myself, I would have loved to be the head teacher. However, I couldn't let myself forget that I was on the Guomingdan wanted list and we had come to Penzhou County to hide. I was grateful to Uncle Zhou, but I insisted that he gave the post to someone local. I also didn't want to upset the present deputy head, who was naturally in line for the job, especially as he was the son of the former town head, in

193

case it caused any bad feelings later on. Uncle Zhou took a little time to think about it but then agreed and appointed me as the deputy head teacher.

When our pupils at the White Cloud Temple School heard we were leaving for the Town Hall School most of them followed us to town. There were about ten pupils left at the Temple School, but they weren't abandoned, as a secondary school graduate was appointed as their teacher.

For the time being, we left Binhua with Mrs Yang whilst we moved to the Town Hall School. This was a brand new building and the classrooms were spacious and bright. It was a primary and secondary school combined and there were more than two hundred pupils and ten teachers with support staff. The difference between the two schools was like the difference between heaven and earth.

It quickly became apparent that the head teacher was an ambitious man and didn't want to stay in such a small place for long, so he was more than happy to take a back seat and let me take over the day-to-day running of the school. There were four teaching posts vacant and I saw this as an opportunity to shelter some of our comrades who were in hiding – more and more of us were having to go into hiding as the Guomingdan closed around us. Guankou had already proved safe for Ninjun and me, so I went to see Father in Chengdu to tell him about this opportunity. I also went to see Shibo who was staying with her niece in Chengdu, but she was ill. She was happy about Binhua and said she couldn't wait to see her and that as soon as she felt better she would come to see us.

A couple of days after I returned to Guankou I had two surprise visitors. Father had sent Second Uncle's daughter, Meixia, and my half-sister, Liuqing, to me for shelter. They told me that the situation at home in Yunan had been deteriorating for a long time, but now things were critical. Second Uncle had long since lost his job and had returned home penniless. He, as well as Big Uncle and his wife, were still heavily addicted to opium, so all income had dried up. Everything of value in the house had been sold and Grandmother had gone to live with Eighth Aunty. Second Uncle's wife was trying to support the whole family by selling salt, but there hadn't been enough money for Meixia's fees so she had had to drop out of secondary school before graduating. So the family decided to send Meixia, as well as Liuqing, to Father in the hope that they would find better prospects in life with him. However, after hearing that there were jobs available at the school, Father decided that they would be better off with me and Ninjun.

It was certainly a surprise to see them, but I was more than happy to have them with me. I gave Meixia a job teaching the primary class and she proved to be as big a hit with the children as Ninjun was. Liuqing helped in the house, especially looking after Binhua.

Father also sent two more people my way for their safety: Uncle Chen Yuping and his wife. In the intervening years, Uncle Chen had become an important member of the Communist Party. His current role was that of special commissioner responsible for identifying and grooming potential defectors from the Guomingdan. His goal was to form a united front line of Communist sympathisers in the southwest region of Sichuan. I had never met his wife before, but she was a university graduate and had been teaching at the First Academy of Chengdu. However, she no longer felt safe there and that's why Father sent them to me, especially as she would be able to fill one of the teaching posts at the school legitimately. Uncle Chen, though, was playing a part. In order to carry out his mission for the Party he was pretending to be an idle and somewhat sickly man who had no interest in holding down a job himself. In the eyes of other people, he was just an affable man who liked to spend his time in the teahouse, chatting to everybody, playing cards and gambling at mahjong. Nobody could guess that he was a senior figure within the Communist Party.

For my part, I was getting along well with the staff and students and still made sure that I didn't draw attention to myself by arranging any anti-government activities at the school. I stuck rigidly to teaching the core subjects.

The long school summer holiday started and all the teachers went home except for our group. This left us alone in the building, which we all enjoyed very much. I accompanied Uncle Chen in travelling around Penzhou County, to learn its geography and gather information, so that we could plan our next move. Whilst pretending to be a layabout, he had learned a lot in his conversations with all and sundry and he pointed out all the key points of the county to me. He told me not to underestimate the area, as it was not only rich in high-quality anthracite, which was much in demand by the power station in Chengdu, but it also had plentiful copper. Copper, of course, went to supply the munitions factories and was used for minting coins.

A few days of travelling around gave us a better knowledge of the whole area and Uncle Chen outlined his plans. He wanted to: (1) use Guankou and the Town Hall School as our headquarters; (2) trade coal, mainly as a business cover, but also to generate income; (3) set up one of the copper mines and surrounding area for our military base; (4) assimilate the local gangs (*paoge*) and to give military training to some of their core members; (5) look at ways of obtaining weapons; (6) foster the coal miners with a view to establishing a guerrilla force; (7) prepare ourselves for a civil war.

Here was yet another exciting project and I couldn't contain my enthusiasm. Soon, our plans were put into action. Gradually I did less and less at the school and Ninjun and Uncle Chen's wife took over from me – then I was free to start trading coal. Meixia became my accountant. We rented a two-storey shop in Guankou with a large back patio where we could store coal. We would buy it from the coal porters who would take either their horse or mule to the mine and load up two wicker baskets each. They could carry about one hundred kilos per trip and made two trips in a day. Then we would bag it up in our yard and try to sell it on. The main market for it was in Chengdu and very soon we were in a position to rent three shops in Chengdu, which Shibo and one other Party member managed.

It wasn't always easy to find buyers, however, especially a buyer who required a large quantity, so it often meant selling it bag by bag to a wide range of customers. Shibo was a good businesswoman, but she was still recovering from her illness, and the other member was a very ineffective salesperson, so it was up to me to do the running around. I went around the streets trying to persuade hotels, restaurants and other businesses to buy my coal. Each day I called on between ten and twenty potential customers, but I was lucky if I managed to find two buyers from that number. Also, it was a buyer's market and I often had to give out a free bag of coal as a sample before anyone was willing to buy from me. It has to be said that there was a great deal of poor-quality coal on the market and people were suspicious. I felt like a horse that never stops galloping. In the end, through a contact, I found a couple of factories to supply. Each month we sold about two hundred bags of coal, which was enough for us all to live on, but not enough to make a profit.

A lot of Americans had come to Sichuan as military and political advisers to the Guomingdan and Chengdu was an established post for the Allied Forces. Father knew someone who worked in the guesthouse at the American base, so I went to see him. This man couldn't have been more frank and he said to me:

'To buy coal from you, my manager will want fifty percent sales commission. It doesn't matter what price you ask and never mind about the quality of the coal – as long as it can be lit. We can take at least two hundred bags a month – you'd be paid on delivery.'

I wasn't a real businessman and I had no idea how to handle a deal like this. I was a serious and earnest man and I couldn't easily go against my conscience to pass off poor-quality coal as high quality and overcharge for it. I didn't dare to agree to his conditions, so I went to ask Shibo about it. She laughed at me and said:

'What are you scared of? Do what they say – it's just business!'

I had an added dilemma, though, because of the Americans. I didn't like them at all, as I often saw them drunk and driving around dangerously in their jeeps. Also, for everybody to see, they dragged young, pretty girls into their vehicles, took them back to their accommodation and, it was rumoured, raped them. The ordinary people, despite our anger, were powerless to stop them and the government turned a blind eye to it. To make matters worse, they were here to assist the Guomingdan and I didn't want to do business with my enemy.

Shibo shook her head and said to me:

'You're too naïve – these Americans are Chiang Kai-shek's

backbone – they're propping up his regime. In order to get America to support him, he and his followers bow and scrape to them like slaves and do anything they're asked to do. At the same time, though, who doesn't want to profit from the Americans? We should join the gravy train too – why not? We can take from the enemy and use it for our own benefit – and who knows, at the same time we might obtain useful information about them. If you don't go into the tiger's den, then how do you get the baby out? Don't worry – there won't be any danger – go for it.'

I felt better about things and went and signed a contract for the first delivery of six hundred bags of coal. Then I rushed back to Guankou to escort the consignment personally to the American base in Chengdu. Our two trucks were stopped at the gate and I had to hand over five yuan to the sentry to let us pass. Then we had to go to the weighing point and the fifty-kilo bags showed up as weighing only forty kilos on their scale, so I had to give five yuan to the man to correct the calibration of the scales to show the true weight. Finally the coal reached the furnace and I watched the stoker shovel some of my good-quality coal into the furnace. I was astonished to hear him announce that the coal was rubbish and that it didn't burn properly and then I found that I had to pay him to 'change his mind' about its quality. As I watched my coal burning fiercely in the furnace I couldn't believe how much money I had wasted and still not pleased anyone. I was angry and I went to find the man with whom I had made the arrangement and shouted at him:

'You said you wanted fifty percent, but *I've* ended up with much less than fifty percent – I had assumed that our arrangement would include everything.'

He laughed, saying: 'Hey young brother! Look – you're new

in this business so let me explain. I took fifty percent to cover what I have to pay to my boss – it's up to you to give the back-handers to all the other people.'

'How can I buy off each person I meet in this business? There is a queue of people all wanting a slice of the profit. I am not making any money on this – we have to pay all our hard-working labourers as well – are you going to allow us to survive or not?'

The man patted my shoulder: 'Little brother – I won't let you suffer – I will tell you how it works and what you have to do next time.'

Then he whispered in my ear the secret of making a profit:

'Just fill each bag with stones and cinders and put a bit of the good stuff on top. Then at each stage at the base, quietly hand over the money without being asked and you'll get through in no time at all.'

I was appalled. I went to Shibo in an uncontrollable rage and told her everything. She wasn't surprised at all, let alone angry. She told me to calm down and started calculating the costs involved with all the added backhanders. She worked out that if we put ten percent good coal on the top of each bag of cinders and stones then we could still make a profit of half a yuan per bag.

I embarked on the second delivery and followed instructions at each stage. No one troubled me at all. When I saw the bags reach the furnace safely I hesitated. The same stoker looked at me and seemed to understand what I was thinking: I wanted to see how the cinders and stones were going to work. At the same moment his boss started walking towards us and the fireman quickly shovelled some 'coal' into the furnace and then threw in some petrol. The furnace exploded into life and the flames flared higher and higher. The stoker turned to his boss:

'Look – such good coal – such high quality!'

The boss continued to stroll past us with his hands behind his back and just nodded. The stoker was very pleased with himself and patted me on the shoulder and said:

'*Hoi*, young man – do you see how it works now? Just continue like this in the future and we all benefit. Those murderous Americans want to eat us, but we can do the same to them too! The Chinese aren't that stupid!'

Some weeks later Uncle Chen and I had a meeting with Shibo in Chengdu. He said to her:

'In the light of the war with Japan being in its last stages and with China expecting victory within days, we now have to think about what will happen next. The Guomingdan never respected our alliance with them during the war against Japan and have repeatedly declared that they ultimately want to destroy the Communists. It is thought that a civil war is now inevitable. The Party feels that the best place to engage the Guomingdan would be in the Huaying Mountain region. The reasons being, firstly the geography of the area would give us the advantage and, secondly and importantly, the people of the region still have the revolutionary fervour and will. The Party recognises that you still have a good relationship with the people there and you are needed to reorganise them into a fighting force once again. You can take this as an official mission from the Party.'

Shibo was speechless. During the years she had been cut off from her link with the Party, which was ever since her trip to Russia had had to be aborted, she had suffered. Being without the Communist Party felt to her as if she were an orphan adrift alone in a vast ocean. And now, sitting in front of her, was a senior leader from the Southern Central Committee giving her an official mission. Uncle Chen continued:

'Shijie, go back to the Huaying Mountains and find the

people, like yourself, who have lost their link with the Party and establish good relations with them – their Party member- ship can be sorted out later. As for you – you are now under Party instructions, so there is no worry about your member- ship. Someone will contact you in due course.'

Shibo was over the moon and she couldn't wait to get back to Yuechi to begin her mission: to prepare for the Third Huaying Mountain Uprising. She laughed and said: 'It looks like I go first – you and Ninjun will follow soon, I'm sure.'

Two Deaths in my Family

August 1945 was a momentous month. The Japanese finally surrendered eight years after their invasion of China. The whole country was in a frenzy of excitement. The high emotions were contagious and we joined the crowds in the streets laughing, cheering, dancing and crying. It had been a long, hard fight to drive the invaders out of our land and victory tasted sweet. It was a new dawn, however, and even as we celebrated that victory, we knew that the time had arrived to reconstruct our country.

Our coal business was struggling. Orders for coal were few, but then when we did deliver, very often we didn't receive payment and our debts were accumulating. We were being chased for payment of our bills and in turn we had to chase our debtors. Day in and day out, we were running up and down for no gain. Our lives were in a terrible fix. Then Uncle Chen said to us one day:

'If business doesn't pick up, just let it go. The Guomingdan have already started to attack our liberated regions and it looks like civil war will be declared at any time. We want you and Ninjun to go back to Yuechi County and help Ninjun's

mother. Take advantage of her foundation work there and prepare the local armed militia for revolution again.'

In October, Ninjun and I travelled to Yuechi, taking our
baby girl, Binhua, with us. This was my third visit and I knew
that I would be staying much longer this time and our lives
ahead would be full of danger. We were, however, thrilled
because it meant a lot to us to have a tough, important mission
loaded onto our shoulders. When we reached Shibo's home,
almost the entire village came out to greet us. Shibo cried tears
of joy to have Binhua in her arms and our little girl, who was
just over one year old, was the centre of attention. She charmed
everyone with her sweet and cheerful smile.

Later that night, when everyone had gone home and Binhua
was asleep, Shibo led Ninjun and me out to the *huangjiao* tree.
This tree had become the holy altar of the family, as under
it lay the bones of Liao Yubi, my father-in-law. It was the
tenth anniversary of his death. Ninjun knelt before her father's
grave and cried and I knelt down and kowtowed three times
in respect of him. On that dark autumn night we sat beside his
grave and made plans for the Huaying Mountain region's third
uprising.

I was eager to tell Shibo about the background picture, as
told to me by Uncle Chen:

'After the Japanese surrender, Chiang Kai-shek put on a
show for the benefit of the whole country, pretending that he
wanted to have peace talks with the Communists. However,
behind the scenes, he sent in a vast army to attack our liberated
areas. He wants to weaken us and gain hold of more territory
before he announces a civil war. Now Central Committee
instructs us to prepare for two scenarios: on the one hand, if
Chiang Kai-shek genuinely wants to have peace talks, we'll
hold off, talk to him and then see what happens. On the other
hand, if he chooses to fight we will be ready for him. We are

in a much better position now than ever before, because we have our own liberated bases with over a million armed men, as well as People's Militias numbering several million. We are no longer afraid of him. What we will need to do is start a revolt against Chiang Kai-shek here, in Sichuan, where he believes he has a safe base. Then we need to cooperate with the Liberation Army to liberate the whole southwest of the country.'

It didn't take much to imagine that my father-in-law was listening to us and urging us to carry on with the work he had started here with Shibo so many years before.

We had to stay with neighbours until something else could be sorted out for us, as it was considered very bad luck for a married girl to live with her maternal family. Even worse was if a daughter were to give birth in the maternal home – and Ninjun was pregnant again.

Shibo went to Liu Yuebo to ask him if we could have a room in his house. He was somebody whom Shibo and her husband had helped in the past and he was glad to do as Shibo asked. The Liu family used to be one of the richest landowning families in the region, but there wasn't much left by the time Liu Yuebo inherited, apart from the family house and a small piece of land. Twenty years previously he was the village elder, but he had abused his position. He sold public grain and stole tax money to feed his opium addiction and consequently he was put under investigation. Luckily for him Shibo's husband was the chief commander of the local force and it was up to him to carry out the investigation. Shibo and Yubi knew that Yuebo had weapons hidden in his house and persuaded him to contribute these to their secret armed defence force. At the time, this defence force was only about thirty strong, but they were gaining support. Yubi made sure that all charges were dropped against Yuebo and this was a turning point in his life. He stopped using opium just in time, because, although he was penniless by then, he still had the family house in his name. He started to earn a living by helping people with their legal papers, family letters and any other reading and writing tasks that the illiterate people of the village needed. He never forgot that Yubi and Shibo had saved his life, so no matter what kind of rumours he heard about Shibo, he would always stand up in her defence. So when Shibo asked if Ninjun, Binhua and I could stay with him, Yuebo didn't hesitate to accommodate us. He cleared out a large room on one side of his family court-yard, furnished it and set up a kitchen for us too.

Although Yuebo was a former opium addict and disgraced landowner, he was still the village 'intellectual'. He was an educated man, who read the newspapers and had a profound interest in the affairs of the country. He hated the warlords and the Guomingdan. With all this in common, we soon became very good friends. He was a glib talker and all he needed was a cup of tea at the Meilin Teahouse to get him started and then he could hold an audience's interest on a wide range of subjects. On market days the teahouse didn't charge him for his tea because he brought in so many people who wanted to listen to his stories. To the people from the countryside, he was like salt and pepper on a tasteless meal. Once we had settled in to his house, he often came to talk to me and, as long as he had his tobacco pipe and a cup of tea, he was happy to chat into the small hours till Ninjun decided it was time to kick him out of the room!

One night the conversation turned to my father-in-law. Yuebo leant back with a long sigh:

'You know, I witnessed his arrest. The heavenly god was blind on that occasion. Such a decent man – an extraordinary life cut short. I remember that tragic day so clearly.'

Yuebo puffed on his pipe and, as he studied the ascending, swirling plumes of smoke, he recalled the event.

'It happened in the late afternoon of 22 February 1935. Unusually for them, because we hardly ever saw them in town, Liao Dage and twelve of his best men came down from the mountain and went to the Meilin Teahouse. I was there too and most people were greeting him warmly. I decided that I would offer to pay for his tea and, just as I was approaching his table, a very short man beat me to it. I watched as he bent to say something in Liao Dage's ear. Liao Dage's expression instantly changed and he sprang up from his chair, beckoning to his men. As he tried to leave he was pulled back sharply because the short man was standing on the hem of his long gown. In the blink of an eye we were all surrounded by dozens of plain-clothes men – there were so many of them in fact that even water wouldn't have been able to flow out of the teahouse. Chairs and tables were overturned and the teacups went flying. Those men were like a pack of dogs as they pounced on Liao Dage. They wrestled him to the ground and trussed him up. A couple of Liao Dage's men were shot and the others were tied up and taken away with him. It all happened so quickly and none of us in the teahouse knew whether we were going to be arrested too – we were all scared to death. I was shaking so much I couldn't move for what seemed like hours. Then overnight I composed a letter, which I co-signed with as many prominent gentlemen of the town as I could rouse in the early hours. In it, we declared that we would be willing to stand as Liao Dage's guarantors and requested that he should be released on bail. We all went to the county court before it opened in the morning to submit the letter, but – aah! – who could have guessed – it was already too late.'

Yuebo faltered, and in the quiet of the night the flickering kerosene lamp cast our shadows grotesquely on the wall opposite. I put my arm around Ninjun. She was silent, but her shoulders were shaking. On the wall I watched how Yuebo's long, skinny fingers sought his cheek to wipe away his tears.

'Who could have known that they would do that to him? They executed him. They cut off his head. They put it in a cage and dangled the cage on the town wall, a sign that he was a common criminal. The Guomingdan made a statement that he was a Communist bandit and head of the outlaws. Nobody dared to contradict their statement, but we all knew that Commander Liao had done many good things for our benefit – he even sold his own land to buy weapons to arm a defence force which protected us, his own local people, from the warlords and bandits who were always preying on us. He was always arguing with the government to try to get the heavy taxes reduced for us. He risked life and limb so that we might lead better, more peaceful lives. How dare they call him a bandit – he and his followers never stole a piece of thread or a grain of rice from a soul! Even more amazing was the fact that he was a scholar – he managed to get to Nanjing University. Do you know how many people from our remote mountain region managed to go to those big cities? None – apart from him and Ninjun's mother of course. I curse that traitor – that cold-blooded, heartless cur – for betraying him. I hope he came to a bad end. Heh! In fact he did get what he deserved – later we found out that the Guomingdan shot him because he was no longer of any use to them!'

Yuebo spat on the ground to show his hatred and contempt.

We felt close to Yuebo and later on, whenever we asked him for any help, he never said no and would do his very best for us. I knew that we needed more friends like him: people who were local and sympathetic towards our goals. We called people like him 'grey characters' – facilitators – people who were not committed Communists but were willing to help us. Mainly, though, we depended on our own people whom we knew and trusted, so we had to continue our search for those members whose link with the Party had been lost and gauge whether they had remained loyal.

Li Chen was such a member on our list. We knew that he had joined the Party in 1932, but after my father-in-law had been executed and the Huaying guerrilla force had been massacred by the Guomingdan, Li had lost contact with the Party. For many years he had been working as a teacher and he had also been made a village elder and, as a result, he was on very good terms with the upper classes. Since Shibo had returned home, he had asked her on many occasions about finding his link back, but she had remained cautious and didn't give him any information. However, we felt it was time to test the water with him and so we paid him a visit.

Li Chen lived with his wife and his brother, whose nickname was 'Ugly Huqin'. He was given this nickname because he loved music and opera and, although he had never had a music lesson in his life, he liked to play the *huqin* – a two-stringed instrument played with a bow. However, only he enjoyed it because other people felt that the noise was an assault on their ears and called it ugly – hence his nickname! Their house was actually an old watchtower, which was set back from the bottom of the high street. Li Chen was surprised and overwhelmed that we should visit him. After exchanging greetings and chatting about the weather, Li asked me about the current situation and I knew he was testing me. I told him what I knew and he was enthusiastic about all the news which he wasn't able to hear about in such a small town. After that visit we saw each other more often, usually at the teahouse on market days. I would talk to him in general terms about the Communist strongholds, and Party policies and activities, but I couldn't divulge any details to him. Obviously by then Li had guessed that I was dedicated to the Communist Party and he asked me if I could link him back to the Party so that he could regain his membership. The only thing I could say to him was:

'As long as you are sincerely looking for the Party, then the Party will come to find you.'

Shibo, Ninjun and I needed to expand our circle and we decided to get a bit bolder. I started to go to the Meilin Teahouse in the high street almost every day. People knew me as Shibo's son-in-law who was knowledgeable and interested in events at home and around the world, so they received me as their respected guest. I always had a crowd around me at the teahouse eager to hear me talk. This was at the time when the war with the Japanese had just ended and the Guomingdan and the Communists were supposedly having peace talks, so there was a certain amount of freedom of speech. I opened up on all sorts of subjects, such as: Joseph Stalin's fight to liberate Berlin, Harry S. Truman, Winston Churchill, the Communists' liberated areas, the Guomingdan-controlled regions, Chiang Kai-shek and Mao Zedong. Within a few days my chatter had earned me a reputation and a few people even came from twenty kilometres away to listen to me. The teahouse owner decided to give me free tea to keep them coming.

We set up a reading corner in the teahouse and we left all sorts of books, magazines and newspapers there – as a consequence, we drew even more people to the teahouse. The owner was very happy! Shibo had organised two uprisings before and she was more experienced about how to proceed from there to rally the people. She knew how important these local groups were and how much strength and influence they actually possessed. To make them feel a unified group she came up with a name for them – the Decent Folks Association – and a motto: 'We strive for happiness and take hardship together – We help one another – We don't bully or terrorise each other – We want to be decent people.' Then we put Li Chen in charge of the association. Within six months Li had convinced sixty people to join. They were mainly people such as town and village elders, school teachers, lecturers and retired military personnel. We normally met once a month and the main topic of conversation was usually the political situation.

By now Ninjun was in the late stages of pregnancy. Shibo had already found a good midwife and had taken care of most of the other necessary preparations. I had, of course, been through the experience of Binhua's birth, but although I felt more confident this time round because Shibo would be there, I still felt it was necessary to read as much information as possible to be better prepared. Once again, finance was a problem, as we had used up all our savings. We had too many outgoings, mainly because we were always in and out of the teahouse and inviting people to eat with us at home, and no income. We needed money before Ninjun had another baby and I started to worry again.

Ninjun didn't seem to find anything difficult and told me not to worry and that she had a solution. Then she asked me to go to Li Chen's house with her and before we left she packed up her cheongsam, the expensive silk velvet gown that Shibo had had specially made for her for our wedding. She told me that two of the buttons were broken and needed replacing. When we got to Li's house, Ninjun went off hand in hand with Li's wife to her room, while I talked to Li. After a while Ninjun reappeared and she was smiling; she came over to me and pulled me by the hand and so we said our goodbyes and left. Without saying anything to me she bought cotton cloth, towels, scented soap, meat, eggs and sugar. I couldn't understand where she had got all the money from. She held back her laughter and said: 'I'll tell you when we get home'.

All the way home I was trying to work out where she had

got the money from and then, just as we arrived at the front door, it hit me – she was no longer carrying her cheongsam. I just stared at her.

'You sold your cheongsam, didn't you?'

'Ah! Yes!'

'To whom?'

'To Li's wife, of course!'

'When – when did you sell it to her?'

She burst out laughing:

'You are a big idiot! Just then – I sold it to her just then in her house! I told her that I had given twenty silver yuan to a friend and asked her to buy it for me from Shanghai. I told her that it was well made, that I had only worn it a couple of times, that after the birth of my daughter I wasn't able to fit into it and now that I am pregnant again, I was never ever going to fit into it. I told her to try it on and, if she liked it, I would sell it to her for only ten yuan. Actually, she looked really nice in it – it looked as if it had been made for her. She didn't hesitate to give me the money from her private savings.'

I knew how much Ninjun loved that dress and she looked stunning in it too. She had been used to wearing beautiful clothes for her stage performances with the theatre and she still liked pretty clothes and always took great care of her appearance. That cheongsam was her only expensive item of clothing and if I had known what she was planning to do, I certainly wouldn't have let her sell it. She was being true to her character, though, and she did it first and then told me about it after. I felt very guilty that I wasn't better at providing the things we needed and smiled bitterly:

'Alright – so you had the solution!'

It was the first day of the Spring Festival and we calculated that Ninjun had another twenty days to go before she was due to give birth. We gladly accepted an invitation from Li Chen and his wife

212

to go to their home for the New Year meal. We went home afterwards and went to bed as usual, but in the middle of the night Ninjun woke in pain. At first, I thought that she must have eaten too much at Li's house, but soon we both realised that she had gone into labour. Once again, I was on my own and it was the middle of the night. Seeing as we had been confident that Ninjun still had another three weeks to go and there hadn't been any prior warning of the onset of labour, Shibo and the midwife weren't standing by. The plan had failed again!

All of a sudden Ninjun started screaming. I jumped out of bed in a panic and fumbled around trying to find the matches, and when I had lit the kerosene lamp I returned to her. She had droplets of sweat on her forehead the size of peas and she wouldn't stop screaming. She had twisted her upper body around somehow and was punching the bedhead. This seemed far more serious than when she had given birth to Binhua, who was also screaming in fright having woken up with all the noise, but I didn't have time to attend to her. The contractions had come on so quickly and so strongly that I was frightened that there was something going wrong with Ninjun and the baby. I was so scared, in fact, that my heart was racing, my legs felt weak, I felt sick and all common sense left me. I simply had no idea what I was meant to do. I rushed outside shouting for help from the neighbours and as I ran back in I heard a sickening thud – the baby had been born, slithered off the bed and dropped onto the footstool by the bedside. As I was dashing over to pick up the baby I knocked over the lamp and it went out, throwing the room into pitch blackness once again. Then Ninjun cried out:

'The cord, the cord – the cord has broken.'

She sounded so frightened and I had read how dangerous it was if the placenta stays inside – it could cost the woman her life. In the darkness, I managed to get hold of the cord in one hand and with the other I started pressing down on Ninjun's stomach, while she also pushed down with all her might. It worked, but Ninjun lay limply in the bed groaning – she was utterly exhausted. The baby was still on the footstool and crying, so at least I knew it was alive. I felt around for it and picked it up, but it was so slippery I decided to put it into a vegetable basket that I'd come across in the dark. I ran outside with the baby in the basket, held it up in the moonlight and shouted at the top of my voice:

'The baby is born – the baby is out – come quickly – come and help – we need some help.'

A cold gust of wind made me realise that the baby was naked, so I went back in, picked up the baby who was covered in blood and still slippery and pushed it under the quilt next to Ninjun.

'It's a boy – it's a boy!' Ninjun shouted, suddenly ecstatic.

At that moment the neighbours poured into the room – thank heavens they had heard us. Within minutes, a lamp had been lit, a fire was started and water put on to boil. Binhua was soothed. Somebody poached some eggs and put sugar on top of them. Someone washed the baby and wrapped him up and somebody else washed Ninjun. The bed and footstool were cleaned. A message was sent to Shibo and, just as day was about to break, she arrived. As Shibo held the baby, she discovered a large lump on the back of his head. I wrote a letter to Father telling him that he had a grandson.

When Father replied, he had a name for the baby: Mingtao, which we all liked. It means 'democracy fever'. At that time peace talks between the Guomingdan and the Communists were in progress and the whole country was demanding democracy.

The peace talks broke down and aggression erupted on both sides. Sichuan was vital to Chiang Kai-shek, being his rear base and bread basket. He came down heavily on the Sichuanese once more by press-ganging the men into Guomingdan army service and imposing high taxes. Shibo led over a hundred men, some of whom were ex-guerrilla fighters, but others were ordinary locals and they armed themselves with long poles, pickaxes, knives and muskets and occupied the rice fields. Firstly, they didn't want to be press-ganged by the Guomingdan and secondly, they wanted to protect their own rice stores. The fields had already been harvested. During this period the Communists sent a large number of members to work in the countryside, recognising that food production could not be interrupted, but also to boost the numbers of local anti-government forces.

In the Huaying Mountain region in particular, feeling was running high against Chiang Kai-shek's latest policies of forced army service and raised taxes and the people were already notorious for being tough, dangerous opponents of the government. Chiang Kai-shek lost no time in sending a 'crack force' to try and put down the opposition from the Huaying Mountain Communist bandits. They swept through the region, killing many people and burning down houses. We had to stop all activities and lie low for a while. Nobody dared to assemble a crowd anywhere and I didn't go to the Meilin Teahouse at all. I only went to visit Li occasionally in his watchtower. Although we had a very good following in Shibo's home area, undoubtedly there were people opposed to us who wanted to see us fail. We heard that Shibo, Li Chen, Ninjun and I had been reported to the Guomingdan as being the Communist leaders in the area, so we had to be even more careful. We never went out without knowing who was on the streets and where the Guomingdan troops currently were. One afternoon I felt it was safe enough to visit Li Chen and his brother was there too. However, I hadn't been there long before we saw someone running fast towards the watchtower and he was shouting:

'Li, Li – it's no good. Run – someone's reported you – you and Lin – said you're Communists – they know where you are – the 'clean-up' team is already on the high street – run – you have to run now.'

Li's brother quickly picked up his *huqin* and bow and started playing and said: 'You two go and hide at the top of the tower. Don't worry about me – I'll deal with them.'

Li Chen and I had just reached the top of the building when more than ten soldiers forced their way in. They cocked their guns and pointed them at 'Ugly Huqin'. One of the soldiers questioned him:

'There are two men – Li and Lin – have they been here?'

Ugly Huqin kept playing and replied calmly: 'Yes, yes they were here – but they left – they went to Heaven-Treasure Village.'

Luckily the soldiers believed him and left, but we waited till nightfall before leaving through the back door of the watch-tower. By following the riverbank, we made our way to the home of one of the members of the Decent Folks Association and hid there.

It was obvious that I was back on the wanted list, so we had to leave Yuechi. The four of us made our way to Ninjun's Second Aunt's home, which was about thirty kilometres away, for temporary shelter. Ninjun had often had to stay with her Second Aunt during her childhood and was close to her. However, we felt that we would be less noticeable in a large city and decided to go to Chongqing. We chose Chongqing because Father was there and so was Liuqing. Because we were on the run, we made the decision to leave Binhua with Second Aunt for the time being and just took Mingtao with us.

In Chongqing I was soon back in touch with the Party. Once we had heard that the Guomingdan's 'clean-up' of the Huaying Mountain region was more or less over, they told me to go back to Yuechi to help reorganise the masses so that all our previous work there wouldn't go to waste.

Before I left, Ninjun told me to buy some of Binhua's favourite sweets to take to her. On arrival in Yuechi I immediately went to find Shibo and it was then that I found out that my little daughter, Binhua, had died. I travelled to see Second Aunt and my heart ached even more when I found out the circumstances. She told me that sometime after Ninjun and I had left, the Guomingdan's 'clean-up' operation reached her area and it was made known that they were also after anyone displaying radical behaviour. She said that she couldn't be sure of anyone's allegiance in her village and was so scared that the Guomingdan would find out that Binhua was the daughter of Communists. She didn't dare keep her in the house, so she took Binhua to hide in the fields and woods, living rough for several days and nights waiting for the Guomingdan to leave the area. The nights, though, were cold and damp and Binhua fell ill with a high fever. Second Aunt didn't even dare to take her to a doctor, in case they were reported. Instead she put all her hopes in a local superstition: many years before, a man known as Carpenter Lou had been held in very high esteem by the local people. He had been made chairman of the local Soviet Association and had helped countless people get out of difficulty. He was eventually murdered and after he was buried a myth grew up around him. People started to believe that even the soil from around his grave had curative powers and could bring people back from the brink of death. So Second Aunt took Binhua to the graveyard, scooped up some soil from Carpenter Lou's burial site, mixed it with water and gave it to Binhua to drink. But, of course, it didn't save little Binhua: the fever didn't go down and she died of pneumonia in Second Aunt's arms. Her last words were: 'Has mama brought my sweeties back home yet?'

I went to her tiny grave and put some more soil on it. Shibo and Second Aunt tried to console me, but it was my fault. Tearfully, I blamed myself and profoundly regretted that we hadn't taken Binhua with us. Of course, it was me who had persuaded Ninjun that the best thing to do was leave her behind. What made it even worse was that pneumonia was a treatable illness. For some reason – and I can't remember what on earth that reason was – we decided together that we should keep this news a secret from Ninjun for as long as possible, even though we knew that paper can't hold back a fire.

I had to get back to the purpose of my journey to Yuechi and that was to give instructions to Li Chen to provide us with information. Firstly, we needed a detailed geographical map of the Huaying Mountain region drawn up. It needed to show all vital communication lines and all the routes used by the guerrillas for transportation of food and other supplies and for combat. Secondly, we needed clearer information about all the local armed forces belonging to the seven towns along the river – including how many weapons they had, whether those weapons were new or old and if they had much ammunition. Also, how many of those forces were sympathetic to us and whether we would be able to take control of them or not.

Li Chen received his mission in a serious and earnest manner. Then I asked him to write his curriculum vitae so that he could get back his Party membership. He was overwhelmed at this news and sighed:

'At last! No matter how hard and difficult it might get, I will work for the Party and never pull out.'

In the following month I went back and forth between Chongqing and Yuechi three times to ensure that Shibo and Li Chen were managing to carry out the orders from the Above. I was the connection between them and we had to make sure that our preparations were detailed, workable and ready for the 'Huaying Mountain Third Uprising', which was planned for 1948.

Each time I travelled, Ninjun gave me sweets and other little presents to take to Binhua and each time I failed to tell her that our little Binhua was no more. She couldn't understand why I never brought her back with me, but the longer it went on the more difficult it was to say anything. It was unbearable.

Then in the middle of June 1946 Shibo received a telegram from Father whilst I was there. It contained just a few words: 'Old friend, looking for you in an emergency, please come quickly to Chongqing.' Shibo took that message to mean that the Party was summoning her to Chongqing for a face-to-face meeting. She felt so happy at that prospect and told me to go first and she would follow as soon as she had made arrangements for someone take over her job.

When I arrived in Chongqing, I straight away went to see Father at his accommodation, but I was met by Liuqing, who was sobbing. She told me that Father was ill, so ill in fact that he was in hospital.

'Why? What kind of illness makes him need to stay in hospital?'

'A few days ago Father came back from work and he was feeling uncomfortable and tired. One of his friends said that he knew a very good herbal doctor and took Father to see him. They came back with four packets of herbal concoctions. His friend handed them to me with instructions on how much to use and said that they were very expensive. I brewed one packet and gave a bowl of it to Father. A while after, he got a tummy ache and became thirsty. Then he started sweating uncontrollably – his clothes were soaked through. He had a high fever and his heart was beating so fast. Then red spots popped up on his hands and face and he was groaning ever so loudly. I was so scared and had never seen anything like it before, so I took him outside, called a rickshaw and took him to the Citizens' Hospital and…'

I couldn't wait for her to finish. I grabbed her arm and we

ran to the hospital. This news was a bolt out of the blue – I had seen him about ten days previously and he had been fine. How come all of a sudden he was so ill? We rushed into the ward and there was Father, lying on a white-sheeted bed with his eyes closed. He was being given oxygen and his face was covered in red spots, just like a child with chicken pox. His face was twisted. I squatted by his bed and gently called:

'Baba?'

He opened his eyes and looked at me briefly and then closed them again. He made a very great effort and asked:

'Is – your – Shibo – here – yet?'

'No, not yet.'

Father turned his head away and said nothing more. I had never seen my father look so ill. I couldn't take this situation in – my head felt empty. A nurse came in and told us off for disturbing his rest. I pulled Liuqing out of the room and went to find the doctor to find out what was wrong with Father and he said:

'Your father is in a critical condition – his blood pressure is still too high. There are abnormal pigment deposits on his skin. His breathing is difficult. He is in a state of delirium. It looks as if his veins are ruptured. You need to prepare yourselves for the worst.'

I don't remember walking out of the hospital, but I do remember that Liuqing couldn't stop crying. A question kept running through my mind – had Father been poisoned? If so, had it been a mistake, or was it on purpose and was it the herbal doctor who did it, or somebody else? We went to the post office and I sent a telegram to Shibo saying: 'Father critically ill, come now.'

Two days passed and Shibo still hadn't arrived. Liuqing, Ninjun and I took it in turns to stay by Father's bedside. On the evening of 22 June 1946 we were all there and Ninjun had brought Mingtao with her. She gently said to Father:

'Baba, your grandson Mingtao is here to see you.'

Father didn't say anything, but we saw tears escape from under his closed eyelids. Ninjun very gently dabbed away his tears with her handkerchief. Then Father opened his eyes and looked around the room very slowly at each one of us, then closed them again and whispered to me:

'Is she here yet?'

I shook my head. Father couldn't wait any longer. At 9.15pm his last words were:

'To... untie... the knot... still... need... the person... who... tied it.'

My dear father had completed his lonely journey through life.

Shibo arrived the day after Father's death. She stood for a long time looking at his body and then she said: 'Brother – I am so, so sorry – I let you down.'

It was a hot summer and we couldn't preserve the body for more than three days, so we couldn't wait for relatives and friends to arrive before we buried him. We only told Uncle Chen Yuping and asked him to inform the Central Committee in Chongqing. They sent a representative with one million 'lawful currency', which equalled one hundred silver yuan, to pay for the funeral. We buried him in the Mingshen Shipping Company's private graveyard under the straggly weeds. Shibo wore a black armband, as a family member would; Ninjun, Mingtao, Liuqing and I wore white hemp mourning garments (white is the colour of mourning in China). Father was penniless when he died and the only thing he left us were memories and the sure knowledge that his heart was honest till the day he died. As Father used to say: 'I came into this world with nothing – I don't need anything for myself and so I will leave it empty handed.'

When I had returned to Chongqing just before Father passed away, once again Ninjun had been expecting me to bring Binhua back and was deeply disappointed that I hadn't. Then when Shibo arrived for the funeral and still Ninjun didn't see Binhua, she kept asking us both why. Shibo and I stammered and procrastinated and wouldn't give her a straight answer, which only served to build up the tension. Of course Ninjun realised that something had happened to Binhua, but still she didn't expect the awful news that we had been trying to protect her from. When we told her, she rained down punches on me and then utterly lost control. Her howl of anguish shook me to the core and she cried until she fainted.

Zhuxi's funeral in 1946

Shattered Dreams

Uncle Chen Yuping brought a middle-aged man named Rao Mengwen to meet us. After greetings, they consoled us on Father's sudden death. They both addressed Shibo as 'Shijie' just as Father used to do – a term of respect as well as affection. It was two years since we had last met Uncle Chen in Jiangyou County and we were both very glad to see him again. Uncle Chen informed us:

'I have now moved on to another position within the Sichuan Branch of the Communist Party and Comrade Rao here will be your new leader. He has just come back from Yanan and he has all the latest information from the Central Committee. We acknowledge that all your excellent foundation work in Yuechi will be invaluable in the future. We must now discuss what both of you are going to do next.'

However, before Rao could start, Shibo felt the need to talk to our new leader about a few things. First of all she wanted him to know how long she had been waiting to get back her Party membership and, although she was so glad that her link had finally been re-established, she wouldn't feel complete until it was official. Then she started to talk about her husband, Liao Yubi. She pulled out a photograph of him from an inside pocket, next to her heart, carefully unwrapped it and showed it to Rao. It was the only photo she had of him and it had been taken in 1925, just after they had come back from Nanjing University. Throughout the years, she had protected that photo come what may. She told him about the last armed uprising and of the days leading up to her husband's execution and then the subsequent massacre of the people of the Huaying Mountains. She described it as a cruel and senseless slaughter and how the blood of the people soaked the very mountains themselves. Then she told him how her journey to Russia had failed and it was then that she had lost her connection with the Party. The tears which she had held under control for so long were unleashed, no doubt made worse by our recent bereavement from the deaths of little Binhua and Father. Rao gently took the photo from Shibo and said:

'Shijie, the Party knows everything that happened to you and Liao Dage in the past. After your husband was martyred, the Party tried to find you on many occasions, but nobody knew where you were. Then, later on, Chen here and Zhuxi often talked about you, so we all know that you have always been loyal to the Party – that has never been in question. The Party has decided to reinstate your membership and you have my assurance that it will be done officially as soon as possible. The Party has also decided to give places at the Yanan Martyrdom School to your two children. They will need to be ready to go no later than the beginning of September – and they can travel on our aircraft to Yanan.'

Both Shibo and I exclaimed with surprise and delight: 'Yanan! That's wonderful!'

However, I suddenly felt lost and devastated that the plan didn't include me and couldn't believe that I was to be separated from Ninjun.

'But what about me?'

Then Shibo said:

'Hah! All those years ago I was told that if the route to Russia via Shanghai wasn't viable, then I would be taken through Yanan instead. Could I still do that do you think – perhaps it is still possible to get to Russia? I have never let go of the dream of studying there.'

'No, neither of you can go anywhere at all – you can't leave now – you're both needed right here. We need experienced people like you. Just in the last few days, the Guomingdan launched a vast attack on our liberated regions and have declared that within six months they will have cracked our main force. It looks like a civil war is unavoidable now. Chongqing is the Guomingdan's main rearguard and with the Huaying region being so close to it, we have to make sure it's protected by sending in more people from our liberated areas. Between you both, you have so much experience in the mountains that we can't let you go.'

Rao turned to me.

'However, we will transfer you to some other job now because you are in the enemy's sights once again.'

Shibo noticed that Rao looked very pale and ill and suggested to him that he should take care of himself and perhaps seek the advice of a doctor. Rao, however, wasn't interested in himself and brushed her remark aside. Instead, before he left, he gave the photo back to her and anxiously said:

'Shijie, you have Liao Dage's photo on you all the time – this is very dangerous, especially with the sentiments and vows written on it. If the enemy finds it then you would be in serious danger. You are an experienced comrade – you should know that this is counter to the Party's secrets regulation. For your own safety – and that of others around you – you know what you have to do.'

When Uncle Chen and Rao left, Shibo looked at me as

she clutched the photo to her. Both of us knew that Rao was not being unreasonable, but then Shibo told me how clearly she remembered the day when Yubi returned home in great excitement and handed her the photo. On one side of it he had written '*Fight Bravely*'; on the other side, '*No More Weak Wills*'; and underneath, '*1925 – the turning point in my life*'. Then he turned it over and showed her what he had written on the back: '*Revolution from now on – it is decided. The meaning of my life is clear. Abandon dreams, abandon romance and abandon weakness. I vow to devote my life, even to give it up, for an equal society.*'

No wonder Rao was so concerned about the photo as the words were clear evidence that Yubi had been a committed Communist. This turning point in Yubi's life set Shibo and Ninjun on a different path too, of course, but one which Shibo embraced wholeheartedly. She couldn't destroy that photo. In the end she peeled away the photo from the writing on the back, wrapped up each half separately in oil-proof paper and told me that she had put them somewhere very safe. It wasn't till 1971, a decade after Shibo's death, that we came across the photo again. One of our old Party connections told us that, thirty years previously, Shibo had given the photo to him and asked him to take care of it for her, so he stuck it to the underside of his dining table.

Ever since we had told Ninjun about the death of Binhua, she had been inconsolable – her tears never seemed to stop. The news of her opportunity to go to Yanan was bittersweet. Had it come at any other time it would have been the culmination of a dream, but to fulfil it meant that she had to leave her baby son and me. However, I knew that she would do well in Yanan. Life there would suit her bubbly character and she would be able to continue with her singing and stage performances. Also, it was well known that anyone who got the chance of going to Yanan, and who tasted the water of the Yan River, which was considered almost sacred, rose rapidly within the Communist Party ranks. To encourage her to seize this opportunity, I told her that I, with Shibo's help, would take great care of Mingtao. In truth, though, I had hard feelings about it. I had been instrumental in sending so many people to Yanan and had always thought that I would get there myself one day. I wanted to go with her. Then the thought of Ninjun leaving me also worried me greatly. Travelling was always unpredictable and, once we were apart, who could tell when we would manage to meet again?

As always, other events intervened. On 26 June 1946 Chiang Kai-shek ordered 300,000 troops to attack our northern Communist-controlled regions. The Guomingdan were now supported by the Americans, who gave them manpower as well as weapons. The civil war between the Communists and Nationalists opened up.

At the end of the summer, we received orders that all Communist-related departments and organisations must make an emergency exit from Chongqing and go to Yanan. However, we, as part of the underground network, had to remain. Therefore Rao Mengwen also left but, because it was an emergency pulling out, there was no space on the same aircraft for Ninjun and Yabin. Rao promised that when he returned, which he predicted might be in December, he would take them back with him then.

We waited and waited, but there was no sign of Rao. Life in Chongqing seemed to get tenser and more dangerous each day. Eight years of war with Japan had hugely undermined the national economy and the civil war brought it near to collapse. The amount of money needed to buy a cow in 1937 was only enough for a box of matches in 1947.

Eventually Uncle Chen turned up in February 1947 with the sad news that Rao had passed away soon after he had arrived in

Yanan. He had indeed been ill and we couldn't help wishing, for his and all our sakes, that he had heeded Shibo's warning to take care of himself. Shibo couldn't stop a rueful sigh:

'It's true, that saying: the road to happiness is strewn with rocks.'

Uncle Chen brought us a new order:

'The Central Committee's orders to all underground fighters in the Guomingdan-controlled areas are: (1) To mobilise the masses, starting in the country areas, by opposing conscription by the Guomingdan. (2) Impose grain levies to alleviate starvation in the cities. (3) Denounce civil war. (4) Denounce the persecution of the civilian masses. (5) Announce that if Chiang Kai-shek wants to fight, we will oppose him to the very end. (6) Determine not only to crush the enemy forces on the front line, but at the same time attack from behind to target their vital organs.'

A couple of days after Uncle Chen left, a liaison, named Yuan Zenyi, arrived with the official reinstatement of Shibo's Party membership, dating back to 1928. This did much to ease the sickness in Shibo's heart. She was then able to return to Yuechi knowing that she was officially representing the Party in preparing for the Third Huaying Mountain Uprising.

Then I received an order to start work at the *Xinhua Daily*, which was our Party newspaper, on 28 February. Unfortunately, on 27 February, the Guomingdan sprang a surprise search at the newspaper's premises. They rounded up all the staff, destroyed the printing machines and closed down the office. They also closed down all the newsagents who sold the *Xinhua Daily*. Much to my regret, a great opportunity for me to work with top journalists, and perhaps to become one myself, slipped me by. However, once more I was lucky not to have been arrested myself. My fate was so different from that of Meixia's husband, who was arrested on that occasion and sent to Zhazidong Prison.

Into the Tiger's Den

In December 1947 I was called to a meeting with our new contact, Zeng Lin. We met in a small village on the north side of the Yangtze River. Zeng Lin was a large, middle-aged man who had joined the Communist Party in 1926. He was originally from Sichuan and so the Central Committee in Yanan had sent him back to lead the Huaying Mountain uprising. As he was much older than me, I called him Zeng Dage (Big Brother Zeng).

Zeng Dage told me that my new task was to urge a former Guomingdan battalion commander, named Yang Shaoyun, to join us. Yang used to command the Five Counties United Defence Force, north of Chongqing. After Yang retired from the military he returned to his home town, Mingyue, and he took control of the local gang there and became its 'snake-head'. They made their own weapons, traded opium and all their business dealings were carried out by force. His strong-arm tactics earned him many enemies and he needed round-the-clock protection by more than ten bodyguards.

Zeng Dage told me:

'The reason I'm sending you to him is that he already has leanings towards our views, but is still not sure. I know him because we used to be in the same army together, but I can't be seen to be too close to him. I told him that I will send someone I trust to help him make up his mind, so when you turn up he'll know why. He will tell everybody that you are the son of one of his former army colleagues and you are going to set up some kind of business under his protection. You have been working as an underground member for a long time now, so you don't need me to tell you what you should or shouldn't do. I will only remind you that you are new to Yang, his family and the many people around him, so tread carefully – they are probably more complex than they seem. Yang is mistrustful of everyone and so stay away from family matters unless he wants to involve you – in which case, help him however you can. Remember that he wields a lot of power locally, but people are afraid of him, so that makes the situation dangerous. Report back to us in Chongqing once a month. Of course, Ninjun cannot know anything about this and you need to cut off all contact with your family and everybody who knows you – you will be totally on your own. We will send Ninjun and your son back to her mother in Yuechi.'

This was a new challenge for me, but knowing that I had the Party's trust was enough to make me feel proud and happy that I had been chosen for the job. I was determined to make every effort to accomplish this mission.

Zeng Dage concluded by saying to me very gravely:

'Junior Lin, this time we are determined to sweep Chiang Kai-shek off the map. After the first shot of our uprising he will send many troops to do the same thing as we are trying to do – that is to join forces with as many local militias as possible. Now let me tell you a little more about Yang – he is a talented military man and a fearless fighter on the battleground, so if he decides to fight on the side of Chiang Kai-shek it will go badly for us. Our first hope is that he will join us wholeheartedly, not only for the number of armed men under his control, but for his abilities too. If he cannot be persuaded to join our side, then the next best thing would be if he abstained from fighting altogether. However, it has to be said that Yang is probably only interested in being on the winning side, so we have to predict all sorts of other possibilities. One of those possibilities is that he may declare he was coerced to fight alongside us, in which case he will not hesitate to sell you in order to protect himself. I have to tell you this so that you can be prepared for any circumstance and the consequences.'

I fully understood what he meant by 'consequences' and I replied earnestly:

'Zeng Dage, I will do everything I can to achieve the first hoped-for result and, at the very least, the second. I am fully aware that the third outcome would be at the cost of my own life. Since the day I became a Communist, I have been prepared to lay down my life for our ideals – it is a righteous cause to die for. I won't let you down.'

As we said goodbye, I felt Zeng Dage's sincerity as he gripped my hands and I saw deep caring in his eyes. We both knew that this could be our last meeting, as he would soon be on the battleground in the Huaying Mountains and I was going to enter the tiger's den.

A few days later I was on my way to start my new mission. Parting from Ninjun had been very hard, especially because I was unable to tell her where I was going or what I would be doing. When I arrived at Mingyue (which means 'Brightening Moon') it was market day and the high street was very crowded. I managed to find a sedan chair to take me to Yang Shaoyun's house.

At the front gate two guards, who had rifles slung across

their shoulders, stopped me and searched me from top to toe. Once I had shown them my introduction letter to their employer, they led me into a sitting room to wait. A short time later Yang Shaoyun entered the room. I respectfully addressed him as 'Uncle Yang' and then, with a bowed head and both hands outstretched, I offered Zeng Dage's letter to him. He took it from me, then casually put it down on the table without opening it and gestured to me to sit down. Yang cleared his throat and asked me where I came from.

I answered him by saying exactly what Zeng Dage had advised me to say and it was obvious that Yang had already guessed why I had turned up at this house and simply said:

'How is Zeng Dage?'

'He is well. He wanted to come here with me, but he was called to the city on business. He asked me to pass on his greetings to you.'

At this point I dared to raise my head to take a look at this famous local 'emperor'. He appeared to be in his mid-forties, was tall and slim and looked very healthy and energetic. His eyes were bright with a sharp look about them and I could tell he was a perceptive, cautious man.

He then took me into his study and closed the door behind him so that nobody could hear us. He then told me very frankly that there were three rules that I had to follow:

'Number one: it is more complex here than you may think. Guomingdan spies come and go all the time and I also have many dangerous enemies who would like to see me dead. Your conduct needs to be careful and cautious. I will tell everybody that you are the son of an old friend and have come here for business reasons and that I have promised to look after you. So you must behave and look like a businessman. Two: you are not to go on your own to places like teahouses and shops. Three: you are not to talk to outsiders about my family, or –

and this is very important – you must not talk about current affairs, the political situation, or anything like that.'

It was clear that he was afraid in case I exposed my identity and also, like most people, he was afraid to talk about the Communists in public.

Yang's bodyguards lived in one large room upstairs in the house. Yang told me that he trusted them and looked after them as if they were family, and that I could stay with them. For the first few nights I couldn't sleep, not just because the men were so noisy, but because they would play around with their guns and I was afraid that one would go off by mistake. Somehow I felt Yang had put me in the same room with his bodyguards either so that they could keep an eye on me, or, more probably, so that I would take the hint to stay under his control. During those first nights, I would pretend to be asleep but my mind was awhirl with worry. I was worrying about how I might deal with every possible situation that might occur. Once I got to know some of the men, however, I started to relax. I listened to their chat and stories and learned about what they were up to and also about some of Yang's shady secrets. They wanted to teach me how to use a gun, but I pretended that I was afraid of guns and didn't want anything to do with violence. I went to teahouses with them and they took me hunting and fishing too. I tried to stay close to them to learn as much as possible about Yang. Although they could see how different I was, I still managed to win their trust and became their friend.

Unusually for a man like Yang Shaoyun, he didn't smoke, drink or gamble. His only pastime was going to the teahouse. It was a place where he was recognised and shown respect, which he enjoyed very much indeed. The locals called him 'Battalion Commander Yang' and would stand up when he entered the teahouse surrounded by his bodyguards and then kowtow to him. They also competed amongst one another to be the one to pay for Yang's tea. Once a week, on market day, the teahouse would turn into a courthouse where people would queue to have their disputes sorted out by Yang. Yang would sit on a dais, listen to the cases presented to him and make quick judgements on them, leaving no room for argument. Some of his decisions were just, others definitely were not, but because people were afraid of him they accepted his verdicts. Yang genuinely thought himself to be above the heads of everyone around him and expected everyone to hang on to his every word. Whilst staying in his household I often attended his 'court', staying behind him at all times, and learned a lot about societal matters, but was careful never to give my view on any of them.

Yang had three sons, who went by the nicknames of Doggy, Sealy and Fauves. They acted like overlords too and did whatever they wished. All three of them used opium. They had racked up many debts between them and to try and settle them they stole valuables from their home or bullied the family's tenant farmers for money. The sons also coerced the family's debtors either to buy opium and guns from them, or to pay the money they owed directly to them, rather than to their father. Yang clearly knew what his sons were up to, but sadly couldn't stop them. His sons failed to live up to his expectations and they were his biggest worry, but then they had learned their ways from a master!

The Yang family had a monopoly on the salt business in the town and the running of the business had been taken over by Sealy, the second son. Sometimes I went to help him, as I knew this business from the bottom up, it having been the mainstay of our family back in Yunan. In my free time I got to know the brothers and we built up a good rapport. I talked to them about their lifestyle and tried to persuade them to give up opium. I also told them that if they worked together with their father, rather than against him, they could build up genuine businesses with good practices, without the need for all their subterfuge. I was being sincere with them, and they recognised that, and we soon became friends.

Yang's latest wife was half his age. She had a round face, big eyes and a very sweet smile. She was very hospitable to me indeed and I wasn't sure whether it was because I was Yang's guest or whether she had something else in mind. At the dinner table she paid me particular attention by always filling up my bowl with delicacies and asking me lots of questions. Sometimes I had to accompany them to play mahjong and she would give me at least three silver yuan to play with and also I could tell that she let me win sometimes. I tried to avoid her as much as possible and only spoke to her when it was necessary. I would address her respectfully as 'Aunty' just to remind her that she was Yang's wife. If I had to sit with her to play mahjong I wouldn't even look at her sideways, never mind looking her straight in the eye. Zeng Dage had warned me that Yang was suspicious of everybody and he had killed two of his former wives for cheating on him. From listening to the chat of the bodyguards, I learned that a friend of Yang's, who had been a regular visitor to the house, had only been suspected of having an affair with one of Yang's wives, but it was enough for Yang to order both of them to be killed.

There were many servants in the household and when I had time I made a point of helping them with their various tasks. I got along well with them too, so inside and outside, upstairs and downstairs, I managed to form good relationships with everyone. It was generally said that I was a quiet, honest, helpful and polite young man. Yang soon dropped his rigid rules where I was concerned and it looked like I had settled in with the Yang family.

I was looking around for a viable business to set up as part of my cover and came to the conclusion that trading wood could work. The region was quite hilly and heavily wooded and quite a few people made a living by selling logs at the local market. This was a small business with hardly any initial over-heads and so easily entered into. I pointed this out to Yang and asked him whether he thought it would be a good idea for me to do. He agreed that I should start with a small business like this first, so he found a trader to help me buy the wood and transport it to Chongqing for the wholesale market there. Yang helped me every step of the way. The best bit about this business was that it would give me a legitimate reason to go back and forth between Mingyue and Chongqing regularly.

It was wintertime and Yang often invited me to sit by the fire with him in the evenings and chat. We covered all the subjects under the sun, but one evening he wanted to talk about his family. He sighed:

'I have been watching you these past weeks and now I tell you the truth – I like a young man like you. Huh! It's a great pity I don't have a son like you – nor do I have a daughter who could marry you into my house.'

I looked into the fire and laughed nervously, as I didn't want to have to respond to a subject like this. When I eventually looked up at Yang, to my surprise I saw that his face was bright red and tears were glistening on his cheeks. When he was calmer he carried on:

'Do you know – for days I have been toying with an idea. I know my sons are useless and I cannot depend on them at all, so I am thinking that I should let you stay here and you could take care of my family and take charge of the salt business. What do you think?'

Yang's eyes were fixed on the fire as he waited for my answer. I was astonished to hear his suggestion. Then I realised that the first step of my mission had been completed – I had won his trust. However, I couldn't even contemplate his suggestion and didn't want to deceive him either, but refusing him outright wouldn't do me any good. I didn't answer him directly, but laughed nervously again and made appreciative noises instead, then fell silent. I hoped I had given the impression that I needed time to think about it and, indeed, he didn't push me.

Under the pretext of doing business, I went to my monthly meeting with Zeng Dage in Chongqing. I was eager to tell him about the progress of my mission. The Party was impressed that I had won Yang's trust in such a short time. Zeng Dage updated me on the current political situation: The Communist Liberation Army had not only stabilised our own areas, but had also widely attacked the Guomingdan regions too. He told me that he felt the time was right to press Yang into making a decision to join the Communists and that I should emphasise the advantages to him personally if he did so. Before I left he gave me some copies of the Communist newspaper *Pressing Onward* saying that, if necessary, I should read the articles to Yang.

I completed my business in Chongqing and returned to Mingyue only to discover that Yang was very unhappy and had a lot on his mind. One afternoon he wanted me to go for a walk with him without any of the bodyguards, which was unusual. We walked quite a long way and took a rest in a hilltop pagoda. As we sat down he asked me:

'Did you see Zeng Dage in Chongqing this time?'

'Yes, and he sends his greetings to you! He also asked me to pass on these copies of the newspaper *Pressing Onward* to you.'

Yang was attentive as I read some of the articles to him. They told of how much ground the Communist Liberation Army had gained as they fought across the country and detailed

237

the battle lines. They listed the names of the Guomingdan's senior officers who had been captured. They analysed the progress of the civil war.

A few days later Yang took me for another walk and asked me questions such as: How long was the civil war going to last? Given that the Guomingdan had all the best American equipment, a stronger army and enough food supplies, why was it that they were losing to the Communists? Was there a list of the Guomingdan's senior officers who had died on the battleground? What was the Communists' policy towards prisoners of war – did they send them to concentration camps, or execute them? How were the Communists going to treat those people who used to fight against them but had now changed their minds? What were the criteria to differentiate between the enlightened gentry who had Communist leanings and the evil landowners? What would the Communists do with those who had blood on their hands? What would happen to the personal property of the richest people?

Of course, each of his questions related directly to himself. Zeng Dage had already answered these questions, but Yang was still unsure about his future. I patiently reassured him over and over again, but in the end I got bold and made a promise to him that I knew was beyond my, or Zeng Dage's, control. I gave little thought as to the consequences if my promises weren't kept – the only thing I considered important at that moment was to do what I had been told to do. I told him that if he took his armed force and joined our uprising, then in the future he would be given a higher rank than battalion commander. I also said that the Communists always kept their word and were reliable. I ended by saying:

'If you don't trust others, then surely you could at least trust Zeng Dage and me.'

Spring Festival and the Lunar New Year came round. It is

always a time for family reunions and visiting friends. Yang's house was full of people, both rich and poor, on each day of the festive holiday. Some people visited willingly and some felt obliged to pay their respects and they all brought gifts for him. Yang told me to make a list of who brought what no matter whether the gift was expensive or cheap and he told me that they all had to be repaid one day. He sent rice spirit and tobacco to all the poor people who came to his house and I was quite impressed with this gesture.

On New Year's Eve the younger generation of the family came to kowtow to Yang, while everyone else bestowed good wishes on him for the coming year. Yang gave out generous lucky red money envelopes, fireworks rent the air and the festive atmosphere rose. After the family dinner, Yang invited me in to his private room and pointed to a chair, wanting me to sit down. Candies, sunflower seeds, nuts, dried fruit and two cups of the best-quality tea were laid out on the table.

'During these last few months, Zeng Dage and you have told me so much and I have listened earnestly. I have thought about it over and over again and I can feel that you are both very sincere and what you have said has come from your hearts. I am not completely lacking in emotion and I can tell who is genuinely good to me, but you know, I still have to consider the rest of my life, don't I?'

He sipped his tea and cracked open some sunflower seeds with his teeth:

'The situation gets tenser between the two sides every day. It looks to me like the Guomingdan are definitely on their way out and the Communists will come into power. I have always worried whether the Communists will really allow a person like me to live under their heaven – seeing as I used to be their hated enemy. But then I see that those Guomingdan officials – whose ranks are much higher than mine and whose cloud of evil hanging over their heads is much bigger – who have been captured by the Communists have all been dealt with leniently, even to the point that when they pledge to join the rebellion they are incorporated into the Communist forces. So, all in all, I believe what you have been telling me. Again, you and Zeng Dage have advised me in all sincerity. I would be foolish if I didn't see the direction I should be heading.'

He then stood up and patted me on the shoulder: 'Please go back and tell Zeng Dage that I have made my decision – when the time comes I will follow his instructions and do whatever he wants me to do and I will continue to listen to him.'

I caught my breath. It was a huge relief to hear his words and I felt very happy. I said to him: 'You have chosen a bright avenue for yourself. Rest assured that our cooperation will be successful.'

Yang opened the door and shouted to his servants to bring out the best ham, smoked sausages and a top-quality rice spirit. When the jar arrived he poured out two large cups of the potent liquid and handed one to me:

'*Gan!*' [Bottoms up!]

'*Gan!*'

He tipped back his head and emptied the spirit straight down his throat. Like Yang, I didn't normally drink at all, but on this occasion I copied my host and drained my cup without hesitation. His wife noticed and called over:

'Hah! My battalion commander never drinks – what happened today – what is the occasion? What makes him so happy that he breaks his pledge?'

'Oh! It is just the spirit of the festival – we should be happy about the good year ahead of us!'

He patted me on my shoulder and we all laughed. Yang laughed because he had finally made the decision which would determine the course of the rest of his life. As for me, I laughed because I had accomplished my assignment.

After the fifteen-day holiday I went to Chongqing to report to Zeng Dage. We all declared it to be good news. However, Zeng Dage told me to make sure that Yang upheld his intentions and to guide him to contact, prepare and strengthen the armed forces under his control in readiness for the uprising.

The 5th, 6th and 7th of April is a period set aside to the memory of our dead and it is known as 'Sweeping the Graves'. Yang used this time to invite notable people, including friends, officials and business associates, for a 'spring drink' to test the reaction to his recent decisions. I didn't make an appearance on this occasion, but Yang told me later that all of the people he had invited had said that they would follow him whatever happened. This was good news and would allow us to estimate how many forces would be under Yang's control.

On the evening of 10 April Yang left, with his bodyguards, to attend a meeting at the town hall. It got late and there was no sign of his return, but we didn't think much of it and everybody went to bed as usual.

A little after midnight there was a loud and urgent banging on the gate which got us all up out of bed. The gate was opened and a man fell in. He was in a state of panic and none of us were able to understand what he was mumbling about. It took a couple of minutes before we understood what he was telling us – Yang had been murdered. None of us could believe this news until the bodyguards appeared carrying Yang's body. They laid him on the ground in front of us and it was plain to see how many bullets had found their mark on his body. The shocked silence was suddenly shattered by screams and cries from Yang's wife and sons as fear and grief gripped them.

Yang was normally very careful about his own safety. However, on this occasion he was apparently keen to make a show of not being afraid for his life and so had told his bodyguards to wait on the ring road, just out of town, while he continued with only two men carrying him in a sedan chair. On his return after the meeting, Yang had been ambushed just before the meeting point with the rest of his bodyguards. No doubt this was a well-planned assassination.

I was shocked and very upset by Yang's death, not only because our well-laid plans would never see the light of day, but also because I had to admit that I quite liked him by then. My heart was filled with hatred for his murderers. I was angry and tense, but I realised that I had to deal with the situation very carefully. Firstly I couldn't leave Yang's house, otherwise I ran the risk of suspicion falling on me – so I couldn't report his death to Zeng Dage. I also didn't know the actual reason behind the assassination, so somehow I had to find out who was responsible.

Yang's sudden death caused his sons' and wife's world to collapse and they had no idea what to do next. They cried all day long and none of them found their backbone. It was left to me, in my capacity as Yang's godson, to make all the arrangements for his funeral, including setting up the mourning hall for the seven-day period prior to the funeral. After the funeral I instinctively felt that Yang's family were in danger too and that whoever had killed Yang wouldn't leave his family in peace either. I had a talk with a few of Yang's most trusted bodyguards and we agreed that something needed to be done to prevent the family from being hurt. They also agreed that we needed to find out who the killers were, so I took Yang's wife and sons to the police headquarters in Chongqing so that they could lodge a murder case.

Whilst in Chongqing, I was able to report the incident to the

Party. It was clear that the forces from the Five Counties had slipped through our fingers, but we had to try and hold on to as much as we could. I persuaded Yang's eldest son to go back home and take control of his father's estate and to pay particular attention to the bodyguards, who were key to the power base there. I reminded him not to forget about their hidden stash of weapons, which was enough to arm over a hundred people. Each and every soldier was vital for our uprising.

Unfortunately, events turned out even worse than I could have imagined. Whilst we were in Chongqing, Yang's enemies looted the house. Everything of value, including the weapons, disappeared. Almost overnight, the Yang family had not only lost their possessions but also their status and the power that came with it. As soon as the bodyguards saw that the family wasn't in control, most of them left to find employment elsewhere.

Once again, such hard-worked-for plans fell by the wayside.

The Third Huaying Mountain Uprising

I cannot express just how frustrated and depressed I felt at the outcome of my mission to get Yang Shaoyun to join us. Not only had I faced much danger in pretending to be his god-son and having to smooth the way between each of his family members, but I had also had to cut off links entirely with my own family and people for months on end. But it had still led nowhere and all my efforts had gone to waste. Later on I heard a rumour that the people responsible for killing Yang were actually from our own committee and had done it for personal revenge. I hated them for their selfish actions, because Yang could have been so useful to us and the mission had been so close to success. I could never have guessed that the plan was thwarted by people from my own side and it was no wonder that I had been powerless to prevent it.

After an appropriate period of time I was told to disappear from Yang's circle and keep an extremely low profile until someone contacted me again. This order was very discouraging and each day of waiting seemed like a year. Then one night there was a knock at my door. I opened it very cautiously and somebody jumped at me and we both nearly ended up on the ground. To my complete surprise, it was Ninjun! Hardly containing her excitement, she gripped my hands and beamed at me. Her cheeks were rosy and glowing and it struck me all over again that she was very pretty indeed! Then she said:

'Zeng Dage mentioned that your last assignment had been a big problem and that you are now jobless. Well, we need people back home on the mountain, so he sent me to pick you up to come and work with us. Also Big Fellow Liu said that we need more intelligent young activists like you to join us.'

I had never heard of this 'Big Fellow Liu' before Ninjun mentioned him, but she seemed to deliberately keep this man mysterious and wouldn't explain anything more about him other than saying:

'He is our leader now and knows you well. He said he is looking forward to seeing you again. Soon you will understand.'

The journey back to Huaying Mountain appeared easy because we were both so happy and excited to be back together again. As we neared Shibo's home the sound of singing filled the air. Several men were singing liberation songs at the tops of their voices:

> The sky in the liberated region is so bright
> The people in the liberated region are so joyful
> The democratic State loves its people
> The Communists' benevolence is boundless
> Is boundless…

'Do you hear that? I taught them lots of songs,' said Ninjun proudly.

We passed many people, including small children, who greeted Ninjun with warmth and admiration. It was obvious that she had become a celebrated figure in these parts.

We walked into the yard of Shibo's house and I caught sight

of her immediately. She had cut her hair short to just below the ears and had a black scarf wrapped around her head. She was wearing a black cotton jacket with a belt around her waist, black trousers and black rubber-soled shoes. She was the epitome of a guerrilla warrior and all the stories she had recounted of her former battles sprang to my mind. I caught my breath.

'Shibo, you look so commanding!'

There were so many people going in and out of the house and the kitchen was especially busy. Two big woks were bubbling away on the stove. In one wok rice was being cooked in four bamboo steamers piled on of top of another and in the other there was a home-cured ham. The food smelled so good and Shibo watched me with a smile as I swallowed my saliva. She explained to me:

'These days we are so busy preparing for the coming battle that we arranged a communal kitchen to cater for all of us. Everyone brings their own meat and vegetables and some of the neighbourhood women do the cooking – it's more efficient this way.'

After dinner Ninjun took me for a walk to show me around. It was nearing harvest time and in field after field the millet stems were heavily laden with seed. We walked along the ridges between the golden fields and then someone shouted out: 'Who's there?'

'We've come to check the sentry post,' answered Ninjun calmly.

In seconds we were surrounded by more than ten young men, with rifles over their shoulders, who had been hiding amongst the millet. They looked relieved to see Ninjun and were happy to chat to her. I quietly asked her:

'They seem very jumpy – why is there so much tension around here?'

'How can we not be tense? Our home is the command headquarters – lots of important people come here for meetings all the time. We have to be on constant alert, ready to fight at a moment's notice – we're only waiting for the order to move out and when it comes we will have to move very quickly.'

Then Shibo joined us and I realised that Yabin, Ninjun's younger brother, wasn't on the scene and I asked where he was. Shibo proudly told me:

'He is now the team leader of this area – and secretary too – he hardly manages to come home, but when he does, he doesn't even have time to eat sometimes. He probably doesn't know that you're both back here yet.'

Whilst Shibo and I were talking, Ninjun's eye fixed on her mother's belt and then she deftly pulled out the pistol:

'Boniang – I have no gun – give me this one!'

Shibo swiftly grabbed Ninjun's wrist and wrenched the pistol away from her:

'How come you are just like me when I was young? That was exactly the same way I took a gun from your father's waist! You're not getting this gun – Zeng Dage gave it to me. You want a gun? Well then, Chiang Kai-shek has plenty – go get one from him!'

I watched the interplay between mother and daughter with amusement because they were so alike.

'Look at you, Shibo – fully armed – are you going to the front line once again?'

Shibo laughed.

'Do you doubt me? Your Shibo has dreamed of this moment on a daily basis for the past ten years or more. Today – finally – my dream is coming true. Don't you dare assume that I'm too old for it – I'm only fifty. Don't you know that older soldiers are better than younger ones? To my mind nothing has changed – I am no less of a person than before – perhaps even a better one. If you don't believe me then let's bet on who can run faster to the Baoding Temple on top of the Huaying Mountain and who can shoot more accurately than me!'

Everyone laughed. Shibo then spoke to the small crowd around us:

'Look around us here – we have created a cohesive village society based on our Communist principles. Apart from a few stubborn landowners, everyone is on our side. The young men and women all have their own role to play – they are the off-spring of our ex-guerrillas, full of enthusiasm to fight today's oppressor – Chiang Kai-shek – and to liberate our country.'

I had been working for quite a long time in underground intelligence by then and, even in my dreams, I wouldn't have dared to say anything so openly in a crowd as Shibo had done. It was as if the country had already been liberated and we were free to express our opinions openly. It was like a shift in the earth's axis and it felt so good to me.

The next day I came across Li Chen and he cheerfully took my hands:

'My old friend Lin – you finally came back.'

Then, without pausing for breath, he poured out his account of what he had experienced in the last two years and how much he had done to prepare for the uprising. Then he pompously announced that he was going to be the Vice Commander of the Seventh Team of our Regional Committee. I didn't get the chance to insert one single word and then, before he left, he whispered that he had some kind of home affair to sort out. By the expression on his face I guessed that his young, pretty wife must have been badgering him about something.

Later, just as we were finishing our dinner, we heard a commotion outside and then, without announcement, a man was carried into the house on a sedan chair. It was one of our leaders of the regional committee, Old Xu. Whilst on his way to our village he had been spotted by the Guomingdan and, in order to escape, he had jumped over a cliff. He had injured his leg badly, but was lucky to be alive. Despite his pain, Old Xu called an emergency meeting and he informed us:

'We are in a threatening situation – we have been betrayed. The traitor is a man on the Eastern Sichuan Committee and he managed most of our Party membership. He was arrested at Guangan and betrayed full information of our plan for the coming uprising and, of course, he spilled names too. The Above wanted us to delay the action and go into hiding, or to transfer to underground activity. The problem is, though, that the enemy has already started to arrest our people. So, in effect, if we don't go ahead we are just waiting to be arrested or killed. Therefore, we have decided to bring our action forward – possibly in the next couple of days – so each team needs to ready themselves for the fight. We need to keep a close eye on enemy movements and seal off our lines of information. Also, there is an order from Zeng Dage: none of our ladies are going to the front line – they must transfer to somewhere safe and wait for further orders.'

Ninjun leaped up from her seat:

'NO! I disagree with Zeng Dage's order. Mother and I have waited for so many years for the day – the moment – to have the opportunity to take revenge on the enemy. Why stop us from fighting on the front line? This is discrimination against the women comrades.'

Old Xu replied: 'Nin Meizi [young lady], don't worry – a hero will always have a time and a place to display their prowess – there will be plenty of things for you to do.'

Old Xu carried on with more instructions for us and then one man stood up and said: 'I request that I be allowed to take my fiancée to the front line with me.'

'Going to the front line is a risky business – you're going

there to fight, not to sleep with your fiancée. Are you really that desperate?'

Everyone laughed and Old Xu dismissed the meeting, but then Li Chen stood up:

'Wait, wait a moment everyone. I have something to declare. My wife said that she doesn't know whether I will come back dead or alive if I go to the front line, so she says that she wants twenty *dan* of grain as her settlement, otherwise she won't let me go. But now I don't have any money left and the only way to give her what she wants is to borrow from my second brother. If he doesn't give me the money then I won't be easy on him, but I will need backup from you to help me persuade him.'

Everyone was shocked to hear such words from a vice commander before the uprising. It was such nonsense that at first I thought it must be a joke. Was he going to fight the enemy or do battle with his brother? I couldn't keep my mouth shut:

'That wife of yours is one track minded and useless, but I suppose we can understand why she feels insecure and perhaps we can talk to her. What I don't understand though is how you think it's alright to force your brother, Ugly Huqin, to give you the money, or grain, that your wife thinks she needs. Your brother is enlightened gentry and he did so much for you, and for me – remember two years ago? If it wasn't for him diverting those soldiers who were chasing us then you and I wouldn't be standing here today, nor would you be in the position of vice commander. At a crucial moment like this why do you want to impose a financial burden on him? In my opinion, you are not at all concerned about the overall situation with the revolution and neither are you concerned about your own brother's welfare. You are a heartless and stupid man. Before you get tough with your brother, perhaps you should consider the possibility that he might not be easy on you first.'

Li Chen went quiet, but he still had no idea how to handle his wife and looked very unhappy. We suspected that she always gave him a hard time and that we would probably have to do something about this matter. Just then Ninjun stood up and said to him: 'Well, I will take care of your wife – I will think of something.'

Next day Ninjun went to talk to Li Chen's wife at their home. After more than an hour she was still adamant that she needed some kind of indemnity. In the end, and with a degree of desperation, Ninjun pulled off her ring from her finger and handed it over to that woman:

'This is pure gold – it's my wedding present from my father-in-law who has passed away. You have it – if you find yourself in a desperate situation you can always sell it.'

My father had had that gold ring specially made for Ninjun as a wedding gift and she had given it away just like that. I was quite upset about her impulsive action and the fact that the ring was now on the finger of Li Chen's wife. I could understand why she did it, but it now meant that two of Ninjun's wedding gifts had been dropped into the lap of that greedy woman: firstly the red velvet cheongsam from her mother and now the ring from my father. Truly, I was so annoyed with the indecisive and weak Li Chen that I was beyond words, but I was even more infuriated by his hen-pecking wife. When I was able to think about it calmly though, I realised that Ninjun's generous, but pragmatic, conduct was also typical of her mother. Shibo was always very considerate and concerned for the individual whilst at the same time knowing what was important for everybody as a whole. They both made me feel very proud of them and I felt blessed to have them in my life.

In private Old Xu told me that he wanted me and Shibo to go to Hechuan for a meeting and that there was a probability of a new mission for us. Also Ninjun and Meixia were told to go back to Chongqing to undertake three things: firstly, to find more young people to join us; secondly, to find a transmitter-receiver and an operator for it; and thirdly, to organise the supply of first-aid medicines to the Huaying Mountain. Shibo had been very quiet since the first meeting with Old Xu and Ninjun wasn't happy either. Ninjun felt that it was her time to prove herself on the battleground rather than being sent back to Chongqing with minor duties. However, orders had to be obeyed.

We had a spare day before we all had to set off, so Shibo, Ninjun and I went to see Mingtao, who was being looked after by Ninjun's Second Aunt. From a distance I saw my son playing with his cousin and Ninjun called to him. He ran over to her and put his arms around her legs, but hid behind her when he saw me. Ninjun coaxed him:

'You silly little boy! Don't you know this is your Baba?'

He stared at me for a minute and then he shyly came to my open arms.

'Don't blame the boy – because of my last mission, he hasn't seen me for quite a few months.'

Second Aunt tearfully watched our family reunion. We knew that she still felt guilty and full of sorrow that our first child, Binhua, had died in her arms and she almost whispered:

'If only little Binhua was still alive, then how wonderful the family would be.'

Second Aunty's home had been like a harbour for us and we sheltered there whenever we needed. She had been Shibo's only support when their family disowned Shibo for marrying a poor, radical young man. Later on Second Aunty had become radical and outlawed herself. We turned to her if we encountered problems or danger, when we needed food or money and when we needed a hiding place. She and her husband never turned us away. We stayed overnight and left Mingtao in her care once again, knowing that she would always do her very best for him. Ninjun made her way to Chongqing and Shibo and I went to Hechuan to meet our liaison.

As soon as we got to Hechuan we started searching for our rendezvous. Before long we spotted an elderly lady sitting by the gate of a yard who was embroidering a shoe; this was the scene we had been told to look out for. Shibo went up to her and they exchanged the passwords. The old lady then led us into the house. A tall man in his thirties greeted Shibo by taking hold of her hands and saying:

'Shijie, here you are! In such tense times you still managed to come on time.'

Shibo turned back to me and said: 'Let me introduce...'

'No, there is no need,' the man said as he laughed. 'We know each other! It's about ten years since we saw each other though.'

I was so surprised to recognise this man, whom Ninjun had called 'Big Fellow Liu': it was Liu Shiquan. He was from my home town and we had been friends in middle school. We had even joined the Communist Party in the same year, but I don't think that I had expected to ever see him again.

He indicated the old lady. 'This is our Revolution Mother – her three sons have all joined our uprising. She passes messages and watches out for us while we have meetings – so we are safe here.'

After we had shared a meal, Big Fellow Liu started talking about the mission:

'The uprising is going to start any day now. It seems that we will have to cover a much wider region than was formerly predicted, which further complicates logistical support. Zeng Dage and I needed to find capable and reliable people to be in charge of logistics, so we decided to let Shijie and you, my old friend, take care of the job. First and foremost, we must stockpile enough grain. We will let you know the identity of all the Qu River liaisons and related people who will be asking you for weapons, ammunition, grain, medicines or any other supplies for the front lines. This is a huge mission – a vital mission – and a hard one too.'

I didn't have any problem with this new responsibility. The truth was that I had never bargained the conditions of any of the missions assigned to me or questioned anything that the Party had told me to do. However, I could clearly see that Shibo's attitude was different to mine and she let out a long sigh:

'I have been running up and down the Huaying Mountains for a good many years – you don't have to tell me about the ditches and trenches because I know them all. I am even familiar with the stones scattered over the ground. *Ai!* For so many years now every time I close my eyes I can see Yubi and all my good brothers – they've all gone – leaving me still alive. The reason I'm still living today is because I always believed that one day I would pick up my gun again and take vengeance for their deaths. Now you are all telling me to step down. Do you really think I'm too old for this? Comrade Liu – last year you and Zeng Dage came here and did I not show you every nook and cranny on the mountain? Did I slow either of you down? In fact, was I not able to run faster than both of you?'

Shibo got emotional and her tears streamed down her cheeks. I could see that 'Big Fellow Liu' felt for her as much as I did, but he sincerely said to her:

'Shijie, please do not take this the wrong way or misunderstand us. It is true that you took Zeng Dage and me up the mountain not only in the summer, but in wintertime as well, to show us the geography. On each occasion our admiration for your knowledge and stamina was boundless. In this uprising it is a fact that having a commander like you on the battlefield to lead our young people, many of whom have no experience of fighting whatsoever except for what they have read, would be invaluable. However, the enemy we face today is very different from those corroded warlords and rotten opium addicts you faced – they are a well-trained and -equipped force made up of local armies, provincial security forces and even the police force from Chongqing – in fact a proper army! Put them all together and they far outnumber us. What's more, they are using American military equipment. Once the battle starts they could come at us from all directions. What would be the point of risking someone like you – even if you weren't aged fifty – by having you running here and there on the front line? You are too valuable to us. But let's also be realistic – we do have to concern ourselves with your health and how much you can really take. Again, you are so good at public relations, planning and organisation that we are really relying on you to take over the rearguard support, which as you know better than anyone, is directly related to whether we win or lose. Don't forget that we are being forced into action long before we're ready. This is not an easy job at all, nor is it a sideline position.'

Shibo listened without comment. She smiled bitterly and turned around to talk to the old lady.

Then Big Fellow Liu patted me on the shoulder: 'There is something else we need you to do – before you take on the next job. Zeng Dage assigned you in particular for this task.'

So Zeng Dage wanted me again, even though my last assignment had ultimately failed. As soon as I thought about it, I felt my anger rise again, but 'Big Fellow Liu' seemed to read my mind:

'Zeng Dage told me that he was angry about what happened on your assignment, but he also stressed that it wasn't your fault. He said that you had been very clever indeed and knew how to act according to the circumstances and so avoided getting yourself involved in any danger. So that's why he wants you to take on Squire Wang. He is a local gangster here in Hechuan – a tyrant in fact. He holds such tight control all along the Qu River Basin that it almost seems as if he is capable of summoning the wind and rain at will. If he decides to oppose us he would be a serious obstacle for us – a tiger in our path. We know that the Guomingdan are pressuring him to stand in our way. It is very likely that he intends to do just that, but at the same time he can foresee the eventual demise of the Guomingdan and doesn't want to make difficulties for himself with the Communists in the future. We're told that he is struggling to make a decision. One of his sons is a Communist and we assumed that he would convince his father, but he is too timid. We have decided to send you to help Squire Wang make up his mind – the principle being the same as for your last mission – meaning that the best result would be that he joins our uprising and the next best thing would be that he steps aside and doesn't oppose us.'

This sounded like a better situation than with Yang Shaoyun as I would have Squire Wang's son as my 'internal link', giving me a better starting point. So I said to Big Fellow Liu that I was confident that I could complete this mission with success.

Time was crucial for all assigned tasks now and Shibo and I started planning straight away. I then went into the town to find Squire Wang's house. I was stopped by armed guards at the gate and so I asked to see Junior Wang, saying that I was a friend of his. Junior Wang received me, took me to a small room and told me not to leave it without his knowledge. He was very uptight indeed. I didn't see him again until the evening when he brought me some food. We ate together and talked about how best to reach his father. He was very hesitant and seemed to have no idea how to approach his father on the subject. I suggested that I should talk to him directly myself the next day. However, Junior Wang insisted that he needed to persuade his father to agree to see me in the first place.

I had to wait until the following afternoon before Junior Wang returned to talk to me. He told me that his father was very angry with someone and had been in a bad mood for the whole day so he hadn't dared to approach him. I was so disappointed that Junior Wang hadn't even asked his father whether I might speak to him, as time was crucial for all of us. I couldn't hide in that tiny room any longer waiting for Junior Wang to overcome his fear of his father. I knew that people like his father were often only strong in appearance and hiding a core weakness, so I said to him:

'During the past years we never knew what the future held for us and the Communists went through so much hardship and risk to carry out their missions. Now we are at the stage where we can actually see our path to victory, so why are you still so hesitant? Again, this is about your and your father's future lives!'

He saw that I was annoyed by his hesitancy and timidity and kept his head down for a few minutes while he was thinking.

'Alright then – I am going to try. I will say that you are my former classmate and have come from Chongqing and wish to see him.'

I had to wait in that small room for several hours again before Junior Wang returned just before midnight. He came in with a smile on his face and said that his father had agreed to see me.

The house was very quiet as Junior Wang led me to his father's room. Squire Wang was sitting on an intricately carved wooden armchair waiting for me. The expression on his face was ghastly and there was a glint of real malevolence in his bloodshot eyes. I was genuinely taken aback and involuntarily shuddered under his icy stare. At any moment I expected him to strike the table with his fist, rise to his feet, point a gun at my head and shoot. No wonder his son was so fearful of him. I tried to stay calm as I greeted him as politely as I could, but he didn't return my greeting. As he glared at me I started to update him on the current state of the civil war and the mood of the masses throughout the country and then I firmly said to him that the Guomingdan were losing their hold on power and would soon disintegrate. I was certain that he had similar thoughts and worries as Yang Shaoyun had had, so I put emphasis on the Communists' policy regarding the treatment of people like him. I gave him examples of how preferential treatment was given to those Guomingdan officials who had pledged themselves to the Communists. Then I detailed what he personally could expect if he did the same thing.

Squire Wang listened intently and, much to my relief, his expression gradually seemed to soften and the frosty, tense atmosphere eased a bit. I allowed myself to relax slightly. He got up from his chair and started to march up and down in the huge sitting room. As he paced the floor he shook his head one moment and then nodded it the next. Obviously he was still indecisive, so I took a chance on being blunter with him:

'We know that you are responsible for many evil deeds, but if you want people to forgive you then you must atone by doing something good. There seem to be two paths in front of you now. Firstly, you can join us in fighting the Guomingdan and, as a consequence, we will dispense rewards in the future according to your contribution now. We will not only protect you, your family and your properties, but also we will give you political status with an official rank. The other way forward is that if you feel you cannot join us, then we should be like well water and river water – they coexist without inundating one another – we mind our own business and you mind yours. In other words, when our army passes through your region you won't make any difficulty for us. For the sake of appearances, though, you can fire blanks to make it seem as if you are opposing us – this would count towards your contribution. However, if you obstinately stick to your own course and still hang on to the hope of joining with the Guomingdan to defeat us, then only death will be waiting for you. We Communists are reliable people and we keep our word. The choice is yours.'

We talked for a couple of hours, but still Squire Wang could not make up his mind and asked me to stay longer to give him more time to think. I couldn't sleep that night. It looked as if this crafty old scoundrel wouldn't be easy to convert, but time wasn't on my side and the fighting could have started already. Squire Wang's decision would directly affect us and the delay was worrying.

After breakfast the following morning Junior Wang came to tell me that his father hadn't slept for the whole night, but had made his decision and had asked him to pass it on to me. He said that, being an old man, he thought it was unlikely that he would follow the Communists to fight the world. He agreed, however, that river water shouldn't intrude on well water and he promised that he wouldn't open fire on us should our army pass through his region. In addition he said that he could give some back-up support, such as providing food, clothes and even first-aid medicines. His condition for this was that when the Communists won power, they should be lenient with him. Then he stipulated that nobody should contact him except through his son.

I finally let out my breath. This wasn't a bad result at all.

I decided to go and give my report to Big Fellow Liu, who would be in Chongqing by then. I left the house with the intention of finding a boat from Hechuan's port, but almost immediately I tuned in to the talk on the street. People were saying that Communist leaders had been arrested and that some

Communists had been killed that morning. I could hardly believe what I heard. I made my way to the high street to see what else I could learn and immediately came across a commotion. There was a lot of shouting and I could see a group of fully armed men coming in my direction. They were escorting a bamboo sedan chair and my eyes fixed on the face of the man who was tied to it – for heaven's sake, it was Old Xu! I had only been talking to him in Shibo's house two days previously and now he was captive. This really shocked me, as it seemed inconceivable that the situation had changed so quickly. I turned away and disappeared into the crowd. I went back to find Junior Wang and said to him:

'The situation has changed suddenly, but don't take any notice of rumours – although we have lost this time, it is only temporary – in the large scheme of things, Chiang Kai-shek is doomed to failure. You need to continue to work on your father and also look out for him.'

I left Squire Wang's house and found a small wooden sailing boat at the port to take me to Chongqing.

We had spent three years preparing for this uprising in Sichuan, but because we had been betrayed, we had gone into action before we were fully ready. The whole engagement, from the first shot fired by Zeng Dage at Guangan on 10 August 1948 to the operation in the Huaying Mountains, only lasted forty-two days.

Before the Dawn

We paid a heavy price for the uprising. During the various skirmishes themselves, forty-five of our men lost their lives and over seventy were arrested, many of whom were killed later. Then during the Guomingdan's 'clean-up' afterwards, countless people were killed in each region of north-east Sichuan. Our leaders had to go into hiding and many of our fighters withdrew to Chongqing.

My family also pulled out of Huaying and we went to Chongqing. Shibo found us a house to rent in the western outskirts and we settled in there as best we could. However, Chongqing was overrun by plain-clothes police and Guomingdan spies and we had to be extremely careful. Like ants they crawled from street to street, into the labyrinthine alleyways and up and down the winding, slippery steps until they had netted every corner of the city in their search for Communists. They stopped everyone they could and asked to see their proof-of-identity card and they went house to house to check registrations. They searched their 'suspects' and they took informers along to identify the Communists, or anyone related to them, and arrested them. The residents of Chongqing were already notorious for being bad tempered, impatient and harsh, but the increased tension in the city caused emotions to erupt. Wherever we went we passed people shouting and fighting. The dangerous political situation clouded our mood and was made worse still by the heavy fog and dirt of the city.

One of the necessary skills we had to learn in order to survive as an intelligence agent, living right under the noses of the Guomingdan, was how to throw off a 'tail'. One day Ninjun found she was being followed. To make sure, she slowed her pace and the tail stopped and when she went faster, the tail quickened their pace too. She quickly changed direction in order to find familiar surroundings and headed for the Seven Star high street. She knew each of this area's alleyways and back doors, having done performances there when she was with the Children's Theatre. She hid until she could safely peep at this tail and to her utter amazement she recognised the short, stocky figure with a round face. With relief she ran up to him:

'Fatty – is it you? I thought it was a spy following me – why didn't you call out to me?'

'Fatty' was one of the liaisons from our committee and both Ninjun and I had had contact with him in the past. After the uprising Fatty had been betrayed and the Guomingdan went to his home to arrest him, but he wasn't there. Instead they arrested his father and younger brother. His mother couldn't take the shock and died from a heart attack then and there. Fatty made his way to Chongqing without any money and wandered the streets like a beggar hoping to find someone he knew. He had seen Ninjun on one occasion, but had quickly lost sight of her. Then Big Fellow Liu had come upon him and advised him to stay on the streets, in the guise of a beggar, to find their comrades who had fled to Chongqing. Fatty was relieved to have found Ninjun once more and told her:

'Thanks to the heavens above! I thought I had lost you again.

You know I saw you three days ago, but at the same time I saw a cigarette end on the ground at my feet and I felt so desperate for it, I took my eyes off you and picked it up. Then I turned and asked the man in the shop behind me to light it for me and when I turned around again – my heaven – you had vanished. You can't know just how much I hated the taste of that cigarette end, but, of course, I only had myself to blame. Today, when I saw you, I didn't dare approach you – you're dressed so fashionably and just look at me! I couldn't decide what to do. Listen – Big Fellow Liu wants to see you all – it's very urgent. Meet him at the usual place tomorrow.'

Ninjun hurriedly dropped a few coins in his hand before they separated.

The following day we met Big Fellow Liu at a teahouse. It was only just over a month since we had last seen him in Hechuan, but we all felt as if the earth itself had shattered since then. We took him back to our home, which was breaking the security rule made for everyone's safety, because nobody could be absolutely certain who was clean. However, we all instinctively trusted him and were so happy so see him alive and safe.

Big Fellow Liu was certainly at the top of the Guomingdan wanted list and we advised him to hide and stop all activity for a while. His own safety was the least of his concerns though, as he was far more anxious about others and said to us:

'There are hundreds of our fighters taking refuge in Chongqing at the moment and most of them have no money and no contacts here. They're all wandering the streets, just like Fatty, trusting to luck to be found by someone they know. What happens when their luck runs out and they're arrested? Apart from the issue of their welfare, it gives all of us more problems and increases the danger.'

He let out a long, heartfelt sigh before carrying on:

'We've suffered enough at the hands of the traitors and now

our people are scattered like grains of sand across the region – from Huaying and Hechuan to Chongqing. We are like a dragon without a head. We are being intimidated on all sides and there is a real threat hanging over our heads. We have lost contact with the Above, but in the meantime I am taking full responsibility. What we need to do now is concentrate on finding our people, then settling them down. As long as they know they still have leadership, they should be alright. Each time we find someone, it means we are all in less danger – every single person counts.'

Liu had first gone to the Huaying region in 1945 to lead the uprising and he had got to know most of the team leaders and fighters, whereas I had got to know our people in the business community in Chongqing. So Liu decided that he and Fatty should go out on the streets to find the people and then bring them to me so that I could find them accommodation and a job, or at least something temporary to tide them over. Within three months we had settled over a hundred people.

In July the Above sent a new man, named Huang, to make contact with us through Shibo. He brought the new order: 'Do everything possible to save our own people. Rescue our comrades in the Guomingdan prisons. Let us stay alive to witness the liberation of the whole country.'

Ninjun had been able to take up working again at the same advertising agency where we had both worked before and she brought back a regular income. Every last fen went towards supporting all of us. We were very happy to have met up with Big Fellow Liu again and Ninjun generously treated us all to a meal at a restaurant to celebrate the reconnection with the Party.

Ninjun said to Liu: 'Big Fellow Liu, every day you are running through the streets across the whole city – do you know how much we worry about you?'

Liu took off his hat and pointed at his forehead and said: 'Do you see the character for "Communist" written here? Even if the enemy uses an X-ray machine they can't see that I'm a Communist. By the way, just to let you know, I have been practising the "tiger bench". I am now able to withstand three or four bricks under my feet without having to make a sound – no problem.'

The 'tiger bench' was one of the tortures that the Guomingdan used on their prisoners. First they tied the person in a sitting position lengthways on a long bench with their back straight against a long pole and then tied the tops of their thighs to the bench. Then they added bricks, one by one, under their feet. It resulted in two broken knees and the pain was terrible. Then I told Liu:

'And some of us have been practising the "duck floating in the water".'

The 'duck floating in the water' torture was when a person's hands were tied behind their back and then they were suspended from a height. Liu nodded:

'Yes, it's best to try and be prepared for these awful tortures – the Guomingdan know how to hurt us. They're an inhumane bunch. Listen – our people are restless at the moment. They don't want to keep fleeing and hiding and having to live like thieves. They want to go back to the Huaying Mountains, pick up their guns and fight again. I have sent a few people back to the Yuechi and Hechuan area just to scout out what the situation is like there now. I also told them to try and find out how many guns and other weapons are hidden there and then just to wait for an order from the Above.'

I could understand how such oppression and inactivity was hard for fighters to bear, but I had always thought that bringing the uprising forward hadn't been a sensible decision. I put forward my opinion that, for now, we should be patient and wait rather than taking any hasty, impulsive action in order to avoid more lives being lost and further damage.

As usual, before we left each other we set up a time and place for our next meeting.

Next day, as arranged, we went to meet Liu. We waited for an hour, but there was so sign of him. The rule was, if the person was five minutes late then everyone should leave the meeting place in case that person had been arrested. If it then became clear that they had already betrayed others, everyone concerned had to move address immediately. As for Big Fellow Liu, we never had any doubts about him and we felt safe enough to go to the meeting point the next day, and the day after that, at the same time each day. However, there was still no sign of him and we were really worried.

The bad news finally reached us that he had been arrested. We heard that, after our meal together at the restaurant, he had gone to meet another comrade. However, that comrade had been arrested the previous day and the Guomingdan spies had laid an ambush for Big Fellow Liu. When Liu turned up for the meeting, he had no way of escape: it was just like getting caught in a spider's web.

We all felt distressed about Liu's arrest, because we were all of the same opinion: he was the most caring person you could ever hope to meet. We were desperate to think of some way of rescuing him, but he had been sent to the Zhazidong Prison, which was Chiang Kai-shek's concentration camp for political prisoners. We all knew that when someone was sent to that prison it meant it had been proven that they were Communist and there was no means of escape.

My job got very much harder without Big Fellow Liu around. There were so many people needing to be fed, housed and fixed up with a job. As winter came upon us it got more

complicated, as warm clothing and more substantial accommodation were necessary.

My old friend Wu Changwen, with his new wife and Big
Sister, also moved to Chongqing. Soon after arriving in the
city, nicknamed 'The Fire City' for its hot summers, Wu's Big
Sister had opened an ice-lolly factory. They eventually found
us and got involved in our activities. By the middle of the following summer temperatures reached 40°C and there was a
high demand for ice lollies, so we were able to place many of
our people to work in the factory. Others sold the ice lollies
on the streets. Once summer passed, though, business tailed off
and the factory had to close until the next May. Many of those
who had worked in the ice-lolly factory turned to buying and
selling fruit and vegetables.

In those days there was no tap water in the city and many
people earned a living by carrying water from the Yangtze and
Jianlin rivers up into the city. We put a lot of our people to
work as water carriers, but only the physically strong could
survive a job such as this. A carrier would take two full buckets
on a pole across his shoulders at a time and the further away
from the river he carried the water the higher the price he got
for it. They covered many miles, including negotiating several hundred hazardous steps up from the river. The steps were
kept constantly slippery by the humidity in the summer and
the damp fog in the winter. Even the strongest men could only
manage two or a maximum of three loads per day and that
would probably earn them one silver yuan. We could only
place the illiterate peasants in this job, however, as anyone else
doing a job like that attracted the attention of the Guomingdan spies. Some of our members were still young enough to be
sent back to university or college to continue their studies. We
also tried to find appropriate jobs for the middle-aged people
so as not to attract attention to them. Those people we couldn't

place in any job were sent to the countryside, or even to different regions. Once again winter was creeping up on us and I had to find extra money to buy the warm clothes and enough food for people to survive the cold. It seemed that I had no cure for the endless ills of those times.

The government forced a new currency, called 'gold yuan', onto the market. They wanted to replace the 'lawful currency' and the silver yuan. However, it wasn't long before hyperinflation devalued their new currency. Then people were desperate to get their hands on silver yuan, because the coins themselves were made from real silver. A black market sprang up around the silver yuan. In Chongqing, the dealers used to congregate at a market called the Rice Pagoda. It was a crowded location with all sorts of people coming and going non-stop, which made it ideal, not only for the black-market dealers, but also for our comrades to meet each other. I decided to join the business. I was a quick learner: I wandered up and down the marketplace watching the dealers and, two days later, I was in business.

I gathered together all our savings from the advertisements that Ninjun had managed to sell, as well as the proceeds from selling off all our leftover herbal medicines, and then I was ready to step into the marketplace. Each day I would take a few silver yuan coins with me, flick them against each other to make them clink and shout: 'Three years, closed eyes!' This meant that my silver yuan had been minted in 1914, which was the third year of the Republic, with the image of Yuan Shikai in profile with his eye closed. Yuan Shikai had been the provisional president after the 1911 revolution. He became emperor in 1916, but his rein only lasted eighty-three days and in history he is known as the 'one-hundred-day emperor'. A large number of these coins had been minted at the time and they were the most valued ones then.

If I was lucky, I made a profit of a few silver yuan per day.

The black market was further undermining the gold yuan and the government needed to put a stop to the speculating, so the police were ordered to clamp down on all money changing. However, the police themselves were key players and the silver yuan they confiscated from the dealers during their spot checks never went further than their own pockets. The police also invented a way of marking the dealers so that they were identifiable as they ran away. They put tar on the end of their batons and smeared the tar over the dealer. One day I was in the middle of negotiating a good deal when I saw some plain-clothes police, with their tar-tipped batons, chasing a couple of dealers. As usual a crowd had gathered to watch the fun. Although I could see the police getting nearer to me, I didn't want the money that was almost in my hand to disappear, so I stood my ground for longer than was wise. Then one of the policemen threw his baton at me. I turned quickly, but it caught me on my back. As the heavy, sticky baton fell it split my new white shirt and marked me on my skin. On that particular day there were police on all the street corners and many of them started running after me as I pushed my way through the crowd. I was still very athletic then and I was able to evade them. When I was sure there was nobody still following me I made my way to Wu Changwen's house. When I told them my story and said it was tar, they couldn't stop laughing! It took a long time for Wu's wife to scrub the tar off my skin and for days after I mourned the loss of my smart white shirt!

Not long after, our liaison brought a man to see me, named Den Zhaoming, who was to be our new leader now that Big Fellow Liu had been arrested. He was one of the planners of the uprising, but after our defeat, he had also lost contact with the Above. He had gone looking for the Party leaders, firstly in Shanghai, then in Hong Kong and then back to Shanghai again where he finally managed to find them. Now he was bringing us the latest news and orders from the Shanghai Central Committee.

He was glad to meet Shibo. He reverentially held her hand and said: 'Shijie, you are part of our respected older generation. I heard your name so long ago – today I finally meet you face to face. It is such an honour for me.'

Then he turned to me: 'I know that all the hard jobs have been loaded onto your shoulders since Big Fellow Liu was arrested.'

We were gathered around him waiting eagerly to hear what the latest news was.

'The Liberation Army is currently marching to the big south west [meaning south-west China]. What we need to do now is change our strategy – which had been to develop armed forces in the countryside. Now we are told to change our focus to the cities – we need "to walk from the country to the city". We must prepare ourselves for liberation – be ready to take over. We must instruct the masses to protect the city's infrastructure – such as factories, schools, supplies and all kinds of archives. We must do our best to prevent, or at least to limit, the damage being brought about by the destructive activities of the Guomingdan. We need to collect as much information about the enemy's military and political movements. We especially need to cultivate and convert anyone willing to come to us. We need to save and reorganise our own forces.'

Den Zhaoming took a deep breath and sadness clouded his eyes.

'The Central Committee particularly pointed out that the principle and method of carrying out the uprising by the Eastern Sichuan Underground Branch were wrong – they called it military blindness – and by rushing headlong into mass action they led it to break down in chaos and so many lost lives.'

The Central Committee's criticism gave foundation to

Shibo's predictions as to what would happen. At the time she had been so worried about all the young people being pushed into battle prematurely, all because of the impatience of some of the leaders. She had been able to foresee that it would end in tragedy and there would be many lives lost, but nobody was willing to listen to her advice. Den Zhaoming looked guiltily at Shibo:

'Shijie, I know we should have listened to you.'

Den Zhaoming turned to me:

'Big Fellow Liu's arrest should teach us all a lesson – we need to be extra careful because our situation grows ever more complex. From now on, you must take over Liu's duties. Carry on with the tasks of settling people and regrouping the force. Remember though, no more armed fighting for the time being – save our strength for the Liberation.'

Everything seemed clearer after Den Zhaoming delivered the instructions and after another couple of months of hard, intensive work we had settled over two hundred more people from the tatters of the uprising. We had also restored the Party branch organisation and set up a new fighting force that could be used to rescue our comrades from Zhazidong Prison.

Then great news came through to us that, on 1 October 1949, Mao Zedong had made a proclamation in Tiananmen Square in Beijing:

'The People's Republic of China has now been established... the Chinese people will stand up for their rights from now on...'

The Communists had finally come to power. We had won China and we felt on top of the world.

By November 1949, the majority of the country was in Communist hands and the Liberation Army had marched down to the south west of the country. Chiang Kai-shek had already fled to Taiwan and left the rest of his people running around like headless chickens. However, seeing as Chongqing had been his headquarters, it was the last place where the Guomingdan were still active. It was their final struggle. Pieces of good news came in one after another and we were counting the days until Chongqing would be in our hands. We planned to do whatever we could to rescue our comrades in the Zhazidong and Baigonguan prisons, which were still firmly under Guomingdan control.

Zhazidong Prison was originally a coal mine and it got its name 'Zhazhi', meaning 'dregs', because the coal was extremely poor quality. It was located on the west side of the city and was surrounded on three sides by mountains. The only access was from the valley and it was well hidden from view. Baigonguan Prison had been the private mansion of a Sichuan warlord, Bai Ju, and it was only two kilometres away from Zhazidong. When Chiang Kai-shek moved his capital to Chongqing in 1937, his chief of police, Daili, found these two places and thought they would make perfect impenetrable prisons. They kicked out the coal miners, bought the mansion and changed both buildings into concentration camps. Each prison was still very heavily guarded.

We had been working on obtaining all the details about the prisons for three months, but the isolated location and tight army security made the prisons very difficult to get to know. Coincidentally, and luckily for us, the Guomingdan recruited some civilian guards to work at the prisons and so we sent Fatty and a few others to apply for the jobs and they were hired. After training, Fatty was made the 'orders courier' and we were very happy when he got that job. Through him we quickly learned that there were three different defence lines. Each line had different passwords, which were changed often, even depending on whether it was daytime or night-time. The closer to the cells, the tighter the security became. Fatty, as

272

orders courier, was able to walk in and out, but strictly using a specified route. He cleverly memorised every detail around him and had drawn a map for us. We sent two people to work in the Twenty-Fourth Military Factory and I infiltrated the Thirtieth Military Grain Depot as the secretary. Both the factory and the grain depot were located very close to the prisons.

At the same time as preparing for an armed rescue, Ninjun came up with the idea that we could try to buy the release of Big Fellow Liu and Meixia's husband. Shibo had met up with an old school friend who had married a journalist, now the Director of the *China News* and, through him, we were able to reach a high-ranking officer at Zhazidong who was open to a bribe. He only agreed to establish the link and the rest of it was up to us to negotiate.

There was a real chance that, once we had made contact with this man at Zhazidong, we would manage to get our people out, for a price, but it was very risky. As Den Zhaoming said as he paced up and down:

'We want to rescue our people, but don't want to jeopardise the lives of others in doing so.'

The talk and questions went back and forth:

'Who is going to go?'

'Is this really a good idea?'

'Who would arouse the least suspicion in the negotiations?'

'It's too risky – we may lose another person – and so close to liberation.'

Shibo asked everyone to be quiet.

'This is the best chance we will have to get Big Fellow Liu and Meixia's husband out, without bloodshed. Of course we are going to do it, but it won't be any of you who will go – I shall go myself.'

Ninjun immediately jumped up.

'Boniang, this was originally my idea – if anyone goes it

should be me. You are getting old now – just teach me a few tricks for the negotiation and how to act in an emergency – you don't need to show your face.'

'What's wrong with showing my face to the enemy? Why does everyone think I'm too old to do anything? Even in last year's uprising I was the one who negotiated with the enemy to stop fighting us – in the end they withdrew their cannons which were already pointing in our direction. I have had plenty of experience of this kind – in case of danger I know what to do. I'm not trying to deny that the years are catching up with me – and perhaps I have to admit that I may not be able to run as fast as I used to – but this is something I *can* do.'

Ninjun yelled back at her: 'Boniang – you look down on me, don't you? But I'm an "old" underground agent myself now – it is so close to liberation I don't believe the Guomingdan can still have much support on their side – it should be easy…'

'What do you know – a young kid like you?' Shibo was getting irritated by Ninjun. 'You only think you have to be brave, but I tell you that bravery is not enough. This is negotiating with the Guomingdan we are talking about – face to face with your enemy – just one wrong word and you could be arrested and killed. Yes, we may very well be close to liberation now, but if anything happened to you, how… how could I face… how could I face your father?'

Shibo turned her head away to hide her red eyes. There was silence in the room. None of us knew what to say, but then Den Zhaoming cleared his throat and said:

'Both of you – mother and daughter – do not fight for the "live or die" card. Ninjun, I think you have been visiting the journalist and his wife and I understand that they like you, so it's best you keep the work going there. As for you Shijie, you are our "big tree" – we rely on you and need to keep you on the safe side of things – if something happened to you, then I wouldn't know how to face the Above. We all ought to be thinking of various different ways of rescuing our brothers and also we need everyone to get some money together – saving even one person is better than none. Time is crucial. Ninjun, you go back to the journalist again to persuade him to negotiate for us – find out how much money we need to buy two of our people. Don't forget to tell him to bargain.'

Indeed, the journalist and his wife, who had no children of their own, had liked Ninjun so much when they met her that they had asked Shibo if they could adopt her! Ninjun happily agreed to become their goddaughter.

Ninjun pleaded with the journalist to negotiate the price for us and he came back with the news:

'They want 500 grams of gold per person. I bargained down the amount by half for you. You need to be really quick in getting the money.'

Ninjun was downcast:

'Good heavens – fifty grams of gold is worth sixty silver yuan – 250 grams is worth three hundred silver yuan. Where on earth are we going to find such a huge sum? Can you go back and bargain more…?'

The journalist was already nervous. He had never wanted to be involved in the negotiations in the first place, but had been talked into it by his wife, and Ninjun had kept pestering him, so he got very short with her:

'Just go – think of some way to get it. Get as much as you can.'

When Ninjun heard him say 'get as much as you can', she knew that there was still room for bargaining. The problem was that everyone around us was poor and many of them were even completely dependent on us for survival. Time was ticking away and the situation was a matter of life or death for our comrades. Everyone searched their own pockets. However, Shibo was still the most resourceful person amongst us: she came up with seventy silver yuan and a gold chain. Everyone placed their contribution on the table, whether it was their own to give or it was something borrowed. In total there was 180 silver yuan, plus a few pieces of gold jewellery. We all stood staring at the pile on the table in silence wondering whether it would be enough and then I watched Ninjun as she unfastened the gold chain around her neck and added it to the collection. A shaft of light was coming through the window. It made the gold glint and Shibo and I exchanged glances. We both knew that this was the last wedding present from my father and in my mind's eye I could see my father's face. Once again, Ninjun had given generously. I had to stop my hands, as if they had a mind of their own, from grabbing that shiny, golden chain back. Ninjun knew what I was thinking, put her hand in mine, gave it a squeeze and whispered:

'Don't worry – after we are liberated, we will have everything we want, won't we?'

Den Zhaoming packed up the money and jewellery and handed it all to Ninjun.

'Ninjun, this mission is different from the ones you have undertaken before – you need to do whatever it takes to save our comrades, but you must prepare for the worst case for yourself. If something goes wrong, rather sacrifice yourself than… you know what I want to say. For the time being you must cut all links with the organisation – we will send someone to contact you when the time is right.'

I stood next to Shibo as we saw Ninjun off. Shibo gently combed through Ninjun's hair with her fingers and lightly brushed her face. Then she took her scarf from around her own neck and put it on Ninjun – there were no words between them. I should have told Ninjun how much I loved her and given her a big hug, but I didn't. I wanted to, but we were in front of other people and I was too shy to show my emotions. At the time I didn't know what might be lying in wait for her and whether I would ever see her again, but I locked up my love and admiration for her in my heart, hoping for her return. She smiled and told us all that she would come back unharmed. We watched her until she disappeared from view. The next thing we had to do, and immediately, was to pack up everything and leave the house. I went to stay at the grain depot for the time being.

Ninjun made her way to the journalist's house, fully expecting him to tell her how to meet up with his contact at the prison, but instead he told her:

'No, no Ninjun – you stay in the house – I can't let you go there. If something happened to you, I wouldn't be able to face your mother and godmother. Those Guomingdan are killing people like flies – they don't even blink an eye. I will take the money – you wait here.'

Ninjun handed him the package with the money and jewellery. He hefted the weight of the package and thought it wouldn't be enough, so in addition he took an expensive set of mahjong tiles and a whole leg of ham.

Ninjun waited until three o'clock in the morning, when the journalist returned. He was highly anxious and his forehead was dripping with sweat. He pulled out the packages from his coat and kept repeating:

'It's too late, it's too late. My contact has just fled to Chengdu. There's nothing, nothing more I can do.'

I worried ceaselessly about Ninjun, because that same night, 27 November 1949, we all heard sporadic shooting from the direction of Zhazidong Prison. Then we saw flames and smoke. It didn't take much to guess what was happening there before the Guomingdan made their escape from the region.

Before the dawn broke, my comrades had been cruelly slaughtered. Amongst the dead lay my brother-in-law, Chen Zuo Yi, my liaison, Yuan Xeng Yi, and my dearest colleague, Big Fellow Liu. We had been meticulously planning for three months to rescue our comrades from the prison, but never got the chance to carry it out.

Meanwhile, before the Guomingdan left their last stronghold – the Chongqing area – Chiang Kai-shek ordered the destruction of the city and the death of all the Communists in the prisons. Some of the important buildings they managed to bomb were the Chongqing Steel Factory, the Fifth and Twenty-Fourth Military Factories, the power station, the gunpowder factory and two radio stations. They also sank a cargo ship on the Yangtze River. By the time the vast Liberation Army reached Chongqing on 1 December 1949, the city was devastated.

On 3 December, Shibo, Meixia and I, along with a few other comrades, made our way to Zhazidong to assess the situation and hopefully to identify our comrades. As we got near, there was an overpowering stench of decomposing bodies, petrol and burning. Spirals of smoke were still issuing from here and there even a week after the massacre. Bodies were lying where they fell. There were eight cells full of burnt remains. Before they had been set alight, the prisoners had been blown apart by machine-gun fire – heads, arms and legs separated from their torsos and turned into blackened lumps. One corner of a wall had collapsed and a heap of what looked like charred wooden planks was piled up by the opening. When we got a closer look, we realised that they weren't planks at all. We found twenty bodies in the latrine pit. There was no way to identify who was who. Beyond the buildings near the first hill we found three huge pits full of bodies. Their open eyes seemed to be full of anger and each one had clenched their right hand into a fist. They were saturated with blood.

This was beyond a nightmare. The images of that day have never left me and I can remember how I couldn't control my shivering – it felt like ants were crawling all over my body. Nobody was able to speak and the silence pressed down on us. I went over to Shibo and put my arm around her. She was wiping away her tears. None of us ever thought we would have to witness horrors like these. There are no words to describe it. Shibo knew what it was like to lose loved ones, but this was something beyond her comprehension and it was wrenching at her heart. We were so resentful that this had happened just before the Liberation: before our dawn.

There were some survivors, but the accounts of the night of 27 November were confused. It seems that the Guomingdan had crowded as many of the prisoners as they could into just a few of the cells and opened fire on them through the tiny windows with machine guns. Spirited calls of 'Long live Chairman Mao' and 'Long live Communism' were quickly silenced. Some of our heroes were killed outright, but others merely wounded and trapped by the fallen on top of them. The soldiers then unlocked the cells, poured petrol over the piles of bodies and set them alight. Many other prisoners were shot as they ran through the courtyards or as they tried to scale the walls. Two hundred and seven people were massacred during the night. In addition, 114 people were executed in the days leading up to the massacre. In the end we learned that only nineteen people escaped, including two children.

I led the work to clean up the prison grounds. There were thirty of us and we looked at each individual body to see if we could recognise anyone, but it was impossible. All we could do was wrap each charred body, or body part, in white cloth and put it into a coffin. We bought up all the white cotton and silk and coffins in the city, but it wasn't enough. I had to send people to the nearest town to collect more white cloth and coffins. Then we buried them all.

Time turned slowly for us and eventually brought us to early spring in 1950. The spring showers interspersed by fog made the city seem so depressing. We waited for the first sunny day then Shibo, Ninjun and I, carrying Mingtao, went to visit Father's grave. Commander Xiao accompanied us. In the three years since we buried him we had never visited his grave. Ninjun eventually found the tombstone amongst the rampant weeds and grasses, which had completely covered the grave. I cleaned the stone and all around the gravesite and lit incense and candles. Ninjun and I went down on our knees and kowtowed three times to Father. Shibo and Commander Xiao stood in front of the grave and bowed three times. I saw tears rolling down Shibo's cheeks. Then she walked in circles around the grave and she was either whispering to herself, or perhaps to Father: 'It's too late now, it's all too late!'

I understood what Shibo meant. The longed-for great day of liberation had come too late for Father. I was sure, too, that she was thinking about her own feelings for my father and of his obvious love for her. Perhaps she regretted never telling him how important he was to her, even perhaps that she loved him. I like to think that Father heard and understood her.

Standing on top of the hill and looking out over the Yangtze River, we were able to see that all the buildings along the riverbanks, and the boats in the water too, were flying red flags. They were fluttering in the breeze and their colour was intense in the sunshine. Red: a traditional colour in China. Red: the symbol of Communism. Red tinged with unbearable sadness, for it is the colour of all the spilled blood of our fallen comrades as well as that of our enemies.

Whenever my friends met up after the events described in my story, we would always greet each other by saying: 'Good heavens! You are still alive!'

Well, yes, I am still alive and in my nineties now. The story I have told here is the first part of my life. The second part is just as full of danger, hardship and turmoil – but for different reasons. The second part of my life was turned upside down and confused by the betrayal of our ideals.

There is only one thing I can say: 'To survive is victory!'

Stories of Survival

Sister Tan

Sister Tan

Sister Tan hadn't heard from her husband Peng Yongwu for more than six years.

At the age of sixteen she married into Peng's family, who had no money and nothing to offer her. The family lived in Yunyang Town, not far from my grandmother's home. She gave up her studies at school so she could look after her husband's elderly parents and she borrowed money so that he could study in the city.

Sometime later they had a son named Zhong, meaning 'loyal'. Peng became a keen political activist and, even though his wife didn't understand his words like 'revolution', 'Communism' and 'democracy', she trusted her husband and whatever he did she was always behind him wholeheartedly. During his radicalisation, Peng had to stay in Chongqing for quite a while, so he sent a letter asking Sister Tan to bring their son and move to Chongqing to join him. Unfortunately at that time she had just set up a textile workshop, in the hope that she could earn enough to pay back the money she had borrowed for his debts. Their son was also suffering from chickenpox just at that time. For these reasons she wrote back telling him that she needed to stay at home for a little while longer and that, just as soon as their debts were paid, they would then be able to join him. After sending the letter she felt enormous guilt that she was not able to take care of him and be there for him when he needed her. Who would cook for him? What would happen when the weather turned cold? That night her tears wet her pillow.

The years passed and dutifully she waited. Nothing! No letters or news of her husband came. Then six years later, on a winter's day in 1948, a letter arrived from her younger brother, Zhuan, who had studied in Chongqing at the same time as Peng.

The letter was carefully worded and it said that Peng had married another woman and that they had a son who was two years old. But now they both had to leave Chongqing and work elsewhere and were unable to take their son with them. They hoped Sister Tan could come to Chongqing to look after their young child.

I can only imagine how Sister Tan reacted, what she was thinking as she read the letter and how she got through the following days.

Zhuan's letter was full of half-truths. For a long time he had been dismayed at having to watch his sister work so hard to pay off her husband's debts, with no knowledge of where he was or what had happened to him, so he determined to trace his brother-in-law, Peng.

Then one day in a street, Zhuan glimpsed a familiar figure suddenly rush past him and he immediately recognised the flustered man as being the person he had long been searching for. For a second Peng looked stunned at being recognised, then he raised his hat to Zhuan and hurriedly said: 'I am in a terrible rush, but perhaps we could meet later – only where?'

Before Zhuan could answer, Peng disappeared back into the crowd. It looked like he was being chased.

Two months passed but there was no further sign of Peng. Zhuan was angry and frustrated with himself for having let Peng run off in mid-conversation.

Not long after, a woman in her late twenties called Jun came to see Zhuan. She introduced herself as Peng's wife and told Zhuan that she knew everything about his sister. She was very apologetic and said Peng and she had had no choice in becoming a couple. However, one day she would give Peng back to his rightful wife. Jun was pleasant, well mannered and sincerely sorry, which really confused Zhuan. Last of all she pleaded with him not to say anything to his sister.

What to tell? How to tell it? It all seemed inexplicable. Zhuan thought about it over and over again. So, to protect his sister, he decided not to say a word.

A year later Zhuan also joined the Communists and in so doing became privy to certain snippets of Party information. He learned that Peng was part of the leadership group of the Chongqing branch of underground agents, who would later go on to lead the 1948 Huaying Mountain Uprising. Because Peng was all alone in Chongqing, the Communist Party sent Jun to accompany him and pose as his wife in order to cover his identity better. Eventually they both fell in love, the Party permitted them to get married for real and they had a baby boy named Yun, meaning 'Little Cloud'.

Peng with his new wife Jun and their baby Yun

In the autumn of 1948 Zhuan received a letter from Jun, which had been secretly smuggled out from Zhazidong Prison. The letter told him that Peng had died during the uprising and that she had been recognised by a traitor who confirmed she was a Communist – she was consequently imprisoned. She entrusted her son, Yun, to Sister Tan and asked if she would bring him up as her own child.

With this devastating news, Zhuan had no choice but to write to his sister and ask her to come to Chongqing. He realised that he would have to tell her the awful truth this time. However, the Party had different ideas and decided not to tell her about her husband's death, so that she would think that Peng and Jun were away working elsewhere, which she would accept as being confidential information. The Party put her up at the YWCA along with her own son, Zhong, and Jun's son, Yun.

This is when I met Sister Tan. She was just in her thirties and looked delicate and pretty, but behind her outward appearance I saw a calm and very capable woman. Sister Tan didn't utter a word of complaint. She quietly looked after the two boys, expecting to see her husband and Jun one day, and she said that when they both returned, she would give them back their son.

A year later, in the autumn of 1949, Sister Tan received a letter from Jun, again smuggled out from the prison. In it she apologised for taking Peng away from her and admitted that she was in love with him. Then she sincerely thanked Sister Tan for looking after Yun for her, but said that in her present situation she could not see herself coming out of prison alive. In which case, she entreated Sister Tan to raise Yun as her own son. She expressed a wish that, when Yun was old enough, Sister Tan would tell him all about his mother. To tell him that what she did was for the Revolution so that he, Zhong and all the children of China would have a better and peaceful life in the future.

Along with the letter, Jun sent a couple of cheongsams she wanted Sister Tan to have.

After the liberation of Chongqing, Sister Tan heard that lots of prisoners had escaped from the Zhazidong Prison, so without further ado she and her brother, Zhuan, went to look for Jun. Sister Tan carried Yun on her back and Zhong ran along behind. They remained there for several days searching in the vicinity of the prison. However, after three or four days they received the terrible news that Jun had been executed some days before the night of the massacre. Evidence of an atrocity had been found several miles further on from the prison. They decided to investigate this site. On their way they came across a local man who told them that about ten days previously, round about sunset, a group of Nationalist soldiers had come past his village ordering that everyone must stay indoors. However, the man watched through a gap in his door and saw about forty people walking down the hill. Some were wearing suits and some were wearing long gowns and it wasn't until he saw the heavily armed soldiers behind them that he realised they were Communist prisoners from the Zhazidong prison.

'Were there any women in the group?' Sister Tan asked desperately.

'Yes, there were two women – one was wearing a bright red cardigan.'

At this point Zhuan felt awful, because when Jun came to see him she had been wearing a bright red cardigan over a dark blue cheongsam.

'They went over the hill that way.' The man pointed behind him and carried on to say: 'Just before dark, we all heard the sound of continuous gunshots and people shouting loudly. Soon after that the soldiers returned with some of the clothes and shoes of the prisoners hanging over their rifles.'

Sister Tan and Zhuan could not wait for the man to finish his story; they ran through the bushes towards the hill and came across a shocking scene. Bodies were strewn all around and some were piled up in a heap. The smell of death filled the air and the soil was dark with the spilled blood. Amongst the bodies, a bright red cardigan stood out. Zhuan cried out. Sister Tan went and stood by her younger brother. She knew straight away this was Jun: a woman she had never met, the woman who had shared her husband and the cherished little boy's natural mother.

That moment was made worse when Zhuan confessed to his sister that her husband, whom she had not seen for over seven years, and whom she still expected to see again, had been killed during the Huaying Mountain Uprising.

From that day Sister Tan decided to send Zhong, her own son, to an orphanage so that she could devote herself to bringing up Yun. We, and the Party, all thought there was no need for her to do that and had difficulty with her decision, but she was resolved. Her words were:

'My husband, Peng, and Jun both died for the revolution, so that they, their children and all of us could have a better life. Jun suffered horrific tortures in prison, including having sharp bamboo sticks inserted under her fingernails. In the end she was executed in secrecy in a horrible way. I believe it is my duty to look after their son – it is the very least I can do. Yun is the flesh and blood of martyrs.'

None of us could say any more but respected her for what she did as an ordinary Chinese woman.

Sister Tan soon joined the Communist Party. There was a job for everyone. She became a nursery school teacher in the first nursery at the City Hall, as she said she just wanted to look after as many children as possible.

On 31 May 1976 we received the upsetting news that Sister Tan had died of a stroke.

Zhuan and Zhong asked me to speak at Sister Tan's funeral.

It was a difficult thing to do. We had enjoyed thirty years of friendship through some of the hardest of times.

'Sister Tan seemed to be an ordinary person, but each of the seemingly ordinary things she did throughout her life served to show just how extraordinary she really was. She was the embodiment of Chairman Mao's description of a true Communist: "noble, truthful, a person without self-interest, devoted to others." Sister Tan was a special wife and extraordinary mother to many of our children. She touched our hearts and gained our respect. She will be truly missed and mourned by many of us…'

My tears fell like rain and I couldn't finish my speech.

Security Commander Xiao

Security Commander Xiao

One afternoon at the Escape Centre, which I set up after
Liberation to help any escapees from the Zhazidong and

Baigonguan prisons and also those people who had lost contact with the Party, Meixia called to us from the courtyard:

'Shibo! Erge! Somebody has just arrived who says he knows you.'

Intrigued, Shibo and I went outside to greet the person. Before our eyes was a small, thin, bedraggled old man. He was leaning on a *dagouguan*, which literally translates as 'beat dog pole', often carried by those who travelled on foot to fight off wild dogs. His neck was wrapped in a bloodstained strip of cloth. His hair was long and matted. He was wearing a tattered, long cotton gown, the bottom of which dragged along the ground. His feet were also wrapped in cloth, with his toes peeping through his broken slippers. He looked like a beggar and he was obviously exhausted. We had no idea who he was.

Immediately the old man saw us, he threw down his stick, shuffled towards Shibo and grabbed her hand:

'Don't you recognise me? I am Xiao! I am Xiao Zhongding!'

As soon as he said his name, Shibo and I gasped with astonishment and I felt a cold shiver run down my spine. I grabbed him to embrace him and Shibo held onto his hand and wouldn't let go:

'Oh, Commander Xiao – you're alive, you escaped, you survived! We were so worried!'

Another friend alive!

Commander Xiao was an old friend of my father. In 1936 he was a Nationalist, like my father, and was the security commander of Wanxian District, and my father's boss. The first time I met Xiao was soon after Shibo was released from Wanxian jail and I was staying with her at her house. One day in 1937, Father brought two people to visit Shibo; one was the famous calligrapher Uncle Menghan, but we had never met the other man before. He was short, slim, had a narrow face and seemed to be in his mid-thirties. He was wearing a smart, dark blue Dr Sun Yat-sen style suit, a grey hat and a pair of gold-framed glasses. His pointed leather shoes were so highly polished they shone like small mirrors. To complete the picture, he was carrying an ornate walking stick and he looked like what we called 'a fake foreign ghost'. Father clasped his hands and proudly introduced him to Shibo:

'This is our famous Security Commander Xiao.'

Xiao took off his hat, bowed deeply and offered his right hand to Shibo.

'Why is Commander Xiao dressed like this?' Shibo asked with a big smile as she shook his hand.

Xiao sighed and said: 'These days people hate officers and people like me are generally in uniform. I can feel their fingers pointing at my back as they scold me – their words are very unpleasant to the ear.'

Shibo laughed: 'Oh really, the masses don't scold Communist officers!'

Xiao grimaced, smiled and said: 'Yes, well it's a pity I am not a Communist officer in that case'.

This broke the ice and everyone sat down and chatted happily.

Xiao complained about the Nationalists not doing enough to fight the Japanese and about the corruption within the government. He then leaned over to Shibo and whispered:

'Lianshi, I hear that you are connected with the other side, how about forming an alliance with us?'

We all heard what he had said, however, and I noticed Father looked shocked to hear Xiao make such a direct request to Shibo. We all knew the 'other side' meant Communist. Being a top Nationalist officer, how could he so nonchalantly mention such a sensitive subject to someone he had just met for the first time?

Shibo just smiled without replying and an embarrassing silence ensued.

I exchanged glances with Father but we couldn't come up with anything to break the awkward silence. Just then Uncle Menghan stood up and said:

'Lianshi, the house is stylish and comfortable enough, but I think it lacks works of art and literature.'

Shibo turned to Uncle Menghan and said: 'Menghan, do I have the honour of your calligraphy?'

The awkward silence was broken and I jumped up to offer to prepare the ink. Then we all moved towards the table to watch Uncle Menghan's skillful calligraphy.

Uncle Menghan was actually on a Party mission. Through Father, he was to try and persuade Commander Xiao to join us, because he had control of nine local Nationalist forces in Wanxian County. In 1937, the Japanese had already occupied Nanjin, attacked Wuhan and Yichang and were making their way up the Yangtze River. However, beyond Yichang the terrain of Sichuan Province starts to get very steep and the Three Gorges form a natural barrier. Wanxian is the first gate into the Sichuan plateau and it was thought that Commander Xiao's forces would make a good first line of defence against any Japanese advance into Sichuan.

Fortunately the plan didn't become a necessity, as the Japanese didn't break through the Three Gorges into Sichuan. Also, Commander Xiao was a willing recruit as he secretly joined the Communist Party in 1938 and became one of us, despite still being a Nationalist security commander.

It was in early 1938 that Commander Xiao received an anonymous letter alleging that my father, who was then a Nationalist local force commander in Zhongxian, was openly using Communist military strategies to train his soldiers, and was a passionate believer of Communism. The letter suggested he should investigate whether Father was a Communist. Xiao destroyed the letter and told me to quickly inform Father to flee Zhongxian, so Father immediately went to Chongqing.

Not long after Father's narrow escape, I received an urgent message from Commander Xiao that the Nationalists had discovered Shibo's true identity and were about to arrest her. I ran back to the house and informed Shibo of her impending arrest and, that night, after dark, I went down to the port with her and saw her onto a small boat which would take her back to her home town of Yuechi. We then lost contact with Xiao for ten years.

In 1948 we (Shibo, Ninjun and I) were in Chongqing and operating right under the noses of the Nationalists. One day, I was pleasantly surprised to bump into Xiao in the street. We headed to the nearest teahouse to catch up on old times. Xiao was saddened to hear of my father's death and surprised that Shibo had become my mother-in-law, rather than my step-mother as most people had thought would happen. He said:

'Do you remember the time when we were in Xishan Park? I first heard from your father that Lianshi could shoot equally well with either hand, but didn't really believe it, so I handed her two guns for a demonstration – and you placed some incense about a hundred paces away. Then I watched her aim both guns at the same time and fire, first right, then left – wow! She didn't miss a single shot – what a woman she is!'

Xiao paused for a moment then carried on and said:

'We all thought she would be your stepmother, it saddens me though that your father left us so soon – far too soon.'

Xiao told me that when my father, Shibo and I all left Wanxian, he too became a suspect and knew that he was in danger so had to flee. The Party sent him to Yichang.

Xiao and I sat there drinking one cup after another of jasmine tea; we kept the tea filler busy till the tea lost all flavour and we were just drinking hot water. We chatted for about two hours and before we parted I gave him two copies of the Communist Party *TingJing Newspaper ('Push Forward')*. On his way home, just as he entered his street, two Nationalist spies grabbed him and took him away to the local police station for interrogation. At this point we didn't know whether he had been betrayed or it was just a spot check, but the two spies had definitely been waiting for him on his doorstep.

He was taken inside a secure office within the police station. However, Xiao wasn't too worried except for the fact that the two copies of the Communist newspaper were prime incriminating evidence. Fortunately one of the officers said he needed to buy some cigarettes and the other needed to use the lavatory. After they both left the room, locking him in the office behind them, Xiao quickly seized the opportunity to hide the two newspapers inside a drawer. Apart from the knowledge that he had formerly been a commander in Wanxian, his past was unclear. There was no evidence of him being a Communist, in which case he should have been released. In spite of this, the two men took him to Zhazidong Prison, such was their suspicion of anyone with Communist tendencies. We all knew that the prison conditions were harsh and getting released was very unlikely. During his incarceration he managed to gain the privileges of a trusted prisoner so he was able to support the other inmates and pass messages between the cells.

In the massacre of 27 November 1949, Xiao and two others survived the first round of shooting. He managed to crawl behind the cell door, pull a dead body over himself, smear the blood from the body over his face and pretend to be dead. Then the guards kicked open the door and used their pistols to finish everybody off. As one of the guards walked past Xiao he fired a casual shot, but the bullet just grazed Xiao's neck. When the cells were set on fire, Xiao and the other surviving prisoners, some from the other cells, ran out through a collapsed wall, but they were spotted. The guards opened fire on them once more with machine guns, firing at their backs. They all kept running, running for their lives. Xiao didn't dare to look back but could hear, and feel, the others falling around him as the bullets thudded into their bodies. Through sheer luck, he survived the massacre. He hid for three days till he overheard some people say that Chongqing was liberated. Now here he was, standing right in front of us.

Meixia and Zuoyi

Meixia and Zuoyi in 1945

Meixia is my cousin and when we were children she was like my little shadow.

In 1944 a fire started in the high street of Yunan Town. In its wake my grandmother's house, along with all of the other Lin family properties, was burned to the ground. My grandmother was saved but she escaped with only the clothes on her back. She moved in with her daughter, my Eighth Aunty.

Meixia and my half-sister, Liuqing, ended up with me in Pen County where, at that time, I was running a school. Since then, Meixia has never really left me. She joined in with whatever I was doing and became 'one of us'. She and I are the last survivors of our generation in the family.

The middle of June 1946 brought one of the saddest days of my life. My father died suddenly and it was a shock and terrible blow to all of us. Meixia brought along a young man to help with the funeral and she introduced him to me as her boyfriend, Chen Zuoyi.

Zuoyi was in his mid-twenties. Intelligence and capability shone through his bright, lively eyes. He had been born into a very poor family. He started his working life at the age of eight in a restaurant and, by the time he was thirteen, he was working down a coal mine. He witnessed his best friend injured in an accident underground and, when the pit owner refused to pay for any medical bills, Zuoyi decided to take revenge. He set fire to the owner's warehouse and then ran away, taking his friend with him. The two of them were taken in by some Communists and later became activists themselves. Zuoyi was taught to read, write and use an abacus, which gave him a good foundation to undertake any job that the Party sent him to do. He had roles such as book-keeper, primary school teacher, hospital bursar and small-business manager. During his short Communist career he had already experienced many narrow escapes from the clutches of the Nationalists. After one arrest he was rescued by his comrades, who knocked a hole through the wall of the building where he was being kept for questioning and pulled him out. Another time Zuoyi was released through lack of evidence because he swallowed the documents he had been carrying. Another narrow escape was when he was being chased by the Guomingdan and he ran to the house of a Party member, whose daughter was getting married that day. The father of the bride hid Zuoyi in his daughter's room where she was being helped to dress for the wedding by the women of her family. It was against social acceptability for a man to be in the bride's room, so when the Guomingdan came to search the house, they didn't dare look in the bride's room and Zuoyi remained safe.

Meixia and Zuoyi married in January 1947 and in May 1948 Zuoyi was arrested. He had been betrayed at a rendezvous and identified as a Communist. He was quickly sent to Zhazidong Prison. We all knew that once our people had been sent to that prison, it was more or less a death sentence.

We tried, tried very hard, to rescue him. Even Ninjun risked her life to buy him out, but to no avail.

It was already a bitterly cold winter at the end of 1948. Our long-planned Huaying Mountain uprising failed. The Communists were routed and most of the survivors tried to flee to Chongqing. Meixia was heavily pregnant at that time and I went to pick her up from Huaying Mountain.

I took her to a small kindergarten in the suburbs of Chongqing where I thought she would be inconspicuous as one of the teachers there. In fact, a new face in a small place is more easily noticed and it wasn't long before Meixia heard that people suspected her of being a Communist. She decided to run and had no time to inform me. She grabbed a couple of her things and told the other teachers at the kindergarten that she needed to see a doctor, before making her way into Chongqing.

As she neared the city centre Meixia realised that she was being followed and fear gripped her. She increased her pace, which wasn't easy in her condition, but she couldn't get rid of her 'tail'. She was desperately thinking of where she could go to avoid arrest and keep her unborn child safe when a flashing neon sign caught her attention. She realised she was outside a nightclub which was run by one of our leading members. His cover name was Erge (Second Brother). Without hesitation Meixia entered through a side door and breathlessly told Erge's wife: 'I have a tail.'

Erge's wife needed no further details. She grabbed one of her own cheongsams and helped Meixia into it. Luckily she was a very plump woman so it easily covered Meixia's swollen belly.

'Where do you want to go?' With the luck of having found this momentary safety, Meixia's brain cleared and she thought of Sister Tan. She would know what to do.

'The YWCA at Seven Star Bridge.'

Within seconds, Erge's wife had led Meixia by the hand out the back door. She called the nightclub's own rickshaw driver and sent Meixia on her way.

Sister Tan calmed Meixia down and settled her to rest on a bed. Meixia was exhausted. Then Sister Tan went to a public telephone to call her brother Tan Zhuan, who worked at Chongqing's *The Masses Newspaper*, and asked him to come as quickly as possible. As soon as he saw Meixia he understood what had happened, but as he quickly closed the door behind him he said firmly:

'No, you can't stay here.'

Sister Tan gaped at her brother.

'But look at her. She can't go anywhere.'

Zhuan had learned to be cautious and simply said: 'The longer she stays here then the more danger you will all be in. Even with just you and the two boys living here it is risky, but with Meixia and her baby here too, that's asking for trouble. There is no time to waste.'

Zhuan took Meixia to stay with a colleague for that night and then the next day took her miles away to the house of Mrs Huo in an outlying area of Chongqing. Zhuan pretended that he and Meixia were married to each other and that they were both good friends of Mrs Huo's daughter. He told her that his wife now needed a quiet place to give birth to their baby.

Mrs Huo was old and lived on her own. She didn't know that her daughter was a Communist. Although she wasn't suspicious of Zhuan and Meixia, she didn't want Meixia to give birth inside the house as she said that it was bad luck for a stranger to spill blood in one's house. However, she finally agreed that only Meixia could stay, but she would have to use the woodshed at the back of the house.

Meixia agreed, although there was no door to the shed and the two windows were broken. It was full of dried corn stalks, straw and wood, which were all used as fuel for cooking and heating, and everything was covered in spiders' webs. Mrs Huo brought in a bamboo board and laid it on the floor for a bed, covered it in straw and an old sheet and also gave her a thin quilt. Then she gave her a stool to sit on and a bowl of water. Zhuan then left, saying that he would return the next day. Meixia couldn't describe in words how relieved she was at that moment to have a bit of shelter over her head and not to have to worry about being chased. She tried to block out the icy wind by propping the corn stalks against the windows and filling the space where the door should have been. It didn't make much difference though and the January air still bit into her bones.

That night, all alone, Meixia went into labour. When she managed to get the baby out she found that the cord was wrapped around its neck. She knew that she needed to cut the cord immediately, but there was nothing to use to do the job. Then she remembered the bowl of water and quickly smashed it on the ground. She picked up a jagged piece of pottery and cut the cord, but there wasn't a sound from the baby. By then Meixia was in a panic and screaming for help. Thankfully, Mrs Huo came in and took the baby from Meixia, held it upside down and lightly slapped it on the back, dislodging the block-age in its airway. It was two o'clock in the morning on 13 Jan-uary 1949 and Meixia had given birth to her son in the worst of conditions. Her thoughts turned to her husband, Zuoyi, who had no way of knowing that he was now a father.

Zhuan gave me the news of the birth the next day and so he, Sister Tan and I went to visit her without delay. Sister Tan had gathered many things together to take with us for Meixia, but she wouldn't let us know what they were. Meixia was relieved to see us.

Zhuan said without thinking:

'If only Zuoyi knew that he has a son, he would be over the moon.' Sister Tan glared at Zhuan and we saw that Meixia's eyes were full of tears, but she managed to hold in her emo-tions. I quickly tried to comfort her by saying:

'Don't worry. The war will soon be over. The Liberation Army has already fought through to the Sichuan border. Zuoyi will be out soon.'

The tradition in China when a baby boy is born is for the father to inform his in-laws by giving them an even number of hard-boiled eggs. This signifies that when the boy grows up he will marry and make a pair back home. The eggs must be coloured red with black ink dotted on each of them, which means 'great, happy news and overflowing joy'. However, if a girl is born the father must give out an odd number of eggs without the black ink dot and this means 'not very happy news, little joy'. This tradition is still in use today in some rural areas.

Sister Tan went to Mrs Huo's kitchen and cooked lots of eggs for Meixia and two eggs for each of us. After she washed the baby, she disappeared outside and we soon heard fire crack-ers exploding and saw their flashes of light. This brief celebra-tion lifted everyone's mood. Meixia lay contently on her 'bed' cradling her baby.

I was reminded of when Ninjun had our first baby girl, Binhua. We had nothing in the monastery, but at least we had each
other. Looking at Meixia I felt guilty that I was unable to look
after her any better than this. Her mother, my Second Uncle's
wife, had looked after me as best she could while I was under
Grandmother's roof and I would have liked to offer more to
Meixia now. As it happened at that time, my business of selling
silver on the black market was doing quite well, so I took out a
silver ten-yuan coin and put it into her hand. Meixia smiled at
me and her dimples looked so sweet as she said:

'Don't worry! I am fine. Really. I am in safe hands. You
know what Sister Tan said to me? She said that life is hard on
all of us, but we share – if I share something with you then I
have less to carry!'

Then Meixia choked back her sobs, but was unable to hold
back her tears from streaming down her face. This was the only
time I saw her cry, no matter how hard life became and how
much danger we were in. At that time there was a Russian
novel called *The Rainbow*. It was a most influential book for
us as we all looked to the Russian Revolution for our inspira-
tion. It was the true story of a woman called Elena in the Soviet
Union and it was published in 1941. The Germans arrested her
whilst she was on her way home to give birth to her baby.
They stripped her, raped her and forced her to run backwards
and forwards in the snow. Whenever she fell or slowed down
they jabbed her with their bayonets. Her blood melted and
stained the snow. They kept her captive until she gave birth,
but they then sunk their bayonets into the baby. The book told
how Elena never betrayed her comrades and never cried.

The Rainbow was Meixia's favourite book. She claimed that
Elena was 'food for her spirit' and said:

'I haven't suffered at all compared to Elena. Revolution
makes us pay in blood and lives. The sooner we win over Chi-

ang Kai-shek the sooner our lives will be better. Then our children won't have to suffer anything at all.' Meixia held up her baby, full of hope.

Mrs Huo happily allowed Sister Tan to prepare a meal for all of us in her house and helped her too. We raised our bowls and said 'cheers' to the newborn baby and 'victory belongs to us, down with Chiang Kai-shek'.

Our lives were never safe. A couple of weeks later Zhuan came to tell me that Mrs Huo's house was probably being watched. It may have been a coincidence, but the mistress of a Nationalist spy moved in next door to Mrs Huo. We couldn't take any chances, so we had to move Meixia. We thought it would be better to move Sister Tan too. Meixia moved in with us in Chongqing, so that Ninjun could help to look after the baby. Sister Tan and her two boys moved to a primary school, also in Chongqing.

On 31 November 1949, just days after the Nationalist massacres of prisoners at the Zhazidong Prison, the Communist Liberation Army had fought their way through to Chongqing and liberated the city. When we went to the prison in the hope of identifying the bodies, Meixia, carrying her ten-month-old son, came along too, desperate for news about Zuoyi. None of the bodies were identifiable, but a few of the lucky survivors were there and one of them gave us his account:

'When the shooting started through our cell window Zuoyi was under one of the beds and I was behind the door. In that first round of machine-gun fire, neither of us were injured, but he was too quick in asking me if I was alright and the soldiers heard his voice and realised that some of us were still alive. So they opened the door and fired on us individually with their handguns. Zuoyi was shot in the leg, but he could see that I still hadn't been hit so he decided to save me by giving me time to run. He knew he couldn't run himself. He stood up in front of the soldiers and taunted them by saying that they were stupid for only managing to shoot him in the leg at such close range. He told them to try again. His final words were: "Long live Communism". Then he was shot in the head several times and he fell on top of the other bodies. He was right there'.

Our tears were pouring out. We all cried for our Zuoyi – a brave young man who had vowed to live with dignity and died for his beliefs. He had been turned to charcoal three days before our liberation and victory. He never saw his son.

Meixia had sunk to her knees and was sobbing. Shibo and Sister Tan encircled her and the baby in their arms. It was a circle of sadness. I looked at the three women, my loved ones, who had all lost their husbands for our beliefs. There were women all over the country like them – what a price to pay. My heart was aching with pain. My comrades, my people – we will remember you forever.

Wu Changwen

Wu Changwen in 1961

Wu Changwen was a good friend of my father's and became a lifelong friend of mine.

He was tall and thin, which earned him the nickname of 'Bamboo Pole'. He was unusual looking in that he had a very long, narrow face and a long, thin nose and he was often mistaken for a foreigner. After he graduated from Shanghai Art College in 1924, he got a job as a correspondent and art editor for the *Communist Youth League Magazine*. He became a Communist in 1927.

In 1932, The Youth League sent Wu and two of his colleagues to JiangXi Province to collect funding. On the way back they were stopped and questioned by the Guomingdan. Wu's two colleagues were revealed as being Communists and shot on the spot. Wu, however, pretended to be a foreign missionary and spoke a few words of English to the soldiers at the checkpoint. He was wearing a traditional gown which was similar to those that the foreign missionaries wore and, luckily for him, the soldiers believed him and let him through. In this guise he managed to get through all the subsequent checkpoints that had sprung up on the roads and return to Shanghai safely.

Then at the end of July 1933, the Youth League sent him to work at the Honghu Lake District Youth League in Hubei Province. Honghu Lake District was a well-known major Communist base and whilst Wu was there, the Guomingdan encircled the area and bombarded it heavily. As the Guomingdan tightened their grip and got closer to them, Wu and his colleagues were left with no other option than to lead the Children's Corps in a withdrawal to the lake. Some of the children were already injured and they didn't stand much chance as they fled to take cover amongst the reeds at the water's edge. The Guomingdan were hot on their heels and mercilessly and indiscriminately gunned down the children. Wu described how there were so many bodies in the lake the water turned red and he could smell the blood of the children in the air. The Guom-

310

ingdan remained in the area for four days and three nights hunting for survivors. The surviving adults each took a group of children to try and lead them away to safety. In the end Wu was carrying two of the youngest, wading through the water in deep, sticky mud. Every time he spotted the soldiers, he submerged himself in the water amongst the reeds and, using a hollow reed to breathe through, he held up the children on their backs, with their noses and mouths just above the surface, as they pretended to be dead. Over that four-day period, sometimes he had to remain beneath the surface of the water for hours at a time. Thankfully, Wu and those two children were rescued by some fishermen. They wouldn't have lasted much longer as, in addition to suffering from exposure, their skin was peeling off.

Together with three other colleagues who survived the massacre, Wu decided to make his way back to Shanghai, which was about six hundred miles away as the crow flies. One of those colleagues was a girl who was still a student and with whom Wu was in love. Although the main attack was over, the Guomingdan were still searching for any remaining Communists. This meant that they couldn't risk taking any form of transport and had to avoid the main roads by only using small paths and trails. One day, they came to a junction leading to a small town and had to make the choice whether to go into the town in the hope of finding something to eat, and so risk meeting with a checkpoint, or to skirt around the town and stay hungry. By having to stick to the small trails, they didn't have many opportunities to obtain food. By this time they were all in very poor health, their clothes and shoes were in tatters and they were down to their last coins. They were all utterly exhausted and were unable to make a decision as to what to do for the best.

They became aware of a little girl, about eight years of age, kneeling down on all fours at the side of the road ahead with some twisted stems of straw on her back. They all knew that the straw on her back meant that she was offering herself for sale. It was impossible to know whether she was an orphan or whether her family had put her there; either way it was a bleak scene. Then, without a word, the young woman in their group detached herself from them, went and knelt down next to the little girl and tucked some straw into her own collar. In no time at all a few men gathered around her and started negotiating a price. In the end she walked back to her friends and put a sum of money into Wu's hands. Still without saying anything she then turned back and followed one of the men. Wu was stupefied and remained motionless for a moment until he dropped the money and fell to the ground. When he regained consciousness he couldn't believe that he had made no move to stop her. He had allowed the girl he loved to sacrifice herself for them.

The money, however, saved Wu and his other two colleagues from starvation and was enough to get them back to Shanghai. Once there, Wu had to be hospitalised. He was suffering psychologically as well as physically. After he was discharged, he remained very weak and in poor health, so the Party decided to send him to his Big Sister in Wanxian to recuperate. This is where I met him.

Years later Wu's wife told me that he had finally traced the girl and found out that, after the Liberation, she had gone to Chongqing and became a Buddhist nun. Wu went to visit her at the temple, which was on the north side of the Yangtze River. His wife accompanied him, but waited outside. When he came out he never said a word about it to his wife and she never even learned the girl's name. Wu never went back to the temple again, but would often go down to the river to a spot from where he could see the temple. I can only imagine the desolation in Wu's heart.

Wu Changwen was a true comrade and had loyally given his whole life to the Communist Party. However, after the Liberation, he was accused of corrupt conduct. He was sacked from his job as head of the government Supplies Department in Chongqing City Hall. His Party membership was revoked and he was sent to a labour camp to be 'reformed'. His wife was forced to resign from her job in the Bureau of Civil Administration and then could only get a low-paid job in a sweatshop. Wu was released from the labour camp after two years, but he went home looking like a walking skeleton. His wife and children cried their hearts out for him. In time he was given a position as librarian at the opera house. He kept a low profile and remained reasonably content with a simple life. In the late 1970s, after the Cultural Revolution, I suggested that he should try to get his Party membership reinstated. He told me that after all that he had gone through, he was too disheartened to be bothered and only wished to live out the rest of his life in peace. However, I felt that I couldn't let this situation be left as it was and that having his Party membership back would vindicate him. Reinstating his membership from 1927, though, proved to be such a lengthy process that I stood as his guarantor to reintroduce him to the Communist Party instead.

For years he and his family had been living in a room measuring ten square metres. After his reinstatement to the Party, he had to wait for two years to be given a flat with forty square metres of floor space. Sadly, he didn't enjoy this for very long as he died, at the age of ninety, one month after moving in.

Dexian and her Children

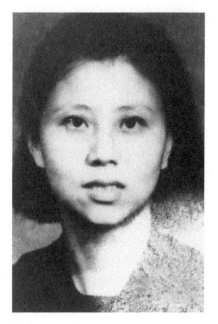

Dexian

After the Communist Liberation Army occupied Chongqing,
I led my family and a few other comrades and occupied the

Nationalist town hall in Peace Avenue in the centre of the city. This was the time we had all been waiting for: Chiang Kai-shek had finally lost control of China. I was so busy at the Escape Centre that my feet hardly touched the ground.

One morning we received a call to say that someone had turned up at the airport who had recently escaped from Zhazidong Prison and could we come and pick them up. I left the office immediately to find transport. I saw a man sitting in a jeep nearby and ran over to him and asked him to take me to the airport to pick up a survivor from the massacre. That's all I needed to say for him to tell me to get in. He put his foot on the accelerator and kept it there, so we covered the twenty miles to the airport in no time at all.

The airport was firmly under the control of our Communist soldiers. They were everywhere in their dark green uniforms and their caps with a red star. I was proud to see them there and proud to see the red flag with five yellow stars fluttering in the wind. We drove around without knowing where to find our escaped comrade, but then one of the soldiers said that a woman comrade with a child was in the headquarters office. I certainly hadn't been expecting to collect a woman and child.

I ran into the office and saw a woman wearing a very muddy, faded blue winter cheongsam sitting on the bench with her eyes closed and her head propped up against the wall. Exhaustion was etched into her face. Above her hung a portrait of Chairman Mao. Her small child was next to her, fast asleep, wrapped in a military coat. At the sound of my entry, she jumped and she protected her child with her own body immediately. When she turned round to look at me her eyes were wide with fright. I caught my breath because I recognised her, but before I could say anything she had run over to me with a loud cry and held on to me. Her name was Dexian.

I had last seen Dexian in 1938 in Yunyang, where she was a

315

student at Yunyang Girls' College. I was twenty-one years old and had already become a Communist – the Party had sent me back there to work at their branch committee. I was responsible for youth and propaganda activities and the Party also got me a position at the Nationalist Education Department. I regularly wrote articles for various newspapers. Dexian was clever – she was also tall and very attractive and many people told me that we would make a good couple.

The Yunyang Girls' College was set up in a monastery and the girls' dormitories were in a small building next to the Boys' College. Rules were strict and the girls weren't allowed out in the evening. However, Dexian and her three room-mates were radical activists, as were some of the boys, and they liked to meet to discuss politics. On several nights per week the girls would secure a rope, climb down from their dormitory window and sneak over to one of the boys' dormitories. One of the boys, named Zeng, used to read out the news from the Communist headquarters magazine to them all. To hide the girls, Zeng pushed one of the beds to the rear door and rigged up a curtain around it so the four girls had an escape route if one of the staff came in through the main door. However, it was the matron from the Girls' College who found them missing one night and the girls got into a lot of trouble.

Dexian and her room-mates hated their matron, who was a Nationalist, and decided to take revenge on her for punishing them. They thought up a very unpleasant prank to play on her. Because toilet facilities were in an outhouse by the side of the building, each dormitory had a communal wooden chamber pot for use overnight. Late one night when they heard the matron walking up the stairs, they carried their full chamber pot to the top of the stairs and tipped the contents of it over the bannister. Their aim was accurate and the unfortunate matron was soaked in urine. She was utterly horrified and humiliated to such an extent that she pulled off her gold ring and swallowed it, crying that she hoped it would kill her. It soon became a scandal in Yunyang because, after Dexian told me about the incident, I wrote an article about it in the *Yunyang Daily*. Having a wicked sense of humour, I also made a joke out of it, saying that two men were found scavenging in the Girls' College cesspit because they had heard that one of the teachers had swallowed a gold ring but hadn't died, and so they wanted to retrieve the ring.

Dexian and her friends hadn't realised that their prank would have such consequences and they regretted their actions. They were even more upset that I had written about it in a newspaper. Dexian came to me and asked me why I wrote about it in the first place and, secondly, why in that way. She was earnest and serious and I'm afraid that I laughed at her and told her that she was a 'silly little girl' and that I was just trying to lighten the whole incident by putting a joke in at the end. Dexian just looked at me darkly and said that I was an arrogant show-off and lacking in compassion. She was furious with me and stayed that way. Even when, later, I offered to stand as her guarantor to introduce her to the Party, she refused. Soon after that I had to leave Yunyang and I never saw Dexian again, but I did hear about her from time to time.

I knew that she had become a Communist and had married Zeng from the Boys' College. I knew that they had left Yunyang and then had two sons. Then I heard that Zeng had been arrested and killed and that his betrayers had led the Guomingdan to Dexian at their home. She and her two children were arrested at the beginning of 1949.

The intervening years since we had seen each other seemed to have passed as quickly as a click of the fingers. I never imagined that I would meet her again and especially under such circumstances.

Dexian was holding on to me as if she were scared that I would disappear. I held on to her tightly too and my heart ached and my eyes filled with tears for what she had been through. Her loud crying woke up the child, who burst out crying at not finding his mother still next to him. I moved quickly to pick him up and suddenly remembered that there should have been two of them:

'But you have two sons, don't you? Where is the other one?'

'Escaped – we all escaped! Mr Zhou was carrying Bo – he ran downhill, but I panicked and ran uphill carrying Ke. We missed each other.'

It was a relief to hear that the other boy had survived the massacre at least. I carried Ke with one arm and held onto Dexian's hand as I led her towards the jeep:

'Let's go – you are safe now. Tell me what happened.'

'From October, the Nationalists started to execute prisoners. We all had to prepare ourselves to sacrifice our last drop of blood for our Communist Party – there didn't seem to be any hope of survival left. The people who brought around the food to the cells told us: "Eat more! There isn't many days' food left." Then around the third week in November, I heard some of the jailers whispering outside my cell: "Three big pits should be enough, shouldn't it?" Every sign pointed to the fact that our enemy intended brutality – before their own deaths, they wanted to wipe us out.

'On the afternoon of 27 November I noticed that all the jailers were fully armed – with handguns on their fronts and rifles on their backs – and there were many new faces amongst them too. I knew it was our time then. Two of the prisoners, General Huang and Li, were taken out of their cells and within ten minutes we heard the shots. Then two more, three more, four more were taken out – they all passed my cell. I looked each one in the eyes through that small window and I shook hands with them – there was no need for words. Each hand I touched was warm and steady. They sang and shouted: "Long live Communism – the victory belongs to us.'"

Dexian was sobbing and had to stop for a few minutes before she could carry on:

'There was one young couple with two children – they were holding on to each other, encircling the children. The wife was holding on tightly to the baby and pleading with the jailer: "We will take all of your bullets – just spare the children – let them live – *please*." But the jailer laughed and said: "Your little ones will soon grow up to be Communists, just like you, and then there will be two more to come back and fight us. There's no point in just killing the grass – we need to clean you from the roots."'

Dexian couldn't say anything else at all. It wasn't until the next day that she managed to tell me the rest of her story. She said that the killing carried on till the middle of the night. All Dexian could do was hold her children tightly – one was four years old and the other was two – and wait for her name to be called. Then, in the dark, her cell door opened slowly and quietly and a man came in. It was Mr Zhou and he picked up her older son and put him on his back and whispered to her: 'Quick, let's run – once we get out of the gate, we must run downhill because there are searchlights up the hill.' Dexian didn't stop to think, but just followed him. As soon as they got out of the gate, however, the searchlights picked them out and she heard gunfire behind them. In a blind panic she just ran, carrying Ke, and ended up going up the hill rather than following Mr Zhou. She didn't know how long she carried on running or in which direction she was going, but she ended up at the house of a peasant who took them in. She stayed hiding there for about two days until the peasant told her that there were Liberation Army soldiers everywhere and she realised that

Chongqing must have been liberated. She had no idea how she ended up at the airport. She also wasn't aware that the soldiers there had informed the Escape Centre that she needed help, so she couldn't believe her eyes when she saw me.

The massacre on 27 November 1949 claimed 207 of our people. Nineteen people escaped, including Dexian's two children. I had led the team to bury the dead at Zhazidong Prison and, although we found it impossible to identify anyone because the bodies had been burnt, we did find the remains of what looked like a family group clinging to each other. One child's arms were tightly around the mother's neck, but both of the child's legs had been blown off. We wrapped them together in white cloth and put them into one coffin.

A couple of days later, Mr Zhou turned up at the Escape Centre with Dexian's older boy, Bo. It was a very happy reunion between mother and child.

Part 2:
Dark Night Falling
(1950–1980)

At the time of the Liberation I was in my early thirties and full of energy and enthusiasm. I remember promising the spirits of all our fallen heroes that they could rest in peace, because we were now going to build up the country in the manner we all fought for and dreamed of. But, my God in Heaven, as I let the events of the 8,000 days and nights of the Revolution flow behind my eyes, it doesn't end in a glorious liberation, it only ends in total frustration.

In our struggle during the Revolution, we had a clear goal and knew who our enemies were: the warlords, the Guomingdan and the Japanese. However, after Liberation and the establishment of the New China, we had to endure countless political movements, which turned us all upside down and inside out. It seemed to start fairly quietly and, as usual, I never questioned my loyalty and obedience to the Party. Then things turned around so fast and it is hard to put into words how much trouble, confusion and fear were unleashed. I was just one of millions of Chinese people who fell victim to unjustified, false accusations and their consequences. Our days were spent somewhere between the land of the living and the world of ghosts, suffering endless humiliation and terrified, day and night, of what might happen next.

We have a saying: 'A moment in time is as precious as an inch of gold.' But how do you measure twenty years of a man's life when that life has been rendered useless? At least I survived, but my tears fall and my heart aches when I think of my dear loved ones and friends who didn't. Thoughts of those years bring lingering horror and distress, which haunt me even today.

Fought through adversity
Welcomed the new life
Thought peace had come forever
Instead, dark nightmares arrived.
Is this right, is that wrong
Is it bad, is it good
All hard to classify
Is it a man or is it a ghost, no one can tell.
To live, to die, is all up to The Slaughterer.
Perpetual conflict, daily struggle
Do I fight for you to die or me to survive?
Too many mothers-in-law, various temple gates
Kowtow to this one, salute to the other.
Speak lies, hide guilt
Tell the truth you will be tackled
Why stir up trouble
Be deaf, be dumb and you may be safe.

After Liberation, all official positions were being reassigned throughout the whole country and it seemed as if half the population was on the move. The highest tier of positions, such as governorships and central government posts, went to military officers. The next tier, such as ministers of departments, went to those who had joined the Red Army on its sweep down through the country, many of whom were barely educated. It was very evident that all of us who had served as underground Communists weren't being given any positions higher than vice-minister of any department. Questions were asked about this division at the time, but nobody could give any answers. It wasn't until thirty years later that the secret policy, which had been decreed by the Central Committee, called 'Sixteen Words Policy' came to light. This policy towards the underground Communists read: 'Reduce their rank, control their use, settle them locally, gradually eliminate them.' Finally, we came to understand why we had been sidelined and treated so unjustly, but it was a shock to discover this treachery and deception. Once I found out, the only words I could find were 'fuck their mothers', and a friend responded with 'fuck their mothers' fuckers'. No words, though, can describe our feelings of betrayal at the most basic level. This policy was the root cause of the ensuing nightmare – the struggle between the proletariat class and the 'exploiting' classes. We, the underground Communists, were all educated people and mostly born into rich families and, unbeknown to us at first, were already being turned into 'the enemy'.

After Liberation

Once we had settled most of the people who had come to the Escape Centre, I was given another job as manager of the Municipal Party Committee staff hostel. This had been set up to house ex-army officers who were waiting to be assigned new positions. My job was to see to the day-to-day running of the hostel as well as help the officers' transition to the next phase of their lives. It was the easiest job I had ever had assigned to me, but I accepted it and started by recruiting my own staff – mainly people from the Escape Centre whom I knew and trusted.

The Party was doing its best to carry out its promise to give jobs and housing to all members. All our basic day-to-day needs were met where food, clothing and toiletries were concerned. Once or twice a month all we needed to do was visit the Supply Department to collect whatever item we needed and sign for it. After several months, I noticed that I was never given the 'hygiene fee' and queried it, thinking that there must have been a mistake. However, the supplies assistant curtly told me: 'No, you can't have it'.

'Why not?' I said.

'Because you don't qualify for it.'

'But it's on the list, so why are other people qualified to get it and not me? This is the New China – we are all equal now. I want to speak to your manager.'

'I am willing to take you to speak to the governor himself, but you still won't qualify to receive the hygiene fee.' Then she turned her back on me and refused to say more.

That evening I told Ninjun about it, saying how unfair it seemed to be. She burst out laughing and swiped me lightly on the nose.

'You are such a foolish man. The hygiene fee is a subsidy for women to buy sanitary towels for their monthly period! Where is your common sense?'

After that I was teased mercilessly by my colleagues, who would ask me whether or not I had collected my monthly hygiene fee!

Everybody's meals were provided in various canteens; I would eat at the middle managers' canteen. In addition, I was given four silver yuan per month to spend how I liked. Housing was more difficult though – accommodation was mainly provided in single-sex hostels and married couples' accommodation was in short supply. My son Mingtao boarded at the committee nursery, but at least he was under the care of Sister Tan. Ninjun's pay and conditions were in line with mine in her job as an entertainments officer.

Ballroom dancing had become fashionable and Ninjun was an expert at it. Her skill on the dance floor, combined with her irrepressible, bubbly character, put her in much demand as a dance partner for the important officials from Beijing, or foreign diplomats, at the weekend activities. I had to content myself with just being in demand for the sporting activities, because Ninjun gave up on me where ballroom dancing was concerned. I wanted to be able to partner her on the dance floor myself, but I was always stepping on her toes or pulling her in the wrong direction!

The Party Committee selected Ninjun to go to the South West Art College to study. This was the top art college at the time and Ninjun had been over the moon to have the chance to continue with the performing arts. However, only two months into the course, Ninjun found out she was pregnant. Her morning sickness was so bad that she had to leave the college and her disappointment overwhelmed her for a while. She was then given a job in the Propaganda Department as entertainments officer and theatre inspector for Chongqing and the surrounding area. After Liberation, the main requirement for all theatre and opera performances was praise for the Communist Party.

Meanwhile my job expanded to include checking every last detail for all Party meetings, whether they were large or small, external or internal. I would also have to greet the important Central Party leaders, such as General He Long, Deng Xiaoping and Chen Yi, wearing full army uniform.

Midway through 1950, the Zhengfeng ('Rectification') Movement was introduced. We were ordered to examine and 'dust off', cleanse, rectify our thoughts and actions. Daily meetings were held where we had to question and criticise ourselves and each other and the goal was to 'cure and save the people'. However, all the retired army officers who now had higher positions with good pay and conditions turned their thoughts to how they might manage to change their old, country wives for new, pretty, younger, city wives. They felt they deserved to start enjoying their lives at last and they said in justification that, now the dynasty had changed, it was also time to change their wives. Some of them went back to their villages to divorce their current wives before they married again; some married again first and then went home to divorce the country wife; and some kept two wives. This raised problems for the Party, which wanted to keep a high moral standard in the New China. At the same time though, Chairman Mao had sent a message to the people to say that in order to build up our new country we needed more hands for construction. He said we should learn from the Russian 'heroine mothers' and have more children and, in return, we would receive benefits from the government for each child.

Shibo in 1951

Shibo was the last one of us to leave the Escape Centre. She remained until it was no longer needed and then closed it down. She was then sent on a short Party member training course – it was from here that the story of her exploits spread further. At that time, China worshipped its heroes and soon the name Double Gun Woman eclipsed her real name. To honour her, she was then offered the governorship of Yuechi, her home town. However, because Ninjun, Mingtao and I were in Chongqing, Shibo opted to stay close to us and instead accepted the much lower post of vice-minister in the Production Department of the Women's Federation of Chongqing. The Minister of the Production Department was an inexperienced woman of twenty-seven years of age.

Shibo earned a good salary of 106 yuan – one yuan could buy fifty eggs at that time. However, she didn't spend anything on herself, as usual, but gave it away to anyone who needed it. Whenever Ninjun and I tried to visit her we hardly ever found her at her accommodation, because she immediately threw herself into tasks over and above her duties.

Using her own initiative, the first thing she did was obtain five sewing machines and organise a group of women into making basic clothing items for sale on the open market. These women were all subsisting on the 'Martyrdom Family Allowance', which was very small, so all the money they made went directly to them and their families to help raise their standard of living. She told the women that whilst they all possessed a pair of hands, why wait for the government to provide everything?

Shibo was in her fifties by this time and we still marvelled at her energy levels, but she told Ninjun:

'Your father fought for this day [Liberation] to come, but didn't survive to see it, neither did so many of our guerrilla force from the Huaying Mountains. Well, I did manage to wait long enough – it is worth it. Hard work isn't going to kill me, but if it does, I will die happy!'

Soon this sewing group developed into a proper enterprise and was turning out clothing and duvets for the troops who were being sent to fight in the anti-American Korean Peninsula War and for those sent to Tibet.

In addition, Shibo was constantly being approached by individuals needing a job or a helping hand. She did her best to assist everyone, keeping in mind how much help she herself had been given over the years, and in her own words:

'Never break the bridge after you have crossed it and always be grateful for everything.'

One of the long-held plans and dreams shared by Shibo and Yubi, her husband, had been to set up a Soviet-style collective farm in the Huaying region. So when a woman came to Shibo to complain that she had not been paid for six months for working on the Jianghua Farm just outside Chongqing, Shibo went to investigate the reasons why the farm was obviously failing. The farm owner had heard rumours about the Land Reform Movement and he believed that the government was soon going to confiscate his land, so he felt that there was no point in continuing to farm it. Seeing that many people were going to lose their jobs and that food production was a priority for everyone's survival, Shibo proposed that the farm should be taken over and run by the Women's Federation. The young minister of the Production Department didn't have much to say about it except to warn Shibo:

'Be careful – if the farm is not successful, it will damage the name of the Women's Federation.'

In order to beat the inevitable loss of his land, the farmer 'willingly' donated his land to the Women's Federation. Despite doing this, however, later on he didn't escape the class struggles and was still classified as being from the 'exploiting classes'. Shibo immediately threw herself into planning, raising funds, selecting key workers, drawing up business plans and much more. She identified where the workers' accommodation, the nursery, the school and the canning and packing factory should be built. The farm was to be run on the lines of pure communalism and she proudly named it 'Huaying's Spring'.

In March 1951 Ninjun gave birth to a baby girl. We named her Kangmei, which means 'Anti-America'. It was during the period of China's fervent support of North Korea in the Korean Peninsula War and many people gave patriotic names to their children. It was only shortly before the birth of Kangmei that we were given married couples' accommodation, but it enabled us to hire a girl to look after both Mingtao and the baby at home and for Ninjun to get back to work.

In the summer of 1951, I was transferred to the United Front Department. My first job, under the banner of the Land Reform Movement, was to take some dignitaries from Beijing down to the south of Sichuan to witness land reform put into action. The goal of the Land Reform Movement was to destroy the exploiting classes and feudalism, categorise the different classes, redistribute land and put communalism into practice. These dignitaries were all from rich families and the purpose of this trip was to re-educate them. We had to make them confess that people like themselves had always exploited the poor. We had to make them cleanse their minds, so that they themselves would be worthy of being part of the proletarian class. At the same time, I had strict orders to protect them from the peasants who harboured so much resentment against the rich. They had to be treated like honoured guests and given whatever they wanted. For instance, one of them was a very heavy smoker and only wanted the best brand of cigarettes called 'China' and I had to send someone to walk to the nearest town, over twenty miles away, to buy them for him. These dignitaries were controversial and they needed armed militia to keep them safe.

331

One of them was particularly unpleasant – Tian, a former warlord – but he was still considered useful to the Party in Beijing. He was in his late fifties and very fat. He couldn't walk very far and so I had to persuade two people to carry him in a sedan chair. Eventually I convinced two radical peasants to do it, but one day they took the opportunity to play a trick on Tian. When nobody was following them they carried him onto the ridge between two rice paddies, pretended to slip and tossed him into the water. Tian limped back to the house supported by a bamboo pole and covered in mud. He shook his head at me and said that he wasn't going anywhere without me by his side, but actually he then refused to leave the house at all.

The south of Sichuan was remote, rural and still entrenched in feudalism, as well as being a pocket of opposition against the Liberation Army. The peasants in this region were exceedingly poor and still at the mercy of powerful, harsh landowners, bandits and warlords. As a form of punishment the peasants were regularly imprisoned, but this was seen as a light punishment and beatings resulting in broken bones and death were common, as was brutal rape. When my team turned up in the area, we were welcomed by the local peasants, who were more than ready to expose the landowners' wrongdoings.

We started by demanding that all landlords and landowners should present their account books for our inspection. We then cleared all the peasants' debts and in many cases gave them refunds. We carried on by burning all the landlords' account books in front of their eyes, thus permanently erasing the record of all their debtors.

There was one landowner whom the locals particularly suffered under. We received more complaints against him than any other landowner in the area. However, we were having a hard time proving anything against him and couldn't make him confess to any wrongdoing at all. I had to change strategy, so I chose two women from my team to spend time with his third concubine and gain her confidence. She told them that, when her husband realised that the Communists would confiscate everything from him, he had buried a coffin containing his riches deep in the forest. When we dug up the coffin we found twenty-four shotguns, fifty kilos of opium, twenty bars of gold, three thousand silver coins and lots of expensive jewellery.

Our team had been very productive overall. I decided to organise an exhibition of our finds to show the masses that the Communist Party could make a difference to their lives and would equalise the difference between rich and poor. However, before I could do so, I was recalled to Chongqing.

From then on, my life turned upside down.

The Three Anti-Movements

When the Communist Party officially gained power on 1 October 1949, many people thought the time had come to start basking in the glory and enjoying themselves. Consequently, corruption and the abuse of power by officials had become widespread. Once the Three Anti-Movements – Anti-Corruption, Anti-Wastefulness and Anti-Bureaucracy – were announced, every official throughout the country had to study 'The Guidance'.

Then in February 1952 there was a public trial, held in the High Court, and seven officials were found guilty of corruption. Two of them, Zhang Zishan, who was the first Commissioner sent to Tianjin, and Liu Qingshang, who was the Party Secretary in Tianjin, had both fought alongside Mao. They had also demonstrated bravery when they had been arrested by the Guomingdan and had made many important contributions to the Liberation. However, once they were in power in Tianjin, they became corrupt and dictatorial and embezzled many millions of yuan. They were both sentenced to death. The mayor of Tianjin pleaded with Chairman Mao to spare their lives, but he refused and said that because they held high positions, they should be made examples of. In this way it would stop twenty, or perhaps two hundred, or even twenty thousand officials from being corrupt in the future. On 10 February 1952 Zhang and Liu were executed by firing squad. Those two gunshots severely shocked the country and made everybody realise that Chairman Mao was serious about stopping corruption.

I wholeheartedly agreed with the campaign at the outset, as, like my father before me, I couldn't tolerate corruption in any form. However, within months, the Central Committee could see that accusations within the Three Anti-Movements were out of control. People were taking 'The Guidance' too far and also using the movement for false accusations, either out of revenge or for personal advancement. False accusations were costing people their lives and livelihoods. Many of the lives lost were through suicide. By October 1952, the Anti-Movements were brought to a close. However, before they ended I was accused of theft and corruption myself.

The day I received my recall to Chongqing I just assumed that I was to be given another job, so I travelled back in a happy frame of mind. When I reached the gate of the United Front Department though, I was met with a sullen and icy stare from the gatekeeper. I had found this man his job and he was normally very happy to see me, so I was a little puzzled by his attitude, but decided not to say anything. Then Secretary Wang stopped me and ushered me into his office.

He had a very serious look on his face and said in a cold voice: 'I called you back urgently because you need to join the current Three Anti-Movements Study Course. Hopefully, you will come to better understand our Party's policy and will earnestly admit your problem.'

My stomach lurched. I knew then that this was serious, but I didn't understand why. Wang was from my home town, Yunyang, and I had been his guarantor when he was admitted into the Communist Party in 1939. I thought we were friends. Even though he was the United Front Department Secretary, I felt he shouldn't be speaking to me in such a manner.

I wasn't happy about it and said to him: 'Hah! We grew up together and during the Liberation we fought side by side – you know what kind of person I am, so there is no need to play the bureaucrat with me.'

Wang was even more solemn and cold and said: 'I am talking to you as a representative of the Party organisation. I hope you calm down.'

There was no way I could accept his insult. During my whole career I had been a dedicated Communist and always managed to earn the Party's praise, even though I had made a few mistakes along the way. I felt it wasn't Wang's place to speak to me in this manner. I lost my composure and shouted at him:

'Don't you dare try and pressure me in the name of the Party – I have no guilty conscience. I have no fear if a ghost knocks on my door in the middle of the night.' I picked up my bag and stormed off.

The door to my quarters was locked, so I went back to the gatekeeper to find out where Ninjun was. The gatekeeper refused to answer my question, but just handed me the key without looking at me.

When I opened the door I found the room was airless, the floor was dirty and the bed was messy; the place looked as if it had been ransacked. The worst thing was that there was no sign of Ninjun and the children; it felt lifeless. I started to feel nervous and stood rooted to the spot with a blank mind. I jumped when Secretary Wang spoke behind me:

'Ninjun and Chen Lianshi (Shibo) are both undergoing a course – they cannot come out – they cannot meet anyone. You will be the same – you cannot go to see them. You need to calm down and give good thought to your own problems

– write a confession. This is the Party's decision – you must obey.' Then he left.

As I sat down on the unmade bed, dust rose and danced in the air around me. I couldn't think straight. What was happening and why? Where was Ninjun? All this must surely be a mistake. It was nonsensical.

A while later the Minister of the United Front Department, Yang, walked into my room with a warm greeting. He asked about how the Land Reform Movement was progressing down south and then said:

'We all have to join in with the Three Anti-Movements – everyone, throughout the whole country. We have to search ourselves and admit if we have done anything corrupt, wasted government resources or are overly bureaucratic. At the same time we can expose others if we think they have done something wrong. This is very like the Rectify Movement, but this time, instead of just brushing off the dust from our faces, this movement requires us to have a full body wash, examine our attitudes and improve our knowledge in order to work better in the future for our country. Rest for a couple of days and then join in with the course.'

Although Minister Yang's tone and attitude were friendly, I didn't trust his words: they belied an abnormal situation, otherwise why wasn't Ninjun allowed home and why wasn't I allowed to see her? There was more to it. I felt I was being segregated, quarantined and investigated, although I really couldn't think of any reason for it.

Next day the 'course' started. Secretary Wang chaired the meeting and Minister Yang brought in several people. Wang stood up and said:

'Today's meeting is a "confess and expose" meeting. Everything needs to come into the light – if anyone has a problem, they need to clear it up. They need to take the initiative and confess, then ask for forgiveness.'

The atmosphere in the room was tense. People looked around at each other in silence. We all remained like that for a full, uncomfortable five minutes and then a man jumped up and pointed his finger at me:

'Lin Xiangbei! Why are you so quiet? Come on – confess your corruption.'

Then I realised that this meeting was all about me. I replied confidently, however:

'I have not been dishonest in any way whatsoever. Exactly what are you accusing me of and where is your proof? I want to hear it.'

Then Wang stood up again and in a harsh voice said:

'Don't think you can get away – we have cast-iron proof of your criminal actions.'

I felt my anger rise. At first I hadn't felt much because my accuser was a stranger to me, and I to him, but Wang and I had known each other for years and I felt wronged by him. I couldn't understand why he should accuse me of anything as he surely knew what kind of person I was. Wang stabbed his finger in the air in my direction:

'Let me tell you what you did. On the second day of Liberation you stole two truckloads of gold bars. Now confess – where did you hide the gold?'

I was stunned. I had absolutely no idea how such a ludicrous accusation could be aimed at me. Wang looked very pleased with himself and continued:

'Before Liberation the Guomingdan were in a hurry to escape. They left silver yuan lying around all over the place in their headquarters. You didn't pick up the coins, but you took the gold bars. Don't try and deny it – you can't hide a crime such as this.'

My fury boiled over and I slapped the flat of my hand on the table and jumped up:

'You are a bloody liar! Stop this absurd attack on me. Bring on your evidence.'

Wang and I ended up face to face, quarrelling fiercely. We were pulled apart before my fists landed on him. The meeting could not continue and Minister Yang said to me:

'Our Party policy is to speak the truth – we would not deliberately wrong anyone – but at the same time we won't let off a criminal. You may be guilty, or you may be innocent – it will become clear. There is no point in denying the truth. Comrade Lin Xiangbei, go away and think carefully about the whole matter. The meeting is dismissed.'

Yang came to me afterwards and said:

'Your attitude today was not good – that sort of behaviour will work against you. There is no need to be so fierce with your own comrades.'

I got angry all over again and said: 'Who do you think I am? You should know me and also know what I am or am not capable of. How can I accept this preposterous accusation? Where did it come from?'

'There are rumours. Someone exposed you. On the second day of the liberation of Chongqing you went to the Guomingdan's Department of Defence and drove away with two trucks full of goods, including gold bars. The Party Civic Committee cannot ignore this and have asked me to set up a special team to investigate the matter.'

My eyes almost popped out of my head. I sighed. The truth of the matter was that when I received the mission to set up the Escape Centre to help the escapees from the prisons, as well as those who were searching for their link back to the Party organisation, it was just a verbal request. I had to start from scratch: there was no office, no workers, no supplies and, of course, no money. I surrounded myself with family and friends to help me, found an empty building as our office and we tried our best to find food, clothing and somewhere to stay for people who had nothing – in the middle of December. So, one of the first things I did was to go the Guomingdan Headquarters to borrow some office equipment. There was nobody there, however, not even a gatekeeper, so I wrote a note to say that I was taking some tables and chairs with me. That was the full extent of my taking something that didn't belong to me.

I was held in detention for two months writing my 'confession'. I wasn't allowed any news of any kind from the outside, which was torment, although one day I heard a voice calling faintly 'Baba, Baba'. I looked out of the window and saw Ninjun, holding Kangmei, in the distance. My heart tightened. All we could do was wave at each other. In the end they couldn't find any evidence against me and so let me go.

Meanwhile, my salary had been suspended, but it was subsequently reimbursed. I used that money to buy new clothes for Ninjun and the children, bought two cartons of one of the best brands of cigarettes (Huafu) for Shibo and took them all out for a meal.

A year or two later I heard what finally befell Wang. Political movements kept coming at us in waves and, during each one, Wang had been a keen activist. Then, during the Anti-Rightist Movement, he heard some rumours about himself: that his political history was 'unclear' and that he had joined in with some anti-Party talk. Wang was so scared of becoming a victim himself that he slit his own throat in the bathhouse.

My experience had been very frightening, but I had escaped the hot water. What happened to Shibo was far worse.

None of us, in our right minds, could ever have guessed that all the things Shibo did towards building up the country would later be called 'crimes' and lead to her being forced out of the Party.

Almost without warning Shibo was called to a 'criticism meeting' in her department and was confronted with a list of her crimes:

1. Wanting to be a capitalist. Evidence of this was the sewing group she had set up, which had become very successful.

2. Being born into an 'exploiting family' – therefore she had no clear line between the enemy and us. The evidence given for this was: the time she was asked to organise a group of women from Chongqing to march in the Victory Celebration Parade, on Chinese New Year's Day in 1950, to mark the New China. The women had to ardently love our Communist Party, be poor and from the working class. Shibo had instructed the local committees to select two hundred women out of a possible six hundred to join the parade. Someone disclosed that one woman had lied about her background and so hadn't met the criteria, for which Shibo was being blamed. Shibo said that there hadn't been time to check every woman's background personally and she had relied on each local committee's selection. Well, that wasn't considered good enough, it seems.

There were a few more similar 'crimes'. For example: there was a request from the South-West Ethnic Committee for a national flag to be embroidered. They wanted it for their representatives to take to Beijing as a gift for Chairman Mao. Shibo got in contact with a woman who used to work for her in the tailor's shop that had been set up in 1935 and who then found twenty

341

specialist embroiderers to work on the flag. They worked on the flag in shifts for four days and nights to get it finished in time. They were praised by the Party and the press. However, apparently one of the embroiderers was a concubine of a landowner and Shibo was blamed for giving such an important job to an enemy of the Party. They described this infringement as Shibo having 'lost her ground and not being able to tell where the line is between the enemy and our own'.

3. Supporting a capitalist's farm and helping the exploiting class – a landowner – escape paying land tax. This was the most serious accusation and it had come from the young minister herself. She had written a long report to the Minister for Party Organisation outlining what she called Shibo's 'bad behaviour' and 'low policy realisation'. She described Shibo as being anti-revolutionary and obviously wanting to be a capitalist. The fact that the owner of Jianghua Farm had willingly donated his land to the Women's Federation was ignored.

Later on these accusations were found to be false, but the young minister and her group were too afraid to lose face and retract the accusations, or to apologise to Shibo.

It was decided, and the decision came from the Above, that Shibo's Party membership should be withdrawn. A man named Xiao Caikuan was then assigned to Shibo's case and he kindly suggested to her that the 'best solution' would be if she willingly resigned her Communist Party membership. In this way, he said, she would avoid any further disciplinary action. It was as if a bolt of lightning had struck Shibo and it nearly broke her – it nearly broke all of us.

Many years later, I met Xiao Caikuan again and he told me that he had thought at the time that the young minister's prime motivation for writing such a damning report had been extreme jealousy. He had tried to put a stop to the process of ousting Shibo from the Party, but nothing he did changed the decision from the Above and he had no choice except to implement it.

Shibo refused to resign her membership and carried on arguing her case. As a result she had to endure endless 'criticism meetings' in which she put forward explanations and made appeals, but nobody listened. Instead they told her that her attitude was making her case worse and that the Above were angry and so was the young minister.

Shibo couldn't eat or sleep and ended up in hospital. Still, though, day and night she carried on writing appeals, staining them with her tears. Each appeal was like a tiny drop in the ocean – they didn't even cause a ripple. Ninjun and I went to see her in hospital and we found her crying. In between heaving sobs, she said to us:

'I was born into a scholar family. I had enough food and clothes, I was educated, I could have lived a very comfortable life – but I went down the road of revolution with your father. During those years we even had to eat soil sometimes – we lived in a cave – death passed over our heads countless times – had enough of hardship since your father's death – pledged my life to our people – swore I would never marry again – I was only in my thirties – protected my two children. I carried on the revolution till the very end – till today. I have kept every word I promised to my people – my promise to your father – all in the name of revolution – now I only want to do more for our New China. I put all my efforts into building our new country – how come – overnight – I became an anti-revolutionary? How come I committed so many crimes? You tell me – I cannot understand it – help me get the answers.'

Still Shibo resisted and then a representative from the Above came to Ninjun and me and urged us to put pressure on Shibo to resign. Of course we knew that Shibo was innocent of all accusations and we didn't agree with the Party's decision, but we had always obeyed, without question, whatever the Party told us to do. So we went to see Shibo. I cannot remember my exact words. I couldn't look her in the eyes and I felt dizzy. Shibo was enraged. I had never seen her in such a state before. She was stabbing her finger inches away from my face and said:

'Other people don't know me – but it seems the two of you don't know me either. You haven't gone to anyone to explain for me or appeal for me – instead you are stabbing me in the back and twisting the knife – do you realise what you are doing at this moment? Did I bring you up to hurt me in such a way?'

I was ashamed, so ashamed that I hoped the ground would swallow me up. I knew that we should never have followed instructions from the Party so blindly, but, at the same time, to disobey the Party was unthinkable. I couldn't forgive myself then for telling her to relinquish her Party membership and still can't today. I even think that I won't be able to face my father and Shibo when I see them in the next life.

Then in 1952 the Above gave the final order to Shibo:

'This is the Party's final decision. You either "willingly" withdraw your membership of the Party, which will leave you with the option of applying to rejoin it later on, or you will force the Party to take disciplinary action. You will be sacked from your job, expelled from the Party and your life will be meaningless and you will have nothing.'

Being sacked and expelled was like a death penalty – for Shibo, it was worse. She said she would rather have been killed by the Guomingdan. We were all scared. Relatives and friends gathered round Shibo to persuade her to back up a bit then see what happened, telling her to save herself.

Shibo was backed into a corner and had no way out. She started to write her letter of withdrawal from the Party and it was heartbreaking to watch. Her tears mingled with the ink on the page. She looked utterly defeated. However, her letter didn't satisfy the Party and she had to change it three times before they accepted it. They wanted to make sure that there was no implied blame on the Party.

As soon as her resignation was accepted, she was ordered to leave the Women's Federation and was sent to Baxian, a small town over a hundred miles from Chongqing, to work in a Women's Reformatory. This institution had been set up to house women who had been classed as 'social trash'. They were prostitutes, thieves or drug addicts.

Shibo had been silenced. She lived in poor conditions in an abandoned, ruined temple. In order to get to work at the Women's Reformatory, she had to walk up and down over a thousand steep steps through the hills, morning and evening. Food was sometimes scarce and many times she only had mouldy rice to eat. Shibo, however, didn't complain but soon became the most respected and loved teacher at the institution. As I write this I'm proud to have in front of me a treasured certificate, issued on 19 January 1953 by the Baxian Town Hall, saying that Shibo had been voted as the people's representative. There is a group photo of that day with it. Shibo is forever everybody's Big Sister Chen, Teacher Chen, the Double Gun Woman.

The Lion Falls Power Station

Once I was cleared of the charges brought against me under the Three Anti-Movements, I was given a new job as the office director in the Chongqing Second District's Municipal Committee. It was a large district north of the Yangtze River. The offices were located in a beautiful, Western-style house set in a large park. The house and land belonged to the Ren family. They were a rich and intellectual family and former supporters of the Guomingdan. As soon as Chongqing was liberated by the Communists, however, the Ren family had given over their property for use as local government offices.

Ninjun, the children and I had our quarters here and we felt lucky to live in these green, pleasant surroundings. Ninjun also changed her job at this time to work in the Propaganda Department of the city of Chongqing.

On 14 June 1953, Ninjun gave birth to a baby girl. I named her Bo, which means 'Wave'.

I chose the name Bo because, after my detention during the Three Anti-Movements, I felt insecure; the ground beneath my feet didn't feel solid any more. The movements from Beijing that we all had to follow were coming at us in waves. I realised that it would be so easy to be engulfed by these waves and be swept away by them. When I had been captured by the Guomingdan and locked up for more than a month, I knew that there were people doing all that they could to save me: Shibo, my father, Ninjun and many friends. But now, this time round, I knew I could not have been saved by our people – instead I was still being watched by 'our' people. So I named my daughter Bo, in the hope that she would be a person who would be able to ride the waves of this life and manage to stay afloat.

Then Shibo came to stay with us for some time. She had become unable to walk up and down the thousand steps in Baxian to go to work at the Women's Reformatory and was sent to hospital. She was diagnosed with tuberculosis. Thankfully, once she had recuperated, she didn't have to go back to the Women's Reformatory, but instead was sent to the Department of Art and Literature in Chongqing. She did her best paintings during this period and many of her bamboo scrolls were exported overseas. In her eyes, this was the hardest time in her life due to the fact that she had been forced out of the Communist Party. She kept writing appeal after appeal for reinstatement, but they were all ignored. The time spent staying with us gave her some comfort, though no one could heal what lay heavy inside her: the injustice.

In June 1954 I was called into a meeting to be told that I had been selected, because I was a model officer, to work at the proposed Lion Falls Power Station, which was to be built about eighty kilometres north west of Chongqing. This power station was the first of 156 proposed projects which were part of the Soviet Union's five-year plan to support China.

We were given three days to prepare. Shibo said that she would take Mingtao to live with her and we would take Kangmei and Bo with us. Ninjun and I both hurriedly handed over our jobs and did the packing. Then we got on the truck, with a

347

few other selected managers and their families, for our journey to Lion Falls and the next phase of our lives.

When we arrived, and much to my surprise, I spotted Den Dage (Big Brother) in the crowd waiting to greet us.

There had been a previous power station at Lion Falls, but it had been bombed by the Guomingdan before they fled from Chongqing and it had been decided to build a completely new replacement. It was to take between two and three years. There was to be a one kilometre-long dam and the resulting reservoir would be four kilometres long, the sides of which would have to be reinforced. It was a huge, technically complicated project, which was expected to be completed without enough time or finance. We had passion and energy, but, in truth, there was also a lot of ignorance.

Den Dage said to me: 'My brother, this is not going to be easy and the responsibility on your shoulders will be very heavy.'

As usual, I thought I could handle anything and said: 'Nothing could be heavier than fighting Chiang Kai-shek.'

He laughed, but said: 'Well, this is a most important project for our country – it has to be a success, we aren't allowed to fail. But the country will give us the best support.'

Next day Den Dage gave a few of us a tour of the area. It was a wilderness. There were a few sheds and other storage buildings and some red-brick houses. There were two groups of technicians already on site. One group was from the north, who had been taking care of a power station under Japanese rule, and the other had been under the rule of the Guomingdan. In only one month's time ten thousand labourers would arrive – there wasn't anywhere for them to live yet and no supplies or materials. Den Dage seemed to know what was on my mind and told me not to worry because supplies and materials were on their way from all over the country and would arrive soon.

Then the Supply Department was established and I was put in charge of it.

The project officially started and workers came from all over the country. The promised supplies, such as cement, dynamite, wood, sand and stones, didn't turn up on time though. This was mainly because the transport system was so poor, so I sent some of my staff to contact the transport departments in different cities to persuade them to prioritise our need. I set up a competition system to encourage them to be quicker in loading and unloading the trucks. For instance, we managed to get down to eight minutes from a previous thirty minutes for one truckload of cement. In this way each truck was able to make more deliveries in one day. There was no crane to lift the heavy equipment, such as a fifty-ton transformer, but we used the primitive method of rolling it on logs. Then the number of workers swelled to about 20,000 plus their families and so the Supply Department became the largest department on the project. We ended up with two hundred officers and over a thousand other workers.

Before we could build accommodation for everyone, even the most basic equipment like carrying poles and baskets had to be sourced. Apart from a roof over their heads, people of course needed food and clothing. My department had to procure everything, from the largest to the smallest item needed. The pressure on me was huge, because if we became short of supplies then it would slow down the work or even stop it completely. I created a policy within the department which said: 'Don't take no for an answer; see a torn seam, stick a needle in it; see a hole, dig it deeper; use any method to get what we need, except for bribery and corruption.' I never had a day off and rarely got more than five hours of sleep at night, but it only seemed to fuel my energy. The workforce was dynamic and non-stop: work was carried out twenty-four hours a day in three shifts. Then, even though it had seemed implausible at the outset, the site of the Lion Falls Power Station became a small town. We had built houses, a school, a nursery, shops, teahouses, a sports centre and a theatre.

Ninjun was in charge of all entertainments and clubs and there were parties every Saturday night, often with ballroom dancing and opera. Ninjun had her best year here too: her management skills and talent for the performing arts shone. I made sure that I supported her with her budgets and manpower. I was still keen to organise all the sporting activities myself.

In March 1955 Ninjun gave birth to our fourth child. It was another girl and I named her He (pronounced *Gher*), which means 'Crane'. This name symbolises 'flying high in life', which is exactly what both Ninjun and I were doing in our own lives at that time.

My salary was 130 yuan per month, plus I also earned a bit more from my articles. At that time, one yuan could buy fifty eggs and four pounds of pork. When we added Ninjun's salary, we were able to live a very comfortable life. I love pomelo fruit and, when it was in season, I bought hundreds of them, piled them up in a corner of the room and gave them out to friends and neighbours. We welcomed friends and their friends to stay, whether it was for one night or for weeks – no questions asked. We were happy.

We completed each work target ahead of schedule, so the completion of the project was brought forward by a year. It was decided to set the power station in motion on 1 October 1956, because it was National Day and it would be the best way to celebrate the Seventh National Day of New China.

Then one month before the official opening, one of the four

main generators still hadn't arrived. We contacted Haerbin Generator Factory, in the north of the country, only to find out that they were short of supplies and hadn't even started to produce it. I couldn't let this happen and I immediately contacted the mayor of Chongqing. I explained the urgency to him and asked for a letter of introduction to the Haerbin Municipal Committee. Then I flew to Haerbin and told them that our generator was crucial for a national project and we needed it as a matter of urgency. The Haerbin Municipal Committee authorised a twenty-four-hour-a-day workforce and it was completed in two weeks.

The next problem was transportation. There was no time to send the generator via ship or train if we were to meet the deadline for the opening. It was too big for civil aviation, so I contacted the military air force. I learned that two of their aircraft had been sent to the aviation maintenance plant for an annual check-up, so then I flew to Beijing, found the Minister for Hydropower and demanded the use of a military plane to get the generator to Chongqing. The minister took me to the vice prime minister and, after a couple of meetings, it was decided to transport the generator before one of the planes went in for maintenance.

On 8 September the military plane flew the generator from Haerbin to Beijing and then the next day flew on to Chongqing and I flew with it. At Chongqing a flatbed truck was waiting at the airport. I didn't waste any time by staying overnight, but drove on in the truck to Lion Falls. When it was safely installed, I could finally start breathing again.

On 1 October, after two years of extremely hard work, the Lion Falls Power Station was switched on and successfully started producing electricity.

Our power station was the first one to be built in China by our own people and it became a model throughout the country. It was celebrated and, almost every day, people came to visit. It quickly became a training location for students, both national and international (from Russia and Asian countries).

After my visit to the Minister for Hydropower in Beijing, an order was sent to the Chongqing Municipal Party Committee for me to be transferred to the Central Hydropower Department in Beijing. However, Den Dage and the other bosses had hidden it from me because they didn't want me to leave. Then another transfer order came through and once again the Party Committee in Chongqing told Beijing that they could have anyone else but me. The minister got impatient and answered them: 'I only want Lin Xiangbei, nobody else. Should I be obeying you, or should you be submitting to me?'

With words like that from the minister, the Chongqing Municipal Committee turned over the decision to me. I refused to accept the transfer. I gave a strange excuse by saying that I didn't like the food in Beijing.

Most people would have thought it was a wonderful opportunity as well as a promotion and, looking back on it now, I find it strange that I refused this chance and challenge. However, even though the two years at Lion Falls had been pressurised and stressful, we were mostly happy. It was one of the most memorable times in my life, because I felt I had achieved something great and had been successful. I also thought it was the best place for me to continue serving my country and people. It was an emotional decision and I allowed my heart to rule my head.

Little did I know that the storm clouds were gathering once more.

The Spring of 1957

I carried on working at the Lion Falls Power Station, but was given the position of the Sichuan Electricity Company Party Secretary. However, I had negotiated to be sent on a training course at the Chongqing Party Institute starting in the following academic year. In all the time I had been a member of the Communist Party I had only had five days of official Party training. All members knew that not only was it an honour to be selected for any Party training course, but it was an important stepping stone to promotion. Ninjun was privileged to receive her chance before me and she joined the current year's course at the institute. She took the girls back to Chongqing with her. I was happy to wait my turn though.

In April of 1957 the Central Committee in Beijing announced another 'rectification movement'. The focus of this one was 'anti-bureaucracy, anti-sectarianism and anti-subjectivism' and was given the name the 'Hundred Flowers Campaign' – its main slogans were: 'Let a hundred flowers blossom and a hundred schools of thought compete' and 'speak out loudly'. The aim was to encourage all of us to voice our opinions of the Communist Party and suggest how the Party could be improved. Open discussions were encouraged where we

353

could speak our minds freely. In May huge posters appeared on buildings, using every available wall space both inside and outside, up and down the country. Workplaces and schools ground to a halt so people could concentrate on making the posters. It was seen as a duty to broadcast thoughts as well as make accusations against perceived enemies. It almost became a competition to produce the largest posters and these notices would be stuck over somebody else's poster until they were many layers thick. Newspaper articles told us: 'The Communist Party is a broad-minded and big-hearted party that is willing to accept all kinds of criticism.'

At that time there were still other political parties in existence, such as the Chinese Democratic League, the Chinese Association for the Promotion of Democracy, the Federation of Three People's Principles and the Chinese Agricultural Workers' Democratic Party. Members of these democratic parties genuinely believed that they were forging a long-term relationship with the Communist Party. They believed that they were trusted by, and could trust, the Communist Party and had a shared goal of taking the country forward. I myself joined in enthusiastically at Lion Falls and set up a committee to organise meetings, especially for non-Communists, under the banner of 'speak out loudly'.

But we were being tricked. The Hundred Flowers Campaign had another name: 'Entice the snakes out of their caves.'

Overnight the *People's Daily* newspaper published the names of the patriotic democrats in Beijing who had spoken their minds, and called them 'Rightists'. So began the 'Anti-Rightists Movement' and it quickly filtered its way to every corner of the country. I, and hundreds of thousands like me, were caught in its sticky web.

In September 1957 the Lion Falls Power Station Company Secretary, Zhao Xiaoting, asked me to hold an 'internal rectification' meeting at managerial level and said that he would join in too. I gathered everyone and sent a messenger to Secretary Zhao to tell him that the meeting was ready to start and he sent back to say that he would be there soon, but that we should start without him. The company director, Guo Ling, was also there. I chaired the meeting, but I managed to say very little and certainly didn't voice any opinion at all. We were all aware of the danger and, by the end of the meeting, I was so relieved because none of us had crossed the line. Secretary Zhao Xiaoting didn't make an appearance at all. I wrote the minutes and relaxed.

However, within days this meeting became known as the meeting where Guo Ling and Lin had led a group in wantonly attacking the Party. Secretary Zhao Xiaoting had set a trap for his chosen victims. He wrote a report accusing five of us, including Director Guo Ling, of being Rightists for a wide variety of reasons. The Above rejected his accusations at first. They said that there was a lack of evidence of our 'vices', especially in the case of Director Guo Ling, who had been appointed to his job by the Central Committee in Beijing and was still in favour. As for myself, I was well aware that I had made an enemy in Secretary Zhao Xiaoting. He had worked under me during the Land Reform Movement and he had had to report directly to me. Then, once we had both got positions at the Lion Falls Power Station, he had tried to get Director Guo Ling ousted from his job. His reason was that Guo Ling wasn't one of us, because he came from Beijing, and wouldn't be able to lead us. I opposed Zhao Xiaoting and offended him by telling him he was a conspirator only interested in getting to the top himself. I had never thought much of him.

Secretary Zhao Xiaoting didn't give up and five of us remained under suspicion of being Rightists, but luckily for Director Guo Ling, he was saved by Beijing and his 'Rightist hat' was removed. This campaign had opened up opportunities for Zhao for self-advancement and he was executing his moves well. He announced to everyone that the remaining four of us, who had all once been model officers, were an anti-Party group and Rightists. Even though it hadn't been confirmed by the Party Committee yet, he let it be known that our status would soon be formalised. Zhao Xiaoting was nothing but a scheming liar.

My life at Lion Falls quickly became hellish. I was shunned, ostracised and lost my right to attend company meetings, to vote or to have my say in any matter. The only meetings I attended were the criticism sessions. My house had once been a shelter for everyone, but friends stopped visiting. They walked around me, or turned in the opposite direction, if we met in the street. People spat on me, or threw their dirty water over me as I passed their doorways. Even children shouted at me and threw stones. I didn't really blame them as they had been told I was the enemy and, apart from anything else, they had to protect their own status, but the humiliation and injustice cut deeply. Then my Party membership was taken away and, as it had been for Shibo before me, that seemed to be the most painful thing of all. All over again, I felt the guilt of having been instrumental in persuading Shibo to relinquish her Party membership. Membership of the Communist Party was the most precious thing for those of us who had strived and fought to bring Communism to our country for so many years. Losing it was like losing a beloved family member.

Meanwhile, on 24 November 1957, Ninjun gave birth to another baby girl in Chongqing. She named her Jihong, which means 'Inherit the Redness'. I was forbidden to go and be with her or to see the newborn baby.

Like many of the other movements, the Anti-Rightist Movement got out of control. Countless people, mostly the intellectuals, couldn't take the shame and degradation suddenly thrust on them and were driven to commit suicide. I held on, firstly because I was a husband and a father of five and secondly because I had the example of Shibo to follow. Even though Shibo's will was almost broken, she still retained a glimmer of hope that the Party would reinstate her one day and that's what I held on to too. There is a saying in China: 'To change your personality is as hard as moving a mountain.' But under such circumstances, there is a price to be paid for holding on to life; I found I had to change. If I retained any pride and dignity at all, I buried it so deeply that it would take me many years to find it again. My energy dissipated. I allowed people to criticise, condemn and demoralise me without retaliating, not even with one word. I lowered my gaze; I bowed my head.

I was required to criticise myself and write down my 'confession', but each time I did so it wasn't enough. I exaggerated my failings and vices for them; I criticised my very soul. Then they gave me the Central Party's guidance – 'Six Criteria for Classifying Rightists' – and told me to link myself to each point. The criteria were anybody who was:

1. Anti a socialist regime
2. Anti a proletarian dictatorship and democratic centralism
3. Anti the Communist leadership and their policies
4. Using socialism and Communism as a way to divide people
5. Organising, or actively joining, any anti-socialist or anti-Communist group; conspiring to overthrow leaders at different levels; inciting anti–Communist or anti-government riots
6. Giving any ideas to the above actions; giving out information to help any of the above actions; leaking government secrets.

The statement also said that one's local Party committee must formalise the classification.

I spent a whole night writing that 'confession'. It was ten thousand words long and, invisible between each line, it contained my fervent hope that they would let me off after I had finished it.

Meanwhile, in Chongqing, Ninjun was being pressured to divorce me in order to protect her own status. Neither of us could believe this was happening. I was thinking: had I been an utterly devoted, fervent, hard-working Communist all this time, or merely a foolish, compliant tool?

Then I was put to work helping the labourers dismantle the construction sheds and workshops now that the power station was completed and running smoothly. The whole site had to be cleared and tidied up. Many of those labourers had worked for me and most of them felt that I was being treated unjustly so were extremely kind to me. They knew though that they couldn't change the situation, except to try and cheer me up, and I felt relieved, acutely so, to be amongst them. I regained a little of my spirit and joined in with their drinking, smoking and banter. Then I regained a little of my intelligence and worked out how to cut down on the time it took to demolish the bamboo buildings. It had been taking about two weeks to dismantle a two-hundred-square-metre workshop and to clear the site. I sent four young men to climb onto the roof and cut the bindings before we simply pulled from each corner and then the building would collapse. The whole process for each building only took a few days.

One cold winter's day, as we were demolishing the club workshop, the gatekeeper came to say that there was somebody waiting outside the perimeter to see me. I couldn't think who it could be and eagerly ran towards the gate to find out. In the distance I saw Shibo standing on a ridge at the edge of the rice field and waving at me. All the pent-up emotion flooded out of me at the sight of my heroine. I shouted her name and could barely see where I was putting my feet through my tears. When I reached her I clasped her hands in mine. She looked so thin and pale, but she calmly smiled at me, extricated her hands from my grasp and tenderly cupped my face in her hands. Then she handed me a jar of pickled tofu:

'Look, I've brought your favourite – it's Zhongxian *tofu rui*.'

Shibo working as an artist in 1958

Then she unfurled a bamboo screen painting she had done for me. It was of the Guanyin Deity sitting on a lotus and there were eight characters on it which read: 'Set Aside the Past, Smile at the Future.' No doubt she was trying to comfort me.

She said: 'Ninjun is still at the Party Institute, but she

couldn't take any time off to come and see you. She asked me to tell you not to worry about her – she is fine – and that, no matter what happens, she will stay with you and that she won't ever change.'

I was sobbing; it was the first time I had cried since Liberation. Shibo's last words to me were:

'Don't be sad. I was accused of even more things than you have been. The time will come when the water clears and we will be able to see the colours of the stones which lie at the bottom of the riverbed.'

Shibo arrived quietly and left quietly. She only stayed about half an hour, but once again her warmth embedded itself in my heart.

Afterwards I realised that I hadn't even asked her how she had travelled to Lion Falls, because it wasn't an easy journey, or where she was staying.

Several weeks later Ninjun came back to Lion Falls, bringing the girls with her. Mingtao was once again left with Shibo in Chongqing so that he could continue at school. After Ninjun finished her training at the Party Institute, she was given the job of director of the Workers' Union. She was still being advised to divorce me, which she refused to do, but the martyrdom status of her father had saved her from my taint. She had also forthrightly told the Above that she couldn't bring up her children on her own and, even if I had vices, they weren't the ones that they were accusing me of having. It was wonderful to have my family back. We weren't as comfortable as we had been before, but we managed.

7 March 1958 was a day I can't forget. Premier Zhou Enlai, and other important leaders, came to visit the Lion Falls Power Station. Normally, I would have been greeting them, but now

I wasn't even allowed to be part of the crowd. The pain of this hit me hard. Back in the 1930s Zhou Enlai and his wife had been the patrons and protectors of the Children's Theatre, which Ninjun had been a part of, and we knew him to be a benevolent and modest man. He was as well loved as Chairman Mao. I longed to be able to run to him and say: 'Beloved Premier Zhou, I am being wronged – accused – please give me justice.' But, of course, I couldn't.

Kangmei, who was seven years old at the time, had been chosen to give the Premier a bunch of flowers. Ninjun told me that Premier Zhou Enlai picked up Kangmei and asked her what her name was. She proudly told him: 'My name is Kangmei.'

The Premier then asked her what she wanted to do when she was grown up.

Premier Zhou Enlai visiting Lion Falls
Power Station on 7 March 1958

'My mum told me that when I grow up I will go and fight the American ghosts,' said my sweet and confident daughter proudly.

Premier Zhou laughed loudly saying: 'Good, very good!'

When Kangmei came home she told me about her happy day. As I held her I was almost in tears and told her: 'Well done, my good girl – you have done a fine job for your Baba.'

Ninjun snorted, however, and said: 'It's a pity that all those photographers didn't take any photos of her presenting the flowers. They claimed that they didn't have any more film left – what rubbish! No doubt they were told not to take any photos of the daughter of a Rightist.'

In May 1958 several of us were called into a small office and told that our 'Rightist' status had been formalised by the Party Committee, as a result of our anti-Party and anti-Revolutionary behaviour. It only took five minutes to label us and fix our fates. Thankfully, this announcement hadn't been made in front of a crowd, so we didn't have to put up with angry jeering.

At another meeting we were given our punishments. I was told that my rank had been lowered by only three levels: from Level 14 to Level 17, due to the fact that I had been put into the 'good attitude and good confession' class. However, one of my neighbours shouted out: 'No! This couple have enough money – their lives are very comfortable. We can't let our enemies live in such luxury – cut his rank down further.'

So my rank went down to Level 19, which meant my salary was reduced from 140 yuan to 74 yuan. My neighbour was rewarded with a promotion to managerial level for 'having his feet on Communist ground', but he didn't last long: he was a drug addict and was soon caught embezzling money to feed his habit. He died of an overdose a couple of years later.

Yu Shoushang was one of the five people who had been

accused by Secretary Zhao Xiaoting at the same time as me. Yu and I were old comrades and had worked together as underground Communists before Liberation. He had fought against his case all along and refused to admit to anything or write a confession. Unfortunately, he was sent to a hard-labour camp immediately and his wage was cut to 40 yuan.

Another of the five accused was Jia Xiyi, another of my old comrades. In fact, he was a hero to me: I had been in his team during the anti-Japanese campaign in 1935-1937. He was also immediately sent to a hard-labour camp: another power station on the Dahong River near Chongqing. He was put to work building the railway track and on 25 January 1960, whilst carrying a section of steel track, he collapsed and died due to exhaustion and starvation.

Sometimes one can say 'What goes around, comes around', because a year later, during the 'Expedite the Anti-Rightist Movement', Secretary Zhao Xiaoting found himself hauled up onto the stage and condemned. During his confession, he admitted that he conspired to get rid of Director Guo Ling so that he could get the top job. He also admitted to going after anyone who tried to stop him. He ended up being labelled a 'Rightist' too. However, his confession didn't make any difference to my case or anyone else's either. I was told that, in all, about five hundred people at Lion Falls had been labelled as 'enemies' for a variety of reasons. I also found out that the Central Party Committee assumed that in every organisation there would be a percentage of 'enemies'. Therefore, Zhao Xiaoting had to accuse five of us in our department in order to fulfil the required numbers.

I constantly struggled to accept that I was a 'Rightist' and was meant to be against the Communist Party, against the Revolution and an enemy of my beloved country. The world had been turned upside down and we had been tipped into hell.

I remember one night I knelt down in front of Mao's portrait and cried in anguish like a small boy in front of his father:

'Chairman Mao! Chairman Mao! You are the greatest leader. I am your loyal subject. I have never deceived you, not even for a minute. You have my whole heart – my life. My accusers are wrong – totally wrong. Please come to save me – rescue me. Tell them they are wrong.'

In a moment of stillness this poem arose in my heart:

Yesterday I was a hero
Today I became a convict
If asking why
No one gives clear reason

Unfortunately, Chairman Mao didn't come to my rescue, nor to others in the same boat as me. I hung my head even lower than before.

Life as a Rightist

At the beginning of 1958 a group of us 'Rightists' were escorted by security guards from Lion Falls to the Zipingpu Power Station construction site at Guanxian, which is on the Upper Ming River in the west of Sichuan. Sichuan was particularly suitable for building water-generated power stations due to its geography. The area around the town of Guanxian was another remote, primitive and poor place.

We knew that life was going to be hard at Zipingpu, so Ninjun left Mingtao and Kangmei with Shibo in Chongqing and the three youngest, Bo, He and Jihong, came with us. Ninjun also asked a distant cousin of hers who didn't have a job to come with us to look after the girls.

There was no welcome for us when we arrived. We had to walk through lines of people who stared at us in silence; their hostility was tangible. We knew they had been informed that we were a group of Rightists sent there to be reformed. I couldn't help comparing our reception here with the one we had received at Lion Falls three years earlier, where banners and flags were flying, drums were beaten and smiles creased people's faces. What a contrast!

Our accommodation was in a row of single-room terraced

'houses' situated halfway up a steep hill. The buildings had been constructed as store rooms originally. The roofs were made of felt and the walls were of clay and straw. Each room only had one window and one door. There was no toilet or even a communal latrine, but each family was given one wooden bucket which had to be emptied into a cesspit each morning. We were given two rooms between the six of us. There were no proper cooking facilities in the rooms except for a small electric ring; we were encouraged to only use the communal canteen. We were given tokens to present in the canteen for cooked food and to collect all our other rationed goods from the stores.

Ninjun was to be the vice-director of the Production Department of the cement factory, which was on site, as well as the entertainments officer for the whole power station.

As a Rightist, I was treated like a criminal and had to attend daily criticism meetings. Usually us Rightists had to sit on the stage facing an intimidating crowd and meekly listen to their condemnation of us. My job was labouring and at times it was back-breaking. I started off as one of the carriers of rocks and pebbles from the quarry to the dam construction site. I had two bamboo baskets and a carrying pole for the task. Before going to work each morning I would go down to the office and, together with the other reformers, stand in front of Chairman Mao's portrait and read aloud some of Mao's words, such as: 'Leniency to those who confess', 'Severity to those who resist'. Then we had to lower our heads to say: 'I must confess.'

Life was harsh for all of us, but at least I had Ninjun and the children with me. Although there was an entertainments programme for the workers, all the Reformers were excluded from this. But because Ninjun was the organiser, the children and I could sneak in to watch the films. They were usually Chinese and patriotic, but sometimes Ninjun managed to obtain foreign films, either Russian ones or ones from other Eastern

European Communist bloc countries. Often she would organise and star in her own theatre and opera productions. Bo, who was five years old at that time, remembers how excited and proud she was to watch her mother on the stage in full theatrical make-up and costume and to listen to her wonderful singing.

In May 1958 another movement was announced: 'The Great Leap Forward.' It was a vast movement aimed at accelerating China's modernisation through industrialisation and collectivisation. It unleashed utter chaos onto our country and brought widespread starvation.

Some of the slogans of the day were: 'One day equals twenty years', 'Running towards Communalism', 'Defeat the Americans and the English', 'Liberate the world' and 'Compete with the speed of the rocket'. We were constantly being told to speed up production and finish the power station so that the country could manufacture more and more steel, which was seen as the most important industry for the modernisation of China. Our project had many aspects to it, however. Before we could construct the dam we had to create a diversion for part of the river so that the existing industries wouldn't be interrupted, such as the timber industry, which floated the logs downriver to Chengdu, and rice production, which relied on the Ming River for irrigation. The plan had been to build a tunnel and channel the water through it, but after digging only thirty metres into the side of the mountain there was an explosion which killed seven people. It seems that the geologists hadn't detected that there was gas in the ground and the tunnel was abandoned. Soon afterwards, construction of a canal was started instead.

Then, to my surprise, in addition to carrying on with the hard labour, I was appointed as one of the dam managers, mainly responsible for supplies, but also in charge of the

Accounts Department. In fact, being the Accounts Department manager was beyond a surprise, it was more a case of being beyond belief! I was used to turning my hand to a variety of jobs and managing to do them well, but I genuinely had no idea about accountancy.

As one of the labourers, I was being given the maximum rations, but they weren't sufficient for any of us. We were all hungry all of the time. People were getting ill and collapsing through exhaustion and then the deaths started. We had to do something for ourselves and so we scouted the surrounding area to find available land to cultivate and grow some vegetables. Many people did the same thing. We were in the mountains, so the ground was hard with very little topsoil. Bit by bit we cleared the stones from several patches dotted all over the place. We would get up before dawn and work until about 7.30am and then go to our jobs. Then in the evenings we would stay until it got dark. The largest allotment we created was about thirty metres square, but most of them were only two or three square metres. Then I started carrying up buckets of excrement from the cesspit to fertilise the thin soil. I would carry two buckets, each weighing twenty kilos, balanced on a pole. Once I slipped right into the cesspit and another time I fell on the ridge and a bucket fell on me! For years after, Ninjun would call me 'stinky man'!

I would make four or five trips with the buckets every day until the ground was ready for planting. I had already established a system of exchange with some of the people in a nearby village by saving up something from our rations, such as salt or sugar, to obtain a little dried meat on occasions. I also went to them for some vegetable seeds, especially of sweet potato and corn. Every spare moment I had I spent tending the vegetables and it even took my mind off being a Rightist, to the extent that sometimes it didn't seem to matter to me any more. I still had to carry up buckets from the cesspit as fertiliser, but fewer of them, and we diluted it with water for the growing stage. We were so happy when we managed to harvest something. Whenever Ninjun got the chance to go back to Chongqing she was able to take some vegetables to Shibo, Mingtao and Kangmei; they were short of food too. Every so often somebody would come and steal from our allotments, which made me so angry that I wanted to lash out, until I remembered how hungry they would be too and so I let them be.

I also obtained a few chicks from the villagers. My little daughter He, who was three and a half years old then, became very fond of them and saw it as her job to look after them. When we wanted to kill one of them and cook it, however, she got very upset. As hungry as she was, she didn't see her precious hen as food. She picked up the bird, tucked it under an arm and tried to run away with it as fast as she could, screaming all the while. Life's lesson was a hard one for her that day.

During that period, although life was grim, Ninjun and I likened our existence to when we were at the White Cloud Temple. We suffered many deprivations then too, but we felt close to each other. Ninjun never mentioned that she was still being advised to divorce me or blamed me for my political status, and I was very grateful she was still my wife.

With the rush of the Great Leap Forward I had noticed that there was a great deal of wastage of materials and tools occurring. It seemed that nobody had the time to look after or repair their tools any more. I set up a workshop and invited those who didn't have a job, such as some of the wives and elderly people, to go around and pick up the abandoned tools and set about mending them. Then we started making new ones too. I encouraged people to make the most of their abilities and to create new ideas. I set up competitions to encourage people to aim for high standards of workmanship. Our workshop became very productive. I was getting praised and my name appeared on the front page of the company newspaper and was broadcast on the company radio station.

I had been doing my utmost best to do whatever was required of a 'repentant' Rightist and this had apparently been recognised. Someone leaked the news to me that the Above were reviewing my case favourably at last and that my Rightist label would be removed soon. Although it was only rumours, I felt happy and dared to look forward to the future.

As always though, life was unpredictable.

Coming up to the middle of 1959, the bad news reached us that Shibo had throat cancer and was in hospital. Ninjun received permission to return to Chongqing to be with her mother and she took He and Jihong with her. Bo, my second daughter, who was six years old, remained with me at Zipingpu.

Then I was unwittingly duped in the Accounts Department. With my general lack of understanding of accounts, I tended to leave the staff in the department to get on with their jobs and only deal with the things which needed my signature and personal seal. One day one of the buyers came to me and asked for 180 yuan in order to make purchases, so I signed the permission and he was given the cash. Months later, the accountant asked me what the 180 yuan had been spent on. I then went to the buyer and asked for his receipts, but he turned a blank face to me and swore that he hadn't spent the money in the end and had, in fact, given it all back to me. He also said that I couldn't prove anything, because I had never asked him for any invoices or receipts. He turned on his heel with his head held high and I'm sure there would have been a smile on his face as he walked off.

One-hundred-and-eighty yuan was not a small amount: it was two and a half times my monthly wage at that time. I tried to clear my name of this latest accusation. I gave my side of the story to every level of management in the company right up to the top, the representative of the Party Committee, but without success and I was rebuked again. In the end I had to 'pay back' the money, but the worst thing was that I retained the label of Rightist.

I was also punished by being put to work down the coal mine, which was several miles away. There were five miners there, who were all kindly people. They taught me how to use the tools properly to dig out the coal. It was exhausting work. However, the coal mine was closed down about two months after I started work there and then I was sent to work on the railway track. One rainy day I slipped on the track, didn't have the strength to stop myself from falling and broke my right arm. I was sent to hospital in Chengdu and stayed there for a month before returning. I was fed properly whilst there and I couldn't help feeling so guilty that my daughter, Bo, was still in Zipingpu, without enough to eat, and having to stay with a neighbour.

There was only one school in the area and the teacher was only a secondary school graduate, but that was all there was for Bo. She had to walk five miles over the mountain tracks to get there and the same back. Each child took their own bowl of food for lunch and they would be steamed all together in large pots at school. I am afraid I could only ever give Bo either a handful of rice or a sweet potato. She didn't have any shoes for the summer months and on the days when it rained the mountain paths were muddy and slippery. She fell often and her legs were always covered in bruises. When she got back to the camp after school, she would have to wash the mud off her legs under the communal standpipe, which was fed directly from the Ming River. The water was icy all the year round because the river's source was in the Himalayas. Unfortunately, her memory of this time was of always being too cold and too hungry.

Our rations got slimmer and so did we. Many was the time that I fainted, due to exhaustion and the lack of food, and was taken to the local clinic and put on a glucose drip. Of course it wasn't just me: it happened to many people, especially the labourers. Each month when I received the salt ration I would fry it up in a little oil to flavour our rice and it tasted so good while it lasted. The only greens we ate were what we could still manage to grow ourselves: leaves from the sweet potatoes and chilli plants and also pumpkin leaves, which are extremely prickly and difficult to swallow. The most difficult thing we ate, however, were the corn cobs: they were exceedingly rough and hard. They really hurt your throat as well as the rest of your system as they made their way through the body. After school Bo would often go searching for the wild edible plants, like wild spring onions, on the hillsides. One time, as a special treat, I bought some sweets made out of imported Cuban sugar, but they gave her terrible blisters on her tongue. We did our best to catch mice, but it was a time-consuming occupation. We rigged up a simple trap of a small bamboo basket, one edge of which was propped up with a stick. At the farthest side of the basket we would lay a couple of kernels of corn to tempt the mice under the basket. Then we tied a long piece of string around the stick and held on to the other end of it. We had to wait patiently and very quietly, and Bo would often fall asleep, until a mouse detected the bait and ventured in. Then we yanked the stick away by pulling quickly on the string and the edge of the basket would fall and trap the mouse. The worst bit was having to skin and gut them. It was a fiddly job and I couldn't help being very squeamish about it. Bo would be squealing about how much blood came out of one small mouse and the fact that it was all over the floor. Then even mice became scarce because everyone was doing the same as us.

One day Bo and some of the other children stole some wheat from the fields. Luckily they didn't get caught, as this was a serious crime, because all the wheat was already spoken for in order to fulfil the agricultural quotas set by the government. Bo and the children tried to cook the grains by lighting a fire, out of sight, inside our room, but the fire got out of control. Luckily some neighbours spotted it and managed to put it out before too much damage was done, but they lost the precious wheat grains in the process. Bo was terrified of telling me about it, thinking that I would scold her. She couldn't stop crying as she kept repeating: 'We are just *so* hungry.'

Both Bo and I were suffering from different levels of oedema. Bo's belly was swollen and so were her hands and feet sometimes, but I think that was mainly due to frostbite in the winter. My legs would get swollen and I had liver damage. I regret not giving more food to Bo in those days, but I was always holding back some of our rations to take to Ninjun and the other children in Chongqing. Whenever I could get away, I would hitch a lift on a truck just to deliver a little extra food to them; they were suffering too. Bo often pleaded with me to keep a bit more of the food for ourselves and maybe I should have done that. Perhaps Bo was the child who was the hungriest. We survived though, in a time when many didn't.

During the period of the Great Leap Forward everybody was in such a frenzy to show that they were being productive that claims about the levels of productivity were being exaggerated to a ridiculous degree. It meant that every single person in the country, from the bottom-most rung to the highest echelon, was living a lie. Once it got started, nobody could stop it. At the Zipingpu construction site, each person was given the task of digging out one cubic metre of stones on a daily basis. Soon, however, it got reported that each person was digging double that amount each day. Then, as the productivity reports carried on their way up the ladder, we were apparently digging out thirty cubic metres of stones each per day, with only a shovel to help us! 'Launch the satellite' was the slogan to speed things up and so at Zipingpu they started mixing soil with the cement; sometimes materials for the cement were too slow in arriving, or were in short supply.

On 23 July 1960, I received a telegram from Ninjun in Chongqing: 'Mother is critically ill, come ASAP.' I knew that Ninjun wouldn't send a telegram unless it was a real emergency. Immediately, I asked for time off and luckily nobody made a fuss, so I left Bo with a neighbour and hitched a lift in a truck to Chengdu. Then I caught an overnight train to Chongqing and arrived the next morning.

I went to the Culture and Literature Association building where Shibo had an apartment on the second floor. Before I even reached the gates to the compound I could see a large notice posted on the wall and I knew then that I was too late; I knew it was going to be Shibo's obituary. My knees were too weak to walk up the stairs and I had to crawl, my tears falling like rain already. The door to the apartment was wide open and I could see Ninjun's cousin tying a white ribbon in Kangmei's hair. Kangmei rushed to me, crying: 'Baba! Why are you so late? Waipo – she died yesterday.'

I sank down on a stool to stop myself from blacking out and put my head in my hands. I knew it, but I couldn't believe it – how was it possible that my dear Shibo was gone?

Ninjun arrived at the apartment with her younger brother, Yabin. We were all crying for a while and then Ninjun told me that Shibo had kept asking to see me and kept calling my name. This made it even worse and my tears were like a waterfall; my heart was aching and my body felt almost paralysed.

Even today, I can't find the right words to explain how I felt. It was an indescribable physical pain and I wondered if I might die too.

I asked Ninjun where Shibo's body was and said that I wanted, and needed, to see her. Yabin answered in a very cold voice that there was no need for me to see her and that in fact the Above had forbidden it. I couldn't believe that people could be so indifferent and inhumane and asked the reason for such a decision. Yabin shrugged his shoulders and said that he didn't know why.

I was inconsolable and hid in one of the rooms and cried aloud. I had lost – I have to say it – the most important and beloved person in my life. I believe that I was the person who knew her best. Since the first day I saw her through the prison cell window my life had been entwined in hers. She was everything to me: she became my heroine, my mentor, a mother, a sister, a friend. We relied on each other more than we ever admitted. If I had known that when she visited me at the Lion Falls was going to be the last time I would ever see her, then I would have striven to say all the things I needed to say and I would have heard everything she wanted to tell me too. It was unbearable to be excluded from the final rituals and denied the chance to say goodbye to her. All I could do was say to her in my heart:

'Beloved Shibo – rest in peace.'

Ninjun holding Shibo's ashes

Shibo's Memoir

Soon after Shibo died, Ninjun was sent to Chengdu to work at the Sichuan Electricity Association as the Entertainments Officer. She took Kangmei, He and Jihong with her. Mingtao had been sent to the top boarding school in Chongqing and he remained there. During the holidays he generally stayed with his Uncle Yabin. Ninjun found accommodation in an old mansion house which had been divided up for several families to live in. Not that we knew it then, of course, but we would live there, Number 94 Trinity Street, for the next twenty years or so.

Bo and I remained at Zipingpu and life there continued in the same way.

In mid-1961 I was given the good news that my Rightist label had been removed. Secretary Zhao Xiaoting had finally admitted that I had been wrongly classified and that, given the fact that he had been *required* to find five of us to be accused, he said that I had been in the wrong place at the wrong time. It wasn't all good news, however, because then I was dubbed an 'Unlabelled Rightist'! I was not reinstated into the Communist Party, I didn't get my former rank back and my wages were still very low. However, it was a very important step in the right direction where my political status was concerned. I felt that I was able to straighten my back a little bit more.

In the first quarter of 1962, much to my relief, I heard that I was going to be sent to Chengdu. I would still be employed by the Sichuan Electricity Company, but both Ninjun and I were going to be seconded to the Sichuan Culture and Literature Association specifically to edit Shibo's memoir. In fact, I didn't know it at the time, but this was part of the reason I had been given the new 'hat' of 'Unlabelled Rightist'.

At last Bo and I were able to pack our few things and set off for Chengdu. This was the best thing that had happened to us in a very long time and I didn't need to take a backward glance as we left Zipingpu. Instead we had something to look forward to: a reunion with the rest of our family. Ironically, very shortly after we left, the whole project at Zipingpu had to be shut down. Just as people were celebrating completion of the dam in front of it, the back of it was being washed away by the powerful Ming River. Putting soil in the cement mixture had never been a good idea.

When we arrived at Number 94 Trinity Street in Chengdu, we apparently resembled a couple of beggars. Ninjun didn't recognise her own daughter. Bo's hair was tousled and full of lice, her clothes were torn and dirty, she had a runny nose and seemingly she was even smelly. She was, in fact, a typical country peasant. In contrast, Kangmei and He were dressed like city girls. It was Kangmei who took control of Bo's plight and immediately fetched a bottle of vinegar and got to work getting rid of the head lice, then heated some water and washed her hair. She found some clean clothes for Bo and destroyed the ones she had been wearing. At first Bo thought she was in heaven being in Chengdu with the family, but then it was evident that she was lacking self-confidence and found it difficult to adjust. Ninjun didn't make any allowances for her and got very impatient when she failed to manage tasks around the house. Ninjun tried to register Bo at the same school that Kangmei attended, but they refused to admit her. Bo didn't pass the entry test. The standard of teaching in the country school had been poor. Consequently Bo was weak at maths and had never been taught the modern Chinese alphabet (called Pinyin), which had been introduced in the 1950s. However, she did get into a school, but it didn't have such a good reputation as the one Kangmei attended.

The director of the Propaganda Department of Chongqing, Shao Zinan, had been instrumental in transferring Shibo from the Women's Reformatory in Baxian to the Chongqing Department of Art and Literature. He had seen the injustice of her situation and did something about it. He had recognised Shibo's great artistic talent, as well as having heard stories about her time as a leader of the guerrilla force in the Huaying Mountains before Liberation. He was also the person who arranged for two people to transcribe Shibo's oral history after she had been taken to hospital with throat cancer. Shao Zinan had seen the urgency of the situation and wanted to get Shibo's exploits recorded for posterity before it was too late. The two recorders, who were young students at the time, told me that they couldn't stop Shibo from talking, but that they were so worried that it wasn't allowing her any peace and rest. Shibo talked animatedly until she was exhausted and spitting up blood. She could recall the minutest details of over two hundred people. She remembered their names, nicknames, families, ages, their heights and builds and their work and hobbies. She told them over a hundred vivid stories about these people and the times they lived through. She described the geography of the Huaying Mountain region in detail, even to the point of how many steps there were in certain areas. The young recorders said how Shibo would laugh with unrestrained joy as she told of the happy times, but would cry like a bereft child as she described the deaths. Shibo knew her time was nearly up and her stories just poured out of her.

One of the recorders told me about a woman who came to see Shibo one day. This woman announced herself as having worked with Shibo in the Women's Federation in 1951. In fact she was the 'young' minister who had written the report denouncing Shibo. Guilt was written all over her face and she cried as she said to Shibo:

'Sister Chen, I am so sorry for what I did...' The woman couldn't continue talking because she was crying so much.

Without saying a word, Shibo took off one of her jade bangles, reached out to the woman and placed the bangle over her hand. The woman tried to refuse the gift and pushed it away, but Shibo was insistent and pushed it over her hand again and gave her a gentle squeeze. This gesture made the woman cry even harder, but in the end she accepted it. As she left she was still sobbing.

During Shibo's last few days, she told Ninjun, as she held on to her hands:

'You and Xiangbei *must* edit and complete my memoir, then there will be no need for a guilty conscience about your father or our fighters who died for the cause. You *MUST*, both of you.'

Then she removed her remaining jade bangle and put it on Ninjun's wrist.

Ninjun and I met the chairman, chief editors and writers of the Sichuan Culture and Art Association, as well as the Party organisation minister, who told us that no one was born to be a writer, but they felt that we would be the best people for the job because of our family ties. My spirits soared again just like in former times and I seriously assured him:

'There is nothing a Communist cannot do. We will learn and it will be a success – failure is not in our vocabulary.'

That was my promise to them, but really it was my silent pledge to Shibo.

Then Wang Yangchen from the Beijing People's Publishing Company was sent to be our editor and team leader. He told us that it had been agreed that we must:

1. Make sure that the memoir was true to life.
2. Let it be known that the Huaying Mountain Guerrilla Unit was acting under the leadership of the Communist Party and that they were not a group of bandits, which they had been called in the past.
3. Describe the social background of the time, for example how the warlords were fighting for power amongst themselves; how there were numerous local forces also fighting each other. Also describe the class struggle and the politics at that time.
4. Describe the local way of life and local customs and include the local dialects.
5. To ensure accuracy, we should do our own research by interviewing people local to the Huaying Mountain region; visit the original scenes of the events described by Shibo and follow in her footsteps; and include other relevant people's oral records.

Both Ninjun and I were overjoyed to be given this task and over the next two years we made about ten trips to the Huaying Mountains, often taking some or all of the children with us, to collect information.

On one of our trips to the region we met Wei Yingan. Wei had been the trusted contact in Yuechi to pass messages and information between the members of the group in the 1930s. He was so excited to meet us, but especially Ninjun, and he grabbed her arm and dragged her into his house. Without a word he crouched down beneath his table and broke open a secret compartment. He brought out a slim package and started unfolding several layers of oiled, waterproof paper and then, with both hands and great emotion, he presented Ninjun with its contents. It was a negative of a photograph of her father. Wei wiped away his tears and said to Ninjun:

'I am returning this to its rightful owner. Your mother asked me to hide it for her – I have kept it for thirty years – today is the day I can set it free.'

None of us could speak.

Towards the end of December 1962, Ninjun found out that she was pregnant again. Life was still very difficult; we had very little money and there was an ongoing shortage of food. We decided it would be better if we didn't keep the child and so we went to the hospital to ask for an abortion. We were surprised when the young nurse asked for our letter of introduction stating the reason why we wanted to terminate the pregnancy. Ninjun and I looked at each other, puzzled. Ninjun turned to the nurse and said:

'What letter?'

'The letter from your company of course, identifying you and giving their permission for an abortion. If you don't have it then you can't terminate the pregnancy – we are all still responsible for carrying out Chairman Mao's directive: "Our heroine mothers should have as many children as possible – we need more hands to build up our country." You only have five children – it's not many.'

'The shortage of food is a big problem and my wife isn't well enough to have another baby – we are having a hard time keeping the children fed – if we have another mouth to feed...' Before I could finish my sentence the young nurse pulled herself up straighter, tossed her head and said haughtily:

'How can you say that? We are living in the new socialist China – how can you claim we don't have enough food for everybody?'

I was enraged. I vaguely heard Ninjun arguing with the nurse as I pulled her up out of her seat. I turned to the young woman and shouted:

'You – you stop lecturing me – you are so young you don't know what you are talking about. My footsteps mark the way through every minute of the Revolution – but you, you haven't even had time to set your feet on the ground. We are leaving. We'll keep the child – I cannot believe we have to get permission from you or anybody else about how many children we have.'

The following September Ninjun gave birth to another baby girl. She was a much bigger baby than is normal and Ninjun had a very hard time. Then the doctors diagnosed Ninjun with diabetes, plus, because of the years of malnutrition, they found that she had cirrhosis of the liver.

I named the baby Ping, which means 'Peace', in the hope that she would have a more peaceful life than we had.

I did the main editing of Shibo's memoir and, in order to concentrate, I worked in the shed at a friend's house. However, in the winter it was freezing cold and in the summer it was like a steam room, full of mosquitoes; the only other place I could go was to a teahouse. I would buy one cup of tea, take a piece of flatbread with me and stay there writing for most of the day. Finally I had it ready to show the editor at the Sichuan Culture and Art Association and then we continued to work on it together until it was finished in 1964. We had written about 400,000 words in sixty-seven chapters and titled it *Huaying Fury*. Then it was turned over to the Association.

The Association mimeographed fifty copies and the plan was to send them to film companies and book publishers. I oversaw the process of producing the copies: the mimeographs were done by etching the characters onto waxed paper with a stylus. I found a young university student to do this and I did the proofreading. I asked Uncle Menghan, the famous calligrapher, to design and etch the title page.

Uncle Menghan in 1960

Then the Association invited some well-known writers – Sha Ting, Ai Wu and Luo Guanbin – to read and review it. Luo commented that: 'The story of Chen Lianshi's life is not only for China, but it is for the world.'

Very soon there were three film companies clamouring for the rights to make a film based on Shibo's memoir: Chang Chun Film Company, Beijing Film Company and Xian Film Company. The Beijing Film Company won the contract and had plans to make a film called *Double Gun Woman*. However, before any film could be produced and before publication of the book could happen, it was put on hold. Another movement was announced, the 'Four Cleanses Movement': clean economics, clean politics, clean thoughts and clean organisation. The emphasis of this one was to root out 'internal Party capitalists'. At this stage all the directors of the Art and Literature Association were accused of being Rightist or capitalists. Any project they were involved with had to be shelved.

Then, in 1966, the largest and longest-running movement was born: the Cultural Revolution. Chaos had been unleashed and it snapped at our heels, jumped on our backs and brought countless people down for the next ten long years.

From Shao Zinan's original idea to record Shibo's history in 1959, we had to wait for forty years to see the book published in China. Finally, in 2000, *The True Double Gun Woman, Chen Lianshi* was published.

We had also collected all Shibo's applications for reinstatement to the Communist Party she had written over the years, starting in 1952 when she had been forced to withdraw her membership. There were forty-two of them and she had never received a single reply. The marks on the paper made by her tears are still visible today. We also found her last painting, which she had been unable to finish in her last days, which was to be for the celebration of the anniversary of the establishment of the Communist Party.

In 1980, Shibo was officially reinstated to the Communist Party backdated to 1928, which was when she first joined. Her home town built a memorial tomb for the reburial of Shibo and her husband Liao Yubi.

The Great Proletarian Cultural Revolution

Ninjun with her six children in 1965

There was a happy event within our family in the summer of 1965. Our son, Mingtao, passed his university entrance exams and was offered a place at Kunming University. This good news lit up the dark days and made us all happy. He was the first one in our family to go to university. Ninjun held up the letter from the university, jumped up and down and chanted: 'Long live Chairman Mao. Long live Chairman Mao!'

Then, one year later, the Cultural Revolution started and all teaching at schools, colleges and universities ceased. Throughout the whole time Mingtao was attached to Kunming University we always denied knowledge of his whereabouts, because we didn't want my status of being a Rightist to impact on him.

The Great Proletarian Cultural Revolution started in May 1966. At its peak, Chairman Mao came to be seen as the 'God of China'. Slogans sprung up everywhere in praise of him. They were plastered on buildings, on street walls and noticeboards, in people's homes, on cups, bowls, towels and bags. The main slogans of the day proclaimed Chairman Mao's 'Four Great Qualities', the 'Three Loyalties' to Chairman Mao and the 'Four Infinities' of Chairman Mao.

The Four Great Qualities were:

- The Great Mentor
- The Great Leader
- The Great Commander
- The Great Helmsman – accompanied by the chant: 'Long live, long, long live, long, long, long live Chairman Mao, our Great Helmsman.'

The Three Loyalties were:

- Loyalty to Chairman Mao
- Loyalty to Mao Zedong's Thoughts
- Loyalty to Chairman Mao's Proletarian Revolution.

The Four Infinities were:

- Infinite Love
- Infinite Faith
- Infinite Praise
- Infinite Loyalty.

Other slogans emerged: 'Right to Rebel – Right to Revolution', 'All the Power Belongs to Rebels' and 'Rebels are the Leaders'. The question was, though, what and whom were they rebelling against? Nobody had an answer, but everybody, young and old, found something to rebel against. It became another movement and fed yet more rounds of accusations. Teaching in schools, colleges and universities stopped because all the teachers, lecturers and professors were labelled as either Rightists, capitalists, anti-revolutionaries, anti-socialists or being from the exploiting classes. Their thoughts and influences were considered poison to the minds of the young generation.

Universities in particular became battlegrounds for different political factions, but also work ground to a halt in factories and other businesses as people formed various opposing groups. People started fighting each other. Weapons and ammunition were even looted from the military. Everyone, however, shared the same motivation, but were coming at it from many different angles, and that was loyalty to the Greatest Leader, Chairman Mao.

Then the 'Red Guard' organisation was created by a group of students at the Qinghua School in Beijing. In a fervent letter to Chairman Mao, dated 29 May 1966, the students set out their reasons for setting up the Red Guard. It was to follow Chairman Mao's theory 'Revolution is Revolt', which was at the heart of Chairman Mao's thinking. In order to join the Red Guards, you had to be from a 'red' family. So children from a 'black' family, like ours, were excluded. Tragically, many young people tried to prove that they were eligible to join the Red Guards by denouncing their own parents, or even by beating up their parents at the condemn and criticise meetings. Soon millions of young people were clamouring to be made a Red Guard, riding on a wave of near-hysterical emotion. The youngest age group admitted were twelve-year-olds. Under twelves joined the 'Little Red Guards'. At the beginning of August, Chairman Mao officially endorsed the Red Guard and then, on 18 August 1966, he inaugurated more than one million Red Guards in Tiananmen Square. For the occasion, Chairman Mao wore full military uniform with a special 'Hong Wei Bing' (Red Guard armband), which would become the symbol for every Red Guard, and declared himself to be the 'highest mightiest commander of the Red Guard'. Seven times thereafter he received over one million Red Guards in the square on each occasion. The children were told that they could travel to Beijing on the trains for free and food and accommodation were provided at specially established reception centres. Because of the huge numbers involved, this all became unmanageable. At the end of November, it was announced that Chairman Mao would no longer receive the Red Guards en masse and the youths were told not to travel to Beijing any more.

Very quickly the Red Guards were given, or took, a great deal of power and ended up being a most malign and out of control group of people who blighted all our lives.

One of the statements issued at the time was of the greatest interest to Ninjun and me: 'Correct the falsification of history.' As soon as we saw this slogan, we took it to mean that we had another chance to legitimise and reinstate the Huaying Mountain Guerrilla Force.

After Liberation power fell increasingly to the proletarian classes, most of whom had joined the Red Army during the Long March, and they didn't understand, and doubted, the 'real purpose' of the Underground Communists in joining the Revolution. Therefore the Huaying Mountain Guerrilla Force was once again classified as a group of bandits. Ninjun and I felt strongly that we couldn't let history be turned upside down; after all, we had been part of the latter-day guerrilla force and witnesses of the sincerity and passion which sustained it.

Firstly we set up a group and called ourselves the Huaying Guerrilla Fighters and then we created a periodical titled *Huaying Fury* (the same title as Shibo's memoir which had failed at that time to reach the publication stage). Each edition's title page was designed and written by Uncle Menghan, which certainly enhanced the journal. Many people were not only interested in reading it, but they wanted to keep his famous calligraphy too.

Once again, Ninjun and I started travelling backwards and forwards to many places in the Huaying region, such as Yuechi, Chongqing and Wanxian, to interview people, just as we had done when we were compiling Shibo's memoir. This time, however, we were documenting how the Huaying Guerrilla Force families were being persecuted by the Red Guards and 'Rebels'. We weren't doing this just to publish it in our magazine, however, but we intended to collect specific evidence in order to lodge appeals with the Central Cultural Revolution Bureau in Beijing in order to 'correct the falsification of history' and to put a stop to the suffering being inflicted on our people.

Violence between all the political factions was spreading to every corner of the country. It had started on a small scale with people using poles and sticks as weapons, but it quickly escalated when the Red Guards and Rebels started looting from the military. They took everything they could: automatic rifles, grenades, machine guns and even armoured vehicles mounted with cannons.

In the Huaying region, we encountered two groups fighting: one was pro-Huaying Guerrilla Force and the other was anti. We had to be very careful not to get ourselves into trouble, as at that time we had no money and we were walking between friends and distant relatives to find free accommodation for the night.

We started writing the appeals on behalf of more than one hundred families who were being persecuted. We had listened to their stories, written them down in front of them and got them to sign, or put a fingerprint, on their statements.

However, before we managed to finish the appeals we were interrupted. I went to visit Uncle Menghan one day. I found him in a very worried and nervous state and he said to me:

'Xiangbei, I don't feel good about the situation at the moment. Have you read the newspapers lately? The mood is changing – I'm sure something big is about to happen... Only yesterday somebody from your company came here asking me all sorts of questions about you. You are being investigated – both you and Ninjun. I don't like it at all. You need to be careful: prepare yourselves!'

After I left Uncle Menghan's house, I went straight home and told Ninjun what he had said. We both agreed that we were indeed at risk and that anything could happen at any time.

At 6.00pm that same evening we heard a commotion outside in the street. Two trucks had pulled up and, within a minute, a unit of armed Red Guards/Rebels from the Sichuan Electricity

Company was battering down our door. They burst in and the leader shouted:

'Lin Xiangbei, Liao Ninjun – we are arresting you both.'

'Why? What for?' replied Ninjun very calmly.

'You are under investigation for your connection to the Huaying Mountain Guerrilla Force – they are a bunch of bandits and traitors.'

The leader gave his orders and one of the guards stepped in between Ninjun and me and turned us so that we had our backs to each other. We were told not to talk. Two more guards pointed their rifles at the girls and pushed them back against the wall. My poor daughters were screaming and crying. Then a guard pushed Ninjun out the door with the butt of his rifle and another very young-looking Red Guard wrestled Ninjun's hands behind her back and tried to handcuff her. She turned and looked him in the eye and said:

'Don't you dare try and put those things on me. You're so young – you're probably still wearing nappies. When I was fighting for the New China, you weren't even born. Kangmei, look after your little sisters.'

I followed Ninjun as we were herded towards the trucks. She was holding her hands behind her back, without handcuffs, with her head held high. I heard my daughters crying behind me and my heart tightened, but a guard prevented me from turning my head to look back at them. Plenty of people had come out of their houses to watch us being taken away.

As it turned out, we didn't have far to go because we were taken to our place of work. Ninjun was pushed into a room with a sign on it saying 'Segregation Room for Female Demon Ghosts'. Next to it was the 'Political Investigations Room' and next to that was to be my prison: 'Segregation Room for Male Demon Ghosts'. I joined seven others from the company there, including the company director, managers and engineers. I also recognised Yu Shoushan, who had been at the Lion Falls Power Station with me. We had lost contact with each other after we were sent to different labour camps. Here we were both given the added name of 'Rightist Death Tiger' – whatever that meant.

Each one of us was taken in turn into the Political Investigations Room for questioning. Behind the table where the panel of 'judges' sat loomed a huge portrait of Chairman Mao. Underneath it was a banner which read 'Leniency to those who confess – severity to those who resist'. All the other wall space was taken up by banners with the slogans of the day written on them, including the usual Four Greatest Qualities, the Three Loyalties and the Four Infinities. The panel of judges were, of course, all Red Guards. None of them looked older than twenty-three, but perhaps some of them were still teenagers. The Red Guards securing the door were heavily armed.

I was charged with trying to reverse the classification of the Huaying Mountain Guerrilla Force from bandits to being members of the Communist Party, thereby tarnishing the name of the Party. Ninjun was charged with the same thing, as well as being a traitor. I was used to being accused of all sorts of things and had always found it best to take the path of least resistance, but Ninjun reacted with her usual mix of fire and passion. She kept denying the accusations with eloquence, extreme stubbornness, pride and scorn and was soon labelled a 'hard-resistance convict'; the Red Guard seemed determined to break her.

One day we were called into the Investigations Room together, but they focused on Ninjun as she was proving to be the harder nut to crack. The Red Guard who led the questioning that day was a middle-aged woman.

'Liao Ninjun, you must confess to being a traitor – you can't ignore this charge. You must confess – we all know you're guilty.'

'I am not a traitor,' said Ninjun calmly.

'You are.'

'I am not.'

'How dare you deny your crime – people's eyes are sharp – you have betrayed Communism – betrayed the People – you are a traitor and our enemy – *confess!*' The woman was becoming increasingly angry.

'What makes you think I am a traitor – what proof do you have? Actually, I know that you are the one who is the traitor,' said Ninjun.

'How dare you say that – you don't know what you are talking about. You don't have any proof of that – I am a proletarian revolutionary soldier and *you* are an enemy of the State.'

'You say people have sharp eyes – well, I have sharp eyes too. I saw you one day at the post office – you sent a telegram to a Guomingdan spy in Taiwan. *You* are the traitor!'

I could have laughed at the way Ninjun wound up those Red Guards, if it hadn't been so serious that is. The interrogator became almost hysterical at having the tables turned on her and threw her notebook in Ninjun's face. I believe if the woman had had a gun at that moment she would have shot Ninjun. As it was the other Red Guards moved simultaneously in Ninjun's direction and some started punching her. When she refused the order to kneel in front of them she was kicked in the back and the back of her legs and held down in the kneeling position. Someone fetched some sharp cinders and put them under her knees and pressed her down. Then they rammed a metre-tall conical hat on her head as an insult. It hurt my heart to watch and I tried to tell her to stay quiet to save herself, and to think of the children, but she remained defiant throughout – too eloquent for her own good.

Then we underwent daily condemnation meetings, either on the company premises or in the streets. We were made examples of in schools and factories and were also paraded through the streets in the back of trucks. There was always a willing crowd to jeer and shout at us and to throw stones. Ninjun was always made to wear a tall hat with insults and her 'crimes' written on it. They also slung a heavy board attached with wire around her neck, which cut into her skin and weighed her down; they stuck her photograph on it and painted a large red cross over it. Loudspeakers constantly blared in our ears listing our so-called crimes and chanting slogans. It was unrelenting and Ninjun became utterly exhausted. We weren't given any food or water during the day, which adversely affected Ninjun's diabetes and cirrhosis. She often fainted but wasn't given any medical treatment. Ninjun was unyielding though, and received far worse treatment than me. I kept pleading with her to change her attitude, but she said she thought I was cowardly for being so meek. Even though Ninjun suffered a great deal I don't know how we avoided even worse treatment, because during those condemnation meetings it was clear that many people were being tortured to death by the Red Guards, egged on by baying crowds. The level of violence during this period of Red Guard supremacy was unspeakable.

There was one consolation in those days, however, in that the children were allowed to bring us some food. We couldn't talk to them, but they hid notes in the rice telling us what was going on in the outside world as well as notes from friends. Thank heaven they didn't get caught doing this and, of course, we had to eat the notes!

After about two months' captivity in the company building we were transferred, without warning, to a labour reform camp farm in Guanxian, which was about twenty miles from Zipingpu where I had been sent in 1958.

We had no idea how long we would be detained so Ninjun managed to arrange for the three youngest girls to be looked after, separately, by some of her distant relatives in Yuechi in the Huaying Mountain region. This left Kangmei and Bo alone together, but at least we knew they were both resourceful people and we could only hope that they would cope.

I was put to work in the fields and Ninjun was given a 'lighter' job of moving bricks. She either moved the bricks in carts, which were very heavy to push, or, if they only had to be moved a short distance, the women would line up and throw the bricks to each other down the line. Ninjun was weakened and she struggled with this job. She often failed to catch the bricks and they would either hit her body or drop on her feet. Many times she collapsed under the hot sun, not only due to exhaustion, but from hypoglycaemia as her diabetes was completely out of control by this time. Then she was transferred to work in the kitchen. At least she got a little more to eat there. Sometimes she took and hid some pickles or dried food, hoping that she would be able to take it to the children when she was released. She kept it until it turned mouldy and eventually completely rotten. Everyone who worked in the kitchen took extra food, but unfortunately Ninjun got caught doing this. They were watching her especially, due to her reputation of being one of the worst 'demons'. It was announced that all food was 'the property of socialism' and Ninjun was charged with stealing. Then she was put to work sweeping the yard, and was out in all sorts of weather.

The condemnation meetings continued unabated at the labour reform camp and no matter how much Ninjun was suffering physically, she still vehemently denied all accusations. In addition to her 'crime' of trying to reverse the injustice done to the Huaying Mountain Guerrilla Force, she was accused of 'spreading poison' to the masses in trying to defend them. She always told the Red Guards:

'I am a Communist – I always have, and always will, defend the name of our Communist Party. I stand on principled ground because my parents were pure and true Communists. My father was executed by the Guomingdan, my mother led us in the fight for Communism right up until the day of Liberation. Let no one deny or manipulate these facts.'

Up on the 'condemnation meeting stage' there was a large picture of Ninjun with a red cross drawn across it on permanent display with the caption: 'Such a demon.'

After six months in the camp, Ninjun had a visit from a military representative of the Central Party in Beijing. His name was Colonel Gao. He and his military unit had been sent to the Sichuan Electricity Company to check up on the activities of the Red Guards/Rebels within the company. The Red Guards told him about Ninjun's case and described her as being the worst, most stubborn 'demon' and that she refused to confess or admit to her wrongdoing. The Red Guards gave Colonel Gao all the editions of *Huaying Fury* to read, thinking these would prove to him that she was spreading poison to the masses via the magazines, as well as through her many visits to the region. The colonel took four days to read everything and then went to the camp to interview Ninjun. In private, he told her:

'This is a true Red Revolutionary venture. You should be proud of your parents – they are good examples of Communists – we should all look up to them. Don't worry – I am here to sort it out.' Then he stood up and saluted Ninjun and called her 'Big Sister Liao'.

He ordered the Red Guards to release Ninjun. He gave them the reason that there were five children at home alone with nobody to look after them. The Red Guards had to obey the colonel's orders and Ninjun went home.

I was sent back home too shortly after.

When Ninjun arrived home she was astounded to see all the girls there. It turned out that, after a few months, the families had returned the three youngest because they didn't want to get mixed up with our troubles. They gave the excuse that they couldn't afford extra mouths to feed, even though Ninjun had given them money to look after the girls. My two eldest daughters were indeed resourceful and able to cope, but also good friends had rallied around to give them a little bit here and a little bit there. One of our friends, whom our children called Uncle Dong, was especially helpful. He worked in a 'scrap shop' and would keep various items, including clothing and shoes, under the counter for our family whenever he could.

When I returned home to Chengdu I was given the job of gatekeeper back at the Sichuan Electricity Company. In addition to letting workers and visitors in and out of the premises, I had to sweep the yard and clean the latrines. It was the lowest of low jobs.

In my spare time, I started keeping goldfish. I made my own fish tanks out of materials that I scrounged and I made new friends through this hobby too. We had always been a hospitable family and our house continued to be a focal point for friends and comrades. If they were passing through Chengdu, we didn't hesitate to feed and house them for however long was needed. I never refused anyone, but Ninjun became more practical than me and quarrelled bitterly with me over how little money and rations were left for the family.

I remember the lengths Ninjun went to in order to feed the children. One time she had managed to buy a chicken and, when I saw it, I immediately invited several friends to come over for a meal the next day. However, the following day I was embarrassed to find that there was nothing to give my guests when they arrived. I asked Ninjun where the chicken was and all she said was:

'Chicken? What chicken!'

I later found out that she had got up in the night, cooked it, woken the girls up at 3.00am and fed it to them! Ninjun admonished me for yet again trying to give away our food. She said:

'Forget about your friends, those dispirited old souls, just like you – don't you realise that the girls are *always* hungry – and why don't you look at yourself, you're as skinny as a lamp post. We ought to be eating those goldfish of yours instead of feeding them too – can't you *see* the situation we're in?'

In the meantime, Ninjun and I finished writing the appeals on behalf of the families of the Huaying Mountain Guerrilla Force. Even though we had been arrested for it, we hadn't given up this cause.

In January 1968, in time for the Chinese New Year, Mingtao came home. Kunming University had become a battleground and all education had long since ceased. He was also worried about us, given our continuing political status, because the Red Guards were still running riot.

In February, Ninjun travelled to Beijing to lodge the appeals with the Central Cultural Revolution Bureau, which was incidentally controlled by Jiangqing, aka Madame Mao – Chairman Mao's fourth wife, later to become known as one of 'The Gang of Four'. Timing is everything, however, and all our efforts came to naught, because on 15 March 1968 Madame Mao made an important speech – this speech is now referred to as 'The 3/15 Speech'. Within this speech was a statement to say that 'the Huaying Mountain Guerrilla Force had never been anything more than a group of bandits and that the

East Sichuan Underground Communist Organisation had too many traitors amongst them'. Heaven only knows whether or not Madame Mao had ever had any knowledge or understanding of the matter, but the next round of damage was done to our cause. Ninjun then decided to try to find a way of getting a meeting with Premier Zhou Enlai to lodge the appeals with him instead. So she sent us a letter to say that she was staying with a cousin of her mother's in Beijing and would probably have to remain there for several months, waiting for an opportunity.

As soon as I heard Madame Mao's 3/15 speech, I knew that this probably meant more trouble for us. I gathered together Mingtao, Kangmei and Bo and told them that we must find a way to hide all our documents. Our house was full of all sorts of political leaflets, but most important of all, we had copies of all the statements of the families of the Huaying Mountain Guerrilla Force, Shibo's original oral record and some of her paintings.

The three of them were very inventive and packed everything up securely and hid it in various places. Some were put deep under the ashes of the stove in the kitchen, some went under the floorboards in the corridor between us and our neighbour and some underneath the piles of straw and wood next to the house's communal latrine. Then Mingtao, without telling anyone, rolled up Shibo's silk paintings and put them in one of the bedposts which he had hollowed out. Even he forgot he had done this, however, and for many years we thought that these paintings had been looted by the Red Guards, until Mingtao recovered his memory!

One week after Madame Mao's 3/15 speech the Red Guards came for Ninjun and me. I was so glad that Ninjun was in Beijing. I was out when they arrived at our house. There were ten of them in a military jeep and truck. When Bo saw them coming, she rushed to smash all the light bulbs in the upper part of the house to make it difficult for them to find their way around.

On seeing Mingtao, who was holding on tightly to Ping (who was four years old), the Red Guards immediately pushed him out of the house and a Red Guard held him there at the point of his rifle. The leader, named Chen Hongbin, which means 'Red Soldier', jumped up onto the table and pointed at the girls:

'Your mother and father want to reinstate the Huaying bandits!' Before he could say anything more, He shouted back at him: '*You* are the bandits.'

Enraged, Chen Hongbin jumped down from the table, punched He hard in the chest and pushed her outside. Another Red Guard hit He with the butt of his rifle and another raised his rifle and pointed it straight at her. Kangmei hastily pushed up the rifle and the startled Red Guard, who was no more than a boy, accidentally shot into the air. People in the crowd that had gathered started screaming. Then Kangmei made an exit in the confusion and ran to the nearest army garrison, about three kilometres away, to get them to come and intervene. In theory it was illegal for anyone to have firearms, even though all the Red Guard units were armed at the time, but the army didn't arrive in time. Meanwhile, the Red Guards looted the house. They took almost everything: our book collection, ornaments, paper, brushes, ink and bedding. They only left the heavy items of furniture which they couldn't be bothered to move. At this point I returned home and the Red Guards fell on me like hungry wolves on their prey.

Chen Hongbin read out the charge: 'Lin Xiangbei, we are arresting you for being the head of the Sichuan "Three Olds Association".'

It didn't make much difference to me what I was being accused of – I was more concerned that I had no idea how long

I might be detained for. With this in mind, I insisted that I be allowed to gather some personal items to take with me and I signalled to Bo to follow me. Before the Red Guards could object, Bo and I hurried inside. I managed to put into her hand all the money I had and thirty kilos' worth of rice tokens without the Red Guards seeing.

I was taken to Sichuan University. All the buildings on the campus, inside and out, were covered in posters from top to bottom. Irate voices bellowed non-stop through loudspeakers. I was kept there in a large, dark room, only furnished with some army camp beds, for the next three or four months. Other detainees came and went in the intervening time.

I was completely cut off from the outside world and had to endure the usual treatment of questioning, condemnation meetings and writing endless confessions. The new accusation against me of being the head of the Three Olds Association had come about as a result of Madame Mao's 3/15 speech. The term 'Three Olds' was meant to mean: the *old* Red Army soldiers, the *old* officers of the Revolution and the *old* Underground Communists. Once again, anything could be made up to look real if it pleased, or suited, somebody in power. Chaos had the upper hand. I couldn't believe that another label had landed on my head, but this time I denied all accusations. However, at the same time, due to all my previous experiences, I did my best not to antagonise my captors. It was my constant fear that the children would bear the brunt of any of my actions.

The group of Red Guards showed me a list of exactly how many visitors had stayed with us, as well as who they were, since Ninjun and I had returned home from the reform labour camp: 151 to be precise. This information showed me that we couldn't necessarily trust all our neighbours; indeed we had heard a few of them calling us a nuisance and saying that we would bring trouble on all of them. None of us knew who to trust any more. The Red Guards described our house as being a 'subversive den for ghosts and demons'. They also pointed out that I had used my children's rice and meat rations to feed the demons. This made me feel very guilty and ashamed indeed. It was exactly what Ninjun had been accusing me of doing and was the source of many acrimonious quarrels between us. I don't know why I had been so blind to the needs of my family and, if I could go back and change one thing, it would be this. In my heart I said to my girls: *'My poor daughters, I'm sorry I kept you hungry whilst I was looking after my comrades. I regret that I didn't put you first. Please forgive me.'*

During one of the particularly long condemnation meetings my requests to use the latrine kept getting refused. Eventually I was allowed to go and I rushed to the nearest one. Unfortunately, in my haste, I hadn't realised that I was about to enter the ladies' side of the latrines and a group of people attacked me with cries of 'You pervert – you evil Rightist pervert'. I was pushed to the ground and kicked and punched until I blacked out. All I was hoping for was that they wouldn't break my bones.

On another occasion I did wake up in hospital. One of the Guards had noticed that I did stretching exercises each morning and one day, being in a bad mood, said to me:

'Wow, you demons! Do you really think your life is normal? If you want to exercise, then I'll give you some exercise – go and run round the yard outside twenty times.'

Each round of the yard was two hundred metres and I managed fifteen before I started seeing stars and collapsed. At the hospital they had to resuscitate me and I remember feeling puzzled as to why the Red Guards had allowed me to have treatment when they had left so many other people to die.

Then, without notice, the Red Guards let me go. I was

relieved to have survived, but frightened to think of what might have befallen the children in the meantime, as I had had no news about them whatsoever.

When I got home I found that Mingtao had been recalled to Kunming University. Before this though, he and Kangmei had decided to try and make an appeal for my release in Beijing. They thought that if only they could see someone 'at the top' then the authorities could put a stop to all the activities of the Red Guards. They tried to travel for free on the train, but got kicked off many times because they weren't part of the Red Guard Youth. They scrounged food from wherever they could. It took them a week to reach Beijing, but then they couldn't find any 'authority' who would listen to them and so had no choice except to return to Chengdu. They were away for one month in all and had slept on the streets and in railway stations. Beijing is many times colder than Chengdu and they were lucky to survive.

Then I was astounded when Bo presented me with the unused rice tokens and all the money I had given her before my arrest. She told me how she had sewn the notes and tokens into her underwear to keep them safe from being looted by the Red Guards. They had returned to the house several times to further ransack the place. Once again Uncle Dong helped the children. One of the functions of the 'scrap shop' was to collect paper for recycling. Whoever brought old paper to the shop was paid according to its weight, so he told the children that before bringing any paper into the shop, they should wet the inner layers of the pile to make it heavier. In that way they earned a bit of extra money. They even went out in the middle of the night to rip down posters for recycling, which was a very risky thing to do. Another friend of mine arranged for them to sell newspapers and that had been their main source of earning money. They had to collect the newspapers at 5.00am and all of them suffered some degree of frostbite, because their shoes and warm clothes had been looted by the Red Guards.

Bo had been terrified of using the rice tokens and money because she didn't know how long they would have to last. Even when Ping, who was only five years old at the time, was rolling around on the floor crying with the pain of hunger, Bo refused to use the tokens. Instead the girls would go to the market and pick up the half-rotten vegetables which had been thrown away. Occasionally Uncle Dong's wife would bring them some cooked food and sometimes a kindly neighbour would give them a bowl of rice. In this way they survived.

I was distressed to find out that my dear Uncle Menghan had been arrested by the Red Guards whilst I was being held at Sichuan University. In fact, many of my old comrades were arrested around this time. We learned that, before the Liberation, Sichuan underground Communists numbered around 18,000; 85 per cent of those had been classified as being Rightist, anti-Party or anti-revolutionists during the 'movements'. By 1968 there were only a few hundred of us left.

Uncle Menghan had joined the Communist Party in 1927. He had been the chief commander of our East Sichuan Underground Communist Organisation and this fact alone was enough for him to be accused of being a feudalist, an academic reactionary, a capitalist and a 'demon ghost'. At the same time as arresting him, the Red Guards looted his house, taking away nearly everything, including his precious pieces of calligraphy and calligraphy tools. Uncle Menghan was in his seventies and it was wintertime and he was taken away and held captive in a dark, damp, bare room. He had to lie on the ground at night with only a thick jacket under him. During the day, he was taken out and paraded through the city in the back of a truck. Like Ninjun and so many others, he had to wear a metre-tall conical hat emblazoned with his 'crimes'. He also had to wear a heavy wooden board, similarly showing his so-called crimes, which bowed him down. At first, Uncle Meng-han wasn't cowed and he would glower in scorn at his accusers and the jeering crowd, who were taunting him, and retort furiously:

'I'm not who you say I am – fucking well go and ask your dead ancestors what kind of person I am! When I was fighting for the Revolution there was no fucking sign of you!'

This retaliation didn't do him any good, because the Red Guards then made conditions much worse for him. They took away his jacket, which only left him with a thin shirt. He wasn't given food or water for long periods. He was refused any visitors. He collapsed many times in the back of the truck. A kindly doctor saw him one day and demanded that Uncle Menghan be allowed treatment in hospital. The Red Guards refused, but did let the doctor take him home, to his near-empty house, and treat him. Once he recovered, however, the Rebels came and took him away again. He received the same ill treatment, day and night, but this time he didn't last long and was eventually taken to hospital. My beloved Uncle Menghan, my lifelong friend and mentor, and dear friend of my father and Shibo, died there on 6 February 1969, aged seventy-five. Liu Menghan stands as a great calligrapher in Chinese history and he was reinstated to the Communist Party in 1979.

Another old friend and comrade, Du Fushen, who joined the Communist Party in 1925, also met a horrible fate. Straight after Madame Mao's 3/15 speech he was arrested, just a few days before me. I knew of his arrest because he came to me in the middle of the night for help. He was bleeding profusely from his head and was limping badly. He told me that the Red Guards had arrested him and kept him captive in a pitch-black room. They only took him out to parade him in the back of a truck and for the condemnation meetings. They put a very large and very heavy black, clay cooking pot on his head and then stuck a huge conical hat on top of it with insults written all over it. Du couldn't take it and he managed to escape from the room, but as it was so dark he didn't know where he was and he fell from the first floor of the building he was being held in. When he got to me, he said:

'Lin, look at what those young bastards are capable of doing – they're completely inhuman. What has come over the people of this country? I am going to Beijing to appeal against these wild animals.'

I bathed his wounds and started to cook something for him to eat. He stopped me and asked only for a cup of tea as he was 'dying of thirst' and said that he must get away as far as possible as quickly as possible. I asked him where he would go now, but he just said: 'Don't worry, I'll let you know when I am settled.'

I gave him a bamboo stick to help support him. I was going to walk out with him, but again he stopped me, saying that he didn't want to get me into trouble and anyway, the fewer the people around him, the less attention it would bring him. When I came home after my own arrest, I learned that he had managed to reach Beijing, but the Red Guards found him there, arrested him again and brought him back to Chengdu. This time around there was no mercy for him at all. His family were finally informed where they could find him, but by the time they arrived the Red Guards had already finished him off. Du had been stabbed several times in the throat with sharpened bamboo sticks. Du's family were heartbroken to find his letters of appeal still in his jacket pocket.

Fan Shoumei joined the Party in the 1930s and was also arrested at the end of 1968. He suffered the usual treatment of being paraded on the back of a truck, but his condemnation meetings were held in the sports stadium. He had an audience of 100,000. He would always call out from the truck and during the meetings:

'Long live the Communist Party – let's overthrow the Guomingdan.'

This seemed to puzzle people, but at least the Red Guard couldn't beat him up for such sentiments. In the end they took him to work in the tannery. Instead of working at the side of the soaking pond, he was made to get into the water with the hides. Day after day, he spent long hours in the corrosive compounds, until eventually his own body swelled up and he died.

We were all relieved when Ninjun returned from Beijing, even though she hadn't made any headway with the appeals. She had never managed to meet with Zhou Enlai or anyone close to him.

Then the 'Distribution Team' caught up with Mingtao. The Distribution Team was responsible for placing all young people in jobs. Mingtao was fervently hoping to be allowed to return to Chengdu after graduating from university, but unfortunately he was sent to work in the Xixia coal mine near Nanjing.

The next movement was the 'Sent-Down Youth Movement'. As a result of the mayhem of the Cultural Revolution, all young people were missing out on their education and also there weren't many jobs available to them. Therefore, Chairman Mao and his cohorts thought that the best education for them was to learn how to live like the 'pure proletariat' in the countryside. A couple of slogans for this movement were: 'Go to the countryside and accept an education from the peasants' and 'the vast countryside has a lot to offer'. Soon, from the age of sixteen, the urban youth were placed in farming communes in the countryside. In the case of my children and those like them, it was also seen as a way of escaping their parents' classification and making a fresh start in life. Kangmei, who had just turned eighteen, registered immediately and was sent to a village near the town of Renshou, about fifty kilometres away from Chengdu.

Bo, who wasn't quite sixteen yet, tried to change her date of birth as she felt she couldn't wait to go. Ninjun prevented her from doing so, but she only had a few months to wait until she was eligible and she registered on her birthday. Soon she was sent to Pujiang, which was the poorest county in Sichuan.

When it came to He's turn, she went to Guanxian Youth Farm.

On one of her visits home in 1970, Kangmei suggested that she should take Ninjun and Ping back to the countryside with her in the hope that Ninjun would benefit from fresh food and some rest. Ninjun was happy to accept as she was constantly struggling with ill health. Several months later Ninjun returned, mainly because she was worried about He and Jihong, but also because she needed urgent medical treatment. For the time being, she had left Ping in the care of Kangmei. Ninjun came back looking like a skeleton and she had lost almost all her hair. The vivacious, chubby Ninjun had gone. None of the hospitals in Chengdu would admit her though; they didn't want the responsibility of looking after her, as they assumed that she couldn't be saved. There wasn't much knowledge about diabetes and how to treat it in those days, but she struggled on.

On 13 September 1971 the whole of China was stunned to hear the news that Vice-Chairman Lin Biao had died in a plane crash over Mongolia. Lin Biao had been one of the closest comrades to Chairman Mao for decades. We were told that he was a traitor to the Communist Party and to China and that he and his son had been trying to escape to Russia when the Chinese military shot down the plane. This shocked the whole nation and was immediately called the '9/13 Event'.

On the same day, I was called in to the manager's office and told that the 'Lin Investigation Officer' had dismissed my case. I was given back all my confession statements: coincidentally, there were 913 of them! I found a flatbed cart and wheeled them all home. I kept some of them as a record of a decade of my life and some were taken to the countryside by Kang-mei and exchanged for dried noodles – there was a shortage of paper in the countryside. At least they were useful for something!

Ninjun's Death

Mingtao came home for a visit in early 1972. He was shocked to see his mother's state of health. He told us that he had heard there was a good hospital in Nanjing called the Nanjing Chinese and Western Medicine Hospital, which was modern and well equipped. He suggested that he should take Ninjun there for treatment. The kind military representative attached to the Sichuan Water and Electricity Company, Colonel Gao, gave permission for Ninjun to go to Nanjing and agreed that her full medical bill would be covered by the company.

In March 1972 Ninjun took Ping with her to Nanjing and was accepted as a patient at the hospital. They had a much better understanding of how to treat diabetes in conjunction with her cirrhosis of the liver; however, it was really the diabetes that was doing so much damage to Ninjun. She entered the hospital weighing only thirty kilos and by the time she came back from Nanjing in the winter of 1973 she was up to forty-five kilos. The climate in Nanjing is much harsher than in Chengdu, however, and Ninjun had found it difficult to cope with the winter temperature of -10–20°C. Chengdu gets cold, but hardly ever goes below zero. Ping hadn't liked the cold either. Ping, now ten years old, had stayed in the hospital with her mother the whole time.

Unfortunately, after only a few months at home, Ninjun's health deteriorated again and she was hospitalised in Chengdu. They didn't know how to treat her except for withholding food and she became skeletal again.

Ninjun insisted on being at home for the Chinese New Year celebrations in 1975. Mingtao came from Nanjing; Kangmei and Bo came back from their respective villages bringing fresh food from the countryside with them. Ninjun planned a party for family and friends. She told the children that they could invite three friends each. Each invitee was told that they had to prepare either a song or dance to perform at the party and that there would be prizes. The girls wrapped up new calendars and books for the winners. Ninjun gave us all detailed orders on how to prepare the food. We were all happy and excited and had a wonderful time.

But we never gave a thought to the obvious fact, which was that this would be Ninjun's last New Year celebration.

Very soon she was in hospital again and fell in and out of a coma a couple of times. The doctors told us to prepare ourselves for the inevitable. On three separate occasions we sent a telegram to Mingtao in Nanjing telling him to come to see his mother for the last time. However, each time Ninjun stabilised and Mingtao had to return to Nanjing.

The medication she needed was only available to the higher-ranking people; however, I did my best to obtain it for her. I used my every contact in every corner of the country to get letters of permission from our Provincial Health Department which needed stamps from the Party Secretary responsible for the hospital in Chengdu. Each official I met was reluctant to help, but I was finally able to hand over the authorisation for the medication to the doctor. It prolonged her life for another three months, but Ninjun had almost lost her sight and hearing by then. We used a small blackboard and wrote on it in large characters in order to communicate with her.

Kangmei, Bo and He took it in turns to be by her side twenty-four hours a day to look after her. I would bring Jihong and Ping during the day.

On 14 May 1975 Ninjun fell into another coma and the doctors did a tracheotomy to ease her breathing, but the doctors told us that they couldn't do anything more for her and said we had to accept that these would be her final hours. I sent a telegram to Mingtao telling him to come.

The five girls and I did not leave the hospital. Then three days later Ninjun woke up and in a very feeble voice asked if we were all there. I told her that all the girls were gathered around her and that Mingtao was on his way. Each girl, sobbing, went close to their mother just to let her know they were with her. Then we barely heard her say:

'Why are you all crying? Believe me, I'm not going to die yet. I am going to sing you a song!'

The Yellow River gushes into the east

The long riv…

Then there was silence until we all started to cry again, even the doctors and nurses. Ninjun started gasping for breath; each breath rattled with an increasing pause between them.

Ping was sobbing uncontrollably and started shaking her mother and begging her:

'Mum, don't go, please don't go. Don't leave me – don't leave any of us. I don't want you to go – Mum – *please…*'

I saw tears escape from the corners of Ninjun's eyes. Ping wiped them away and carried on screaming. We all called to Ninjun, waiting for her to take another breath, but then the doctors shook their heads and left the room.

I wanted to bang my head against the wall. Ninjun had left

us two days away from her fiftieth birthday. Ninjun! My brave, daring Ninjun. My dearest wife and lifelong friend. My comrade. A warrior to the very end. How like her to die singing. The day I first met her, she sang to me.

Over two hundred people came to Ninjun's funeral.

The Cultural Revolution was brought to a close by the death of Chairman Mao on 9 September 1976 and the trial of the Gang of Four in October.

I was reinstated to the Communist Party in 1978 and consequently given the job of chairman of the Workers' Union at the Sichuan Electricity Company. Two years later, at the age of sixty-three, I retired.

I will say, once again, to survive is victory.

Lin Ping

Epilogue

By Lin Ping

Father doesn't want to say any more. He has had enough of the pain some of his memories cause him.

On the night of my mother's death on 17 May 1975 I don't know how long we all remained by her bedside stricken with grief, but eventually some staff returned to say that she had to be moved to the hospital morgue. My sisters insisted on laying out my mother's body. They tenderly washed her and then dressed her. But when it came to the final garment, they paused and four pairs of eyes held mine. I had wrapped myself up in my mother's dark brown corduroy jacket for comfort and didn't want to relinquish it. New waves of tears engulfed me, but Erjie (Second Sister) Bo gently helped me to take it off and put it on Mother. Then Dajie (Big Sister) Kangmei led us as we accompanied Mother to the morgue. Father had remained leaning against the wall in silence all the while. As we passed him, I grabbed a stool and gave it to him. He distractedly waved his hand above his head as he sat down and we left him there next to Mother's empty hospital bed.

We had to inform people of Mother's death and it was Erjie Bo who ran backwards and forwards to the post office to send the telegrams to relatives and friends. The first person to arrive

417

was Uncle Yabin: Mother's brother. By this time he had been appointed chief of police in Chongqing. He arrogantly ordered us all around and didn't try to disguise his contempt for Father.

Many friends and relatives turned up to comfort us, bringing wreaths or small gifts and food with them and quite a few of them would have to stay with us until after the funeral. Soon we had amassed about 150 wreaths which had to be laid in the street as we quickly ran out of room in the house. My brother, Mingtao, set up a desk and a calligraphy set and recorded everyone's messages of sympathy on strips of yellow paper which were then pinned onto the wreaths. The postman was kept busy delivering countless telegrams of condolence to us. Dajie Kangmei liaised with company officials to sort out the funeral arrangements. Sanjie (Third Sister) He was busy looking after the people who were staying with us. Sijie (Fourth Sister) Jihong was making black armbands for all the relatives to wear and I was making white paper flowers for all the other mourners to pin onto their clothing. Father managed to greet everybody and remained deep in conversation with old friends and comrades whom he hadn't seen for a long time. Various aunties busied themselves in the kitchen and food was provided for everyone.

More than two hundred people turned up to the funeral service to pay their respects to my mother. The secretary of the company Communist Party organisation stood to say a few words and it was ironic that he described Mother as 'a good, loyal Communist Party member' and, in so doing, my mother was reinstated into the Communist Party – what a pity she couldn't hear him. Erjie Bo made a very moving speech on behalf of the family. In the afternoon we gathered at the crematorium, which was outside the city. The memory of my mother's cremation is still raw. I will never forget how her body, which was merely placed on a thin board, was inexorably drawn towards the gaping doors of the furnace, the awful sound of the flames bursting into life and how the blinding, molten heat was already consuming her so brutally, even before the doors to the furnace clanged shut. We were all screaming and crying out for her. There was no coffin, no soft music or any curtains to shield our sensibilities, just a metal barrier to separate us from the beast-like furnace. Half an hour later my mother's ashes were handed over to us.

Life carried on without my mother:

Brother Mingtao remained assigned to a manganese mine in Nanjing.

Dajie Kangmei was still stuck in the countryside; she had already been there for eight years as one of the 'sent-down youth'. By that time, most other young people had been allowed to return to the city to find a job, but this was part of my family's punishment because my father was still classified as a Rightist. A few months later though, she was given permission to replace my mother in the Sichuan Electricity Company, so she returned to Chengdu at the end of 1975 to work in the engine factory.

Erjie Bo was in her final year at a teacher training college.

Sanjie He continued at the company's collective farm in Guanxian, not far from the Lion Falls Power Station. She went so far as to join a group of enthusiastic young people in swearing, under Chairman Mao's portrait, to stay there forever, sacrificing their youth to build up the farm for the good of the country.

Sijie Jihong was a senior at secondary school, but she had had a very chequered school career right from the start. Sijie Jihong had always been a bit of a tomboy and was labelled a troublemaker in her own right, quite apart from being from a blacklisted family. Even when Mother was still alive, she often got into fights at school and one of those fights had been so serious that she ended up in hospital in fear for her life. One of the girls she had been fighting had kicked her so hard in the back that one of her kidneys was crushed. She often remained at home rather than attending school. After Mother died though, it seems that Sijie Jihong couldn't handle the bullying at school any more, or life at home, and she ran away. She had no money and so she hitchhiked around the country seeking out all the distant relatives she had met at Mother's funeral, going from one to the other. Most of the time, however, we didn't know where she was or how she survived.

I was twelve years old at the end of 1975 and about to finish primary school. All children from 'wrong families' were bullied at school and I certainly missed my mother's advice and sometimes her intervention. I remember that much of the worst bullying I experienced was meted out by my teacher.

Each day, I would have to get my lunch from the company canteen and I hated having to do so. It wasn't that it was a long walk to get there and back from my school, it was more because I dreaded meeting Father there. He was still the gatekeeper, sweeper of the yard and cleaner of the toilets and still shunned by everybody at the company. He was as skinny as his broomstick in those days. People would walk past him quickly averting their eyes as if he might be contagious and I'm afraid I tried to avoid him too. I felt I had enough troubles of my own.

1976 was a Year of the Dragon. Chinese people believe that in a Dragon Year one receives either the best of luck or the worst of luck; nothing in between. It turned out to be one of the worst years.

On 8 January 1976 Father got up early as usual to make his tea and listen to the 7.00am news broadcast. I heard Father shout out and Dajie Kangmei scream. The volume of the radio was turned up and I heard the music of lament. Then, in a deeply sad voice, the newsreader announced that our beloved Premier Zhou Enlai had passed away. It wasn't long before people started filling the streets and posters went up all over the city with the announcement. Other posters went up praising him in poetry and prose. On the day of Premier Zhou Enlai's funeral, all flags were flown at half-mast and people all over the country mourned him. We heard how, when his hearse was driven through Tiananmen Square in Beijing, the crowds fell silent. After the cremation, his wife scattered his ashes in the sea.

On the morning of 6 July 1976, the same music of lament started to be played over the radio. This time it was Zhu De, the great general, who had passed away. His name had been even bigger than Mao's in the twenties and thirties. In his time he had been the Supreme General.

At about 3.00am on 28 July 1976 we felt the ground shaking beneath us. Later in the morning it was announced that the epicentre of an earthquake, which measured 7.6 points on the Richter Scale, had been in Tangshan, a city in the north of China. We learned later that over 242,000 people had been killed and countless others badly injured. In fact, the actual numbers could never be confirmed. The aftershocks were felt over a huge area of China and kept occurring. Everybody in Chengdu moved out into the streets and main roads. There was no transportation because no vehicle was able to get through the rows of beds and temporary shelters all over the place. Throughout the whole summer people slept in the open or in buildings, such as schools, which were deemed to be safe. Gradually the aftershocks died down and everybody returned to their homes.

On 9 September 1976 I turned thirteen. Usually on my birthday I would receive enough money to buy a couple of books; that year 0.5 yuan would have been enough. I was also allowed to ask for one of my favourite foods, such as two spiced rabbit heads, or a bowl of noodles from the noodle bar at the top of our street. But on that morning, I awoke to the sound of the music of lament on the radio once more and Father calling to all of us. I was scared to know who it was this time. Then the newsreader began the announcement; he was almost sobbing:

'We are utterly heartbroken to make this announcement. Our Party's, our military's and our nation's greatest leader, international proletarian, the leader of oppressed nations' struggle and the people's greatest adviser, the Chairman of the Chinese Communist community, the Chairman of the Chinese Military…'

I didn't hear the rest because Dajie Kangmei and Erjie Bo were screaming and crying:

'No this cannot be – he cannot die.' Father was mumbling over and over:

'Heaven – Heaven! What are we going to do now? What will happen to China? We've lost our greatest leader – he should have lived a much longer life.'

We were all truly sorry and we were crying as if it was our own father who had died. The whole country went into mourning for about a month and there was no entertainment of any kind for that period. A vigil, or guard, was set up beside each official portrait of Chairman Mao twenty-four hours a day. Even children weren't allowed to wear any patterned or colourful clothing. Unfortunately, I didn't have the appropriate white shirt to wear at school and I had been singled out and humiliated for 'not showing enough loyalty and respect for Chairman Mao' and wasn't allowed to take my turn at standing guard beside his portrait.

Every person was like a lost lamb waiting to be found. We were waiting to find out who the next leader would be. Then it was announced that before he died, Chairman Mao had appointed Hua Guofeng as his successor. Very swiftly, at the beginning of October, Chairman Hua denounced the Gang of Four, one of whom was Chairman Mao's widow. They had tried to overthrow the succession as soon as Chairman Mao died. Then, once the 'Gang of Four' had fallen, and much to everyone's surprise, Deng Xiaoping was reinstated into the Communist Party. For many years he had been dubbed the 'topmost Rightist'. This gave us huge hope and we knew the country was going to undergo massive change once again. We waited for it with bated breath.

After Chairman Hua announced that the Great Cultural Revolution had officially ended, Father seemed to come alive. The radio was switched on most of the time and friends starting visiting regularly. Every week Father would host a dinner for all those Rightist 'Uncles and Aunties'. Dajie and Erjie had to do the cooking and I was kept busy doing the food shopping and most of the washing-up.

At the beginning of 1978 it was thought that all the 1957 Rightists were going to be reinstated into the Communist Party. When it finally happened it was a boost to all our egos, not just to Father's, and it felt as if we had regained our dignity. However, there was no compensation for the lost twenty years' worth of wages. Only a small group of people received reimbursements, but Father didn't even try to claim anything. He was just so happy to be a member of the Communist Party once more.

One evening Yu Shoushang, a close friend of Father's, paid us a visit. After dinner Father remarked:

'Life is such a joke – in 1957 someone simply said to me "Now you are a Rightist" and my life dissolved into hell. Twenty years later someone equally simply said "Now your Rightist hat is off" and I'm suddenly reinstated. They were such unassuming words, but they held such power. Twenty years –

twenty years of suffering for my loved ones and me. I'm having difficulty making my head and my heart deal with all the different emotions.'

Yu's voice was suddenly so loud that I jumped a bit:

'Yes, that's right – is it any wonder? – and you know it! Tell your daughters what you did!'

We all looked questioningly at Father, but he shook his head and closed his eyes, so Yu continued:

'Your father knelt down in front of Chairman Mao's portrait and, with tears in his eyes, *thanked* Chairman Mao for reinstating him!' Then Yu jabbed his finger in Father's direction, shaking his head, and said:

'Your father is still stupidly loyal to the very regime that nearly destroyed him and did destroy millions – he has become a brainless tool!' Father remained quiet.

Father was fifty-nine years old when his political status changed and because he was so close to retirement age, which was sixty-three at that time, the company didn't give him a very important position. Father didn't mind though as he was no longer interested in titles and levels of importance; he just wanted a normal job, where he could sit next to normal people who were full of energy for the job in hand. He was appointed chairman of the Company Workers' Union and remained there until his retirement. He still often remarked however:

'What a pity! I could have made so many contributions to build my country – twenty years have been totally wasted.'

After Father's retirement he was invited to work at the Sichuan Party History Department to document the Sichuan underground Party organisation. He also started to publish his articles on different subjects in magazines, newspapers and Party journals.

Father became an important focal point for people who needed to prove that they were once members of the Communist Party. In order to be reinstated written proof was required, but so many records had been destroyed or lost in the intervening years that many people were being left in limbo. The only course of action left for these people was finding someone – a Party member – who could vouch for them. There was another reason for wanting to prove Party membership: if you could prove that you had become a member of the Party, or you were an activist, before 1938 then you were entitled to receive a full salary pension. In addition, you would have a more prestigious status. Father managed to help about two hundred people get reinstated.

By 1977 my brother, Mingtao, finally managed to move back to Chengdu having found work in a factory which manufactured aeroplanes.

Dajie Kangmei had become a journalist on the *Chengdu Mercantile Newspaper*.

Erjie Bo was the only sibling to have joined the Communist Party and was in line to become principal of the Teacher Training College of Chengdu.

Sanjie He had graduated from Sichuan University with a degree in agriculture and worked at the Sichuan Agriculture Research Institute. None of her group had stayed on at the collective farm.

Sijie Jihong had returned to Chengdu, but because she had never had much of an education, only found work in a warehouse.

Also, by the early 1980s, all of my siblings had got married and some of them had started a family. Each family had one child each, which was in line with the 'one-child policy'. It was actually more of a recommendation because having two children was allowed. However, Erjie Bo considered herself a good Communist Party member and went so far as to terminate her second pregnancy, in order to set a good example to other people.

In 1982 I was enrolled at the Science and Technology University of Chengdu, studying digital communication.

Father had started doing a lot of travelling around the country and was often in Chongqing in 1982. One day, out of the blue from my point of view, Erjie Bo told me that Father had just got married and would soon return to Chengdu with his new wife. I was shocked and couldn't believe that nobody had told me that this was likely to happen. It was well known, though, that I had been against Father marrying again; I felt it would be a gross betrayal of my mother, even though I very well knew that Father was lonely. Erjie Bo showed me the letter Father had written to her. In it he asked her to break the news of his marriage to me gently and said that his new wife, Feng Liqing, was within our circle of friends and that they trusted each other and were both happy to be together. He also wanted her to remind me that our mother had passed away ten years previously and that it was more than a decent period of time to wait before getting married again. He described Feng Liqing as being in her fifties, very elegant and very pretty. He added that he would never settle for anyone who wasn't good looking. It was evident that my father had got his confidence back! I held on to the letter and went away quietly to think. When Father and his new wife returned to Chengdu I did behave myself, but I couldn't bring myself to call her 'Mama' as Father requested; instead I respectfully called her Feng Ma (Mother Feng). Feng Ma had been married before and had three sons. Her former husband had been headmaster at the top middle school in Chongqing and had been one of the casualties of the Cultural Revolution. Feng Ma died in 2017 at the age of ninety having lived with Father for thirty-five years. They used to divide their time between Chengdu and Chongqing.

After I graduated from university in 1984 I started working at the City of Chengdu Electricity Supply Company; although in my spare time I was studying art. Art was my greatest passion and it was all I really thought about.

Almost ten years of Deng Xiaoping's open economic policy had changed China dramatically. There was a focus on making money and it gave many people the opportunity to start up their own businesses. One of Deng Xiaoping's sayings was: 'It doesn't matter whether you are a black cat or a white cat – as long as you can catch mice, then you are a good cat.' None of my family, however, managed to be a 'good cat' and go into business.

In 1989 students started demanding democracy; it was another huge movement. I was excited and talked about it openly and went out onto the streets to demonstrate too. In the first few days everything was fine, but then the situation got tense and Father warned us all not to go out in case we got caught up in any trouble. We couldn't stay still though and I know that Erjie Bo and Brother Mingtao were very active. Father warned us again, saying that he had been in countless similar situations and knew the danger. On numerous occasions he stood by the door with his arms outstretched to prevent me from leaving the house.

In 1990 I was commended as an 'excellent worker' at the Electricity Company and this made Father very proud. He said:

'Good – good! Well done! So now it's time you wrote your applications.'

'What applications?' I was puzzled.

'Your applications to become a member of the Communist Party *of course*.'

I laughed in his face.

'Baba – I am not interested in politics – I only want to become an artist.'

Father let out a very long and very disappointed sigh.

'All the family have been committed Communists. I assumed and fervently hoped all my children would be too.'

In 1992 I resigned from my 'perfect' job at the Electricity Company because I had decided to go to the UK to chase my dream of becoming a portrait artist. I had been accepted to do a course at London Guildhall University.

On the day I left Chengdu, my whole family and many friends came to see me off at the railway station. My flight was leaving from Beijing. Father was pacing up and down the platform, but hadn't said very much to me at all. I had boarded the train and was waving at everybody through the window when my father suddenly broke into a run and grabbed my hands. He ran with the train a little way and with tears in his eyes kept saying: 'Write to me – write home.'

Eventually my hands slipped away from his and tears blurred my own vision till I could no longer see my family and friends on the platform.

A few years later I brought Toby Eady, a British literary agent, on a visit to China to meet my father. Toby Eady was interested in the story of my grandmother's life: the Double Gun Woman. Having met my father, Toby urged me to persuade him to write about his own life. He said that my father was a wonderful man, but too modest. Father was eighty-four years old then and he did indeed start to record his story and he carries on writing even today: prose and poetry.

Many years later, here we are, and, with my friend Ellen's help, we have finally put my father's life story into English.

Now Father lives sometimes with Dajie Kangmei and sometimes with Erjie Bo, who take it in turns to look after him. Father has six grandchildren and five great grandchildren. He still, of course, has his son and all his daughters – his 'five golden flowers'!

Chronology and Family Tree

Year	Family history	Major events in China
1900	Chen Lianshi (Double Gun Woman/Shibo) born in Sichuan	Boxer uprising in Beijing
1901	Lin Zhuxi (Lin Xiangbei's father) born	
1912		Republic of China established
1918	Lin Xianli (name later changed to Xiangbei) born	
1920	Lin Zhuxi leaves home to become Dr Sun Yat-sen's loyal follower	
1921		Chinese Communist Party (CCP) established in Shanghai
1925	Ninjun born; Lin Xiangbei leaves Grandmother's home to live with his father	Death of Sun Yat-sen
1927		Chiang Kai-shek comes to power within Guomingdan

1931		Japanese gain military control of northern China
1934-1935		The Long March
1937	Lin Xiangbei meets Chen Lianshi (Shibo), who was imprisoned in Wanxian. He works at the *Wanzhou Daily* newspaper as trainee journalist	
1937-1942		The War of Resistance Against Japan (WW2 in East Asia) begins with Marco Polo Bridge incident
1938	Lin Xiangbei becomes a Communist	
1939	Lin Xiangbei meets Ninjun (Shibo's daughter)	
1940	Lin Zhuxi becomes a Communist	
1943	Lin Xiangbei and Ninjun marry	
1944	First child Binhua born in Penzhou County	
1945		The Japanese Army surrenders
1946	Binhua dies; second child, Mingtao, born; Lin Zhuxi dies	
1948		The Third Huaying Mountain Uprising

1949		The People's Republic of China is established; massacre at Zhazidong Prison in Chongqing; Chongqing liberated by the People's Liberation Army
1950		Rectification Movement
1951	Daughter Kangmei born	Land Reform Movement; China supports North Korea in the Korean Peninsula War
1952		The Three Anti-Movements
1952	Shibo forced to withdraw her Communist Party membership	
1953	Shibo sent to Women's Reform Institution in Baxian	
1953	Daughter Bo born	
1954	Lin Xiangbei appointed as supplies manager at the Lion Falls Power Station	
1955	Daughter He born	
1956		Hundred Flowers Campaign/Movement
1956	Lin Xiangbei promoted to Party Secretary at Lion Falls	China's first power station opened
1957		Anti-Rightist Movement
1957	Lin Xiangbei accused of being Rightist and shunned; daughter Jihong born	The Great Leap Forward

1958	Lin Xiangbei sent to the Zipingpu Power Station at Guanxian	
1960	Chen Lianshi/Shibo dies	
1962	Lin Xiangbei released from labour camp and returns to Chengdu (with Bo); rest of family now living at 94 Trinity Street	
1963	Daughter Ping born	
1966		The Cultural Revolution
1971		Vice-Chairman Lin Biao dies in a plane crash over Mongolia
1975	Ninjun dies	
1976		Zhuo Enlai, General Zhu De and Chairman Mao die; Gang of Four arrested; Tangshan earthquake; Cultural Revolution ends
1978	Lin Xiangbei reinstated into the Communist Party	

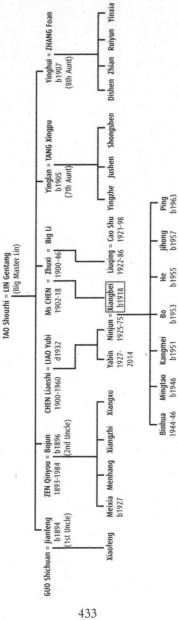

Unbound is the world's first crowdfunding publisher, established in 2011.

We believe that wonderful things can happen when you clear a path for people who share a passion. That's why we've built a platform that brings together readers and authors to crowdfund books they believe in – and give fresh ideas that don't fit the traditional mould the chance they deserve.

This book is in your hands because readers made it possible. Everyone who pledged their support is listed at the front of the book and below. Join them by visiting unbound.com and supporting a book today.